OPERATION SOLO

OPERATION SOLO

The FBI's Man in the Kremlin

John Barron

Regnery Publishing, Inc.
Washington, D.C.

Library of Congress Cataloging-in-Publication Data

Barron, John, 1930–
      Operation Solo : the FBI's man in the Kremlin / John Barron.
        p. cm.
      Includes bibliographical references and index.
      ISBN 0-89526-486-2
        1. Childs, Morris, 1902-1991.   2. Intelligence officers–United
States—Biography. I. Title.
      JK468.I6B39 1996
      327.1273 '092–dc20
      [B]   95-25755
                              CIP

Published in the United States by
Regnery Publishing, Inc.
An Eagle Publishing Company
One Massachusetts Avenue, NW
Washington, DC 20001

Distributed to the trade by
National Book Network
4720-A Boston Way
Lanham, MD 20706

Printed on acid-free paper.
Manufactured in the United States of America

10 9 8 7 6

Photos courtesy of Eva Childs
Text design by Dori Miller

Books are available in quantity for promotional or premium use. Write to Director of Special Sales, Regnery Publishing, Inc., One Massachusetts Avenue, NW, Washington, DC 20001, for information on discounts and terms or call (202) 216-0600.

THIS BOOK IS DEDICATED to all who contributed to Operation SOLO and kept it secret. Specifically, it is dedicated to Morris Childs, Eva Childs, Jack Childs, Alexander Burlinson, Carl Freyman, Walter Boyle, John Langtry, James Fox, and Ivian Smith, all of whom represented the United States Federal Bureau of Investigation.

By their deeds, all exhibited a shared conviction: "Freedom never comes free. Freedom at any price always is a bargain."

CONTENTS

ACKNOWLEDGMENTS

IN ADDITION TO THANKING benefactors named in the Foreword, I thank others, without implying that any of them necessarily endorses the accuracy or concurs with the conclusions of what I have written.

William Gunn was a research assistant to every FBI Director from J. Edgar Hoover to William Webster. After retiring from the FBI, he worked with me as a researcher and helped conduct the initial interviews with Morris and Eva Childs in the early 1980s. He also interviewed other sources by himself.

Former Assistant Director Raymond Wannall supervised SOLO from FBI headquarters during the last years of his career and saved the operation when congressional committees were about to inadvertently destroy it. He favored me with unique perspectives of the operation as it was viewed from headquarters.

Former FBI Agents Edward Miller, Donald Moore, William Brannigan, and Edward Jones confirmed the broad history of SOLO and provided details of various aspects of it.

Herbert Romerstein, formerly a staff member of the House Intelligence Security Committee and the U.S. Information Agency, briefed me about personalities prominent in the American and Soviet Communist Parties, and constructively critiqued the manuscript.

Professor Harvey Klehr of Emory University made available his excellent history of the U.S. Communist Party, *The Heyday of American Communism*, and generously shared with me references to Morris Childs that he discovered in the Moscow archives of the Comintern.

Former FBI Agent Wesley Roberts facilitated my many interviews with Eva Childs and advised me as to how I could communicate with other primary sources.

Chicago attorney Charles Goodbar, in ably representing Eva, greatly facilitated publication by solving or dissipating a number of legal problems.

William Shulz, managing editor of the *Reader's Digest*, out of personal friendship reviewed and beneficially critiqued the manuscript.

Alfred Regnery, president of Regnery Publishing, Inc., agreed to publish this book at a time when other publishers expressed no interest in "a book about the Cold War." Throughout its preparation, he encouraged me.

Richard Vigilante, senior editor at Regnery, expertly edited the manuscript and counseled me on deficiencies that needed my attention.

FOREWORD

WHILE WRITING A BOOK about the Soviet KGB during the early 1970s, I interviewed many former FBI agents and, in ensuing years, some favored me with their friendship. In 1977 one of them outlined to me what he described as a great espionage operation that the FBI had long conducted against the Soviet Union. The principal American spies were Morris Childs, his wife Eva, and his brother Jack Childs. The retired agent said that all three were elderly, that both brothers were in very poor health, and that the FBI was ending the operation. An accurate account of it would benefit the public and the country; an incomplete or distorted account could be harmful. Accordingly, he and other former agents, for whom he purported to speak, recommended that I ask the FBI if someday I could write the story and begin research while the three main protagonists were still alive.

Without confirming or denying the information imparted to me, the FBI said that the subject I broached was extremely sensitive and highly classified. It requested that I pledge never to mention or allude to the subject in any writings or conversation. If I could not freely make such a commitment, the FBI needed to know that, then and there. I promised to say nothing. A few weeks later, a senior FBI executive asked to talk to me about "a vital national security matter." He stated that because of new developments and because American lives were at stake, the FBI had to be sure I would honor my pledge never to say anything about the subject I had raised at headquarters. I gave him my assurances. There is nothing remarkable about not publicizing classified information whose disclosure would imperil the lives of American spies, and I mention these incidents only because they are relevant to what subsequently happened.

The operation about which I learned in 1977 continued well beyond 1977, and Morris and Eva Childs were aware that I had suppressed my knowledge of it. That is one reason why they indirectly approached me in 1982 through FBI Agent Michael Steinbeck. He said that the operation in which Mr. and Mrs. Childs were involved finally had ended and they wished to discuss with me the possibility of my writing a book about their experiences. The FBI stated that it would neither oppose nor contribute to such a book; however, if I desired, it would facilitate an initial meeting between me and the Childses, who were in hiding under government protection.

We first met in Santa Monica, California, where we were joined by former FBI Agent Walter A. Boyle. For an unprecedented eighteen years, Boyle had served as the "case agent" closest to Morris and Eva. Morris looked upon him as a son and invited him to participate in our beginning interviews. Steinbeck was present as an escort but did not take part in the interviews. I found Morris, Eva, and Boyle fascinating and saw each as a striking character in a drama. Never have I enjoyed interviews more. Morris and Eva later came to Washington, and in a Georgetown suite we talked many hours a day for the better part of a week about the history in the making that they had witnessed and at times had helped to make. We became friends and very much looked forward to working together on a book.

We were about to begin work full time when the FBI advised Morris and Eva that the Justice Department had ruled they could not tell their story to me. No one from the Justice Department ever spoke to me, and I received only a hearsay explanation of the rationale behind the ruling. Supposedly, a relatively junior Justice

Department attorney reasoned thus: Many of the details Morris and Eva would necessarily reveal in recounting their espionage careers remained classified top secret, and the government still refused to release these details to anyone. If the Justice Department allowed Morris and Eva to tell their story, it in effect would be sanctioning release of top secret data exclusively to me. That would represent unacceptable favoritism toward one journalist. More important, the release of such secrets through Morris to me would make it difficult for the Justice Department to resist demands that had been filed under the Freedom of Information Act requesting that other secrets be revealed.

Morris was disappointed and angry but there was little he could prudently do. He was eighty-one; his health was terrible; he believed, probably correctly, that the KGB and Communist Party were hunting him; he needed the protection and support of the government; and he had to consider the welfare of Eva. Still, he retained hope that Americans someday might learn of his secret life and its meaning. And we continued to see each other, particularly when the FBI brought him to northern Virginia for consultations or to lecture at its academy in Quantico.

In 1987 Ronald Reagan ordered the National Security Medal bestowed upon Morris and awarded posthumously to his brother Jack. The president offered personally to decorate Morris at the White House and to host a luncheon or dinner in his honor. The FBI persuaded the president that security considerations made a White House ceremony imprudent, and so Director William Sessions presented the medal at FBI headquarters. At the insistence of Morris and Eva, I was invited to a private, unofficial reception afterward.

Gathered in a hotel suite on Pennsylvania Avenue were Morris' best FBI friends. I was privileged to meet and speak with some of them: Walt Boyle; John Langtry, who for twelve years was the case agent of Jack Childs; Carl Freyman, who long ago persuaded Morris to ally himself with the FBI; and Assistant Director James Fox, a patron of Morris and Eva since 1971.

Morris had been so near death so many times that I think he had lost fear of a natural death; he did dread death in a Soviet execution chamber or from an assassin's exploding bullet. He once remarked to me, "I hope I can die quietly and peacefully without any of them knowing." On June 2, 1991, eight days before his eighty-ninth birthday, Morris died just that way in a hospital bed with Eva and a rabbi at his side.

In the judgment of Eva and me, Morris' death and the disintegration of the Soviet Union removed any justification for further withholding his story, and in 1992 I began work on the book, with Eva's indispensable help.

Upon marrying Morris in 1962, Eva became his full and equal partner in espionage and thereafter accompanied and assisted him on almost all his many missions into the Soviet Union and eastern Europe. She sat by Morris during the pre-launch briefings and the post-mission debriefings. She was a confidant of the head of the U.S. Communist Party and his wife; she was a friend of the FBI agents who ran the operation. Eva alone was an extraordinary, original source.

In addition she made available a rare trove of papers, records, files, and notes assembled and kept by Morris. Among them were copies of Soviet documents he and she smuggled out of Moscow; copies of reports from Morris and Jack to the FBI; detailed notes reconstructing secret briefings the Soviet rulers gave Morris; notes recording conversations with these rulers; and memoranda Morris submitted to the Politburo.

In 1987 FBI Agents Charles Knox and James Milburn spent eleven days with Morris and Eva recording on tape Morris' reminiscences of a lifetime. The FBI made handwritten transcripts of these conversations and gave Eva, a party to them, copies of most of the transcripts, and she gave those she had to me. Eva also supplied from Morris' memorabilia numerous photographs, some of which appear in this book. One in particular had significant consequences; it shows Morris and Leonid Brezhnev together in the Kremlin.

Before her death, Eva stated her intention to bequeath these files and records to the Hoover Institution at Stanford University in the hope that they will be useful to future researchers.

Beyond documentary data, this book is based upon hundreds of hours of interviews with FBI participants in the operation, including James Fox, Carl Freyman, Walter Boyle, and John Langtry. They appear as major characters in the book, and the narrative provides ample means for readers to assess their qualifications to testify as expert eyewitnesses to history. The special qualifications of Boyle and Langtry merit mention.

From 1962 on, Boyle embarked Morris and Eva on and recovered them from every mission and wrote the mission reports. When they were in the United States, he talked to them almost every day. He made the daily operational decisions and was consulted at all the major operational conferences in Washington, New York, and Chicago. No one was closer to Morris and Eva; no one knew more about them and the operation than did Boyle. Fortunately for history, Boyle kept a log of his career.

Langtry in New York administered an elaborate clandestine communications system designed and built by the Soviets. Through this system the FBI regularly received messages from the Kremlin and, in the name of Jack or Morris, sent back whatever the United States wanted the Soviets to hear. Langtry handled many millions of dollars smuggled into New York by the KGB, and he drafted the reports of what the KGB and communist leaders told Jack. After he retired, the FBI recalled Langtry to write a secret "in-house" history of the operation and put at his disposal all the documents he required. Langtry personally saw much of the operation; he read everything about it.

Boyle and Langtry, in countless interviews and conversations, generously shared with me their unique knowledge and insights. They took time to scrutinize, criticize, and correct the manuscript. Certainly I alone am responsible for any errors or defects in this work, but the book could not have been written without such gifts from Morris, Eva, Boyle, and Langtry. The names and contributions of other important benefactors are cited in the Acknowledgments.

There are four appendices. Appendix A lists the dates and destinations of each of the fifty-seven missions into enemy territory Morris, Eva, or Jack accomplished under FBI control. Appendix B lists, year by year, the amount of money the Soviet Union illicitly supplied the U.S. Communist Party from 1958 to 1980. Appendix

C identifies the KGB officers who worked in the United States with Morris and Jack from 1958 to 1982. Appendix D replicates documents that illustrate various phases of the operation.

A minor caveat. Eva proved herself to be the kind of source a researcher covets, the kind of witness a lawyer likes to put on the stand. Many times she had said, "No, it didn't happen that way," or "I can't remember," or "I don't know." In short, she was a stickler for facts.

However, Eva now and then had a problem recalling dates. She vividly remembered an intimate dinner with Fidel Castro at the Cuban embassy in Moscow, down to the menu (steak) and the smell of cigar smoke; however, she could not remember the date she and Morris dined there. There was one date she adamantly refused even to discuss: the date of her birth. I had to know how old Eva was, so I inquired of government sources who said that Eva Lieb Childs was born March 24, 1900. Asked if that was correct, Eva indignantly exclaimed, "No! I'm not *that* old." I then asked, "All right, Eva, in which year were you born?" She said 1910.

Doubtless, some clerk got it wrong and Eva is right. Regardless, anyone caring to read further will meet a lady who, at whatever age, for nearly two decades served alongside valorous and daring men with equal valor and daring.

OPERATION SOLO

one
___

WE WON

THE FBI EFFACED RECORDS of the death, and no newspaper made mention of it. The United States had kept the secret for thirty years, and the FBI intended to keep it still. The communists never knew what had happened to Morris after he vanished, and they hunted him in vain; let them keep looking for him, and wondering.

Elaine Fox overheard her husband, Assistant FBI Director James Fox, say over the phone, "When did it happen?... Yes, I will be proud to do it."

Reading the sadness on his face, she asked, "Is the old man gone?" Fox nodded yes and said he had agreed to speak at the funeral, then he retreated to his study to reflect and compose.

If Jim Fox could have arranged the funeral, it would have been like a state funeral. He envisioned a long line of FBI agents and troops standing at attention on a ridge in Arlington National Cemetery overlooking Washington. He saw and heard the Marine Band marching and playing a dirge in front of a horse-drawn caisson bearing the casket draped with a new American flag. Perhaps even the president would be there. After all, Ronald Reagan had offered personally to decorate 58[‡] at the White House.

Had Fox been at liberty to tell the real story of the greatest espionage operation in FBI history, he could have justified such a funeral and he might well have begun the eulogy by saying, "Here lies the greatest of American spies."

Morris risked his life on fifty-two missions into the Soviet Union and other parts of its empire, most lasting several weeks. For more than twenty years, the highest Soviet rulers—from Nikita Khrushchev, Leonid Brezhnev, and Yuri Andropov on down—treated him as an intimate friend. They confided to him their innermost thoughts, ambitions, and apprehensions; their strategy and plans; what they would do and dared not do; their reactions to world events; and their real attitudes toward the United States and its leaders. Often they solicited his opinions and advice, and often they heeded it. The Soviets so trusted and esteemed him that on his seventy-fifth birthday, Brezhnev hosted a banquet at the Kremlin in his honor. The Soviet dictator eloquently thanked Morris for more than half a century of service to the Soviet Union and international communism, then awarded him a medal, the Order of the Red Banner.

In the United States, Morris secretly served as the principal deputy to the head of the American Communist Party, Gus Hall. In effect, an FBI spy was the second-ranking figure in American communism. The Soviets smuggled money to the U.S. party through Morris and his brother, Jack Childs, and over the years they received from Moscow more than $28 million, which the FBI counted down to the penny.

The voluminous secrets Morris stole from the Kremlin for more than two decades enabled the United States to read the minds of the men who ran the Soviet Union, to anticipate their actions, and to exploit their problems, most spectacularly their problems with

---

[‡] In the most guarded FBI files, Morris Childs was listed as CG-5824S*. Among themselves, FBI agents referred to him simply as "58." CG meant Chicago; S meant security; and the asterisk meant that the source could never testify in court or be otherwise identified.

China. It was like playing poker knowing which cards everyone else at the table held.

By elaborate ruses, the FBI concealed the identity of Morris and the nature of the operation from everybody—the State Department, the CIA, the Defense Department, and the National Security Council. FBI agents personally took the most sensitive reports from Morris to the offices of these and other agencies. There a few people were allowed to read the reports in the presence of the delivering agent, but they had to hand them back. Not until 1975 did the FBI finally inform the president and secretary of state of the source of the intelligence for which they and other policymakers clamored.

Even now, at the funeral, Fox could disclose few of these facts. But he resolved to hint at the truth by telling as much of it as he could.

In the foyer outside the chapel of a funeral home in northwest Chicago, Fox bent down to embrace a tiny, elegantly coiffed woman who in her late eighties remained unbowed, trim, and lovely. Officially, she was CG-6653S*; Fox called her Eva because he revered her. How many elderly women would hide with their husband underneath bed covers in Moscow copying secret Soviet documents, one holding a flashlight while the other wrote? How many would smuggle out copies encased in plastic wrapped around their bodies? How many would carry hundreds of thousands of dollars in shopping bags through the streets of New York and Chicago? How many so late in life would give up their life to espionage?

Two old friends, Carl Freyman and Walter Boyle, joined them. Freyman, in his late seventies and limping slightly, reminded Fox of a courtly grandfather; Boyle looked as lean, tough, and darkly handsome as he did forty years before when the commanding general of the first Marine Division decorated him on a Korean battlefield.

The four of them—Eva, Fox, Freyman, and Boyle—belonged to the small American team that challenged the Soviet empire on its own territory and terms; they were teammates. Morris always credited Freyman with saving his life. In 1952, while Morris lay near death, Freyman persuaded him to be a partner of the FBI, put him in the Mayo Clinic, and restored his will to live. Freyman was the first to perceive that Morris someday might penetrate the highest

Soviet sanctums, and he recast the operation accordingly. And Freyman rescued Boyle's career and brought him into the operation at a time when nobody else in the FBI wanted anything to do with him.

For eighteen years Boyle embarked Morris and Eva on their every mission, and wherever they alighted back in the United States, he was there, waiting to lead them past customs and to a hideaway to draft the first flash report to Washington. He saw or talked to them every day that they were in the United States, and he was at their call night and day. Always he carried a weapon, and they knew he instantly would use it in their defense. To them, he was as a son. In consequence of a false allegation of misconduct, FBI headquarters proposed removing Boyle from the operation. To the FBI, Eva, at the behest of Morris, spoke dulcet words whose import was not sweet: If Walt goes, we quit and the operation ends. Boyle stayed.

Fox started working with Morris and Eva after being appointed Boyle's supervisor in 1971. He incidentally mentioned that his unexplainable absences at night or on weekends caused his wife to fear that he was seeing another woman. Eva's blue eyes smiled at him. "Why don't you introduce her to the other woman?" Morris and Eva became like relatives of the Fox family, and the children called them "Aunt Eva" and "Uncle Morris." Eva in turn called Fox, who was part Sioux Indian, "my favorite Baptist Indian." Although his ascent into the leadership of the FBI later separated him from the operation, he remained their friend and patron throughout his FBI career.

Eva asked if another team member, retired FBI Agent John Langtry, was coming to the funeral. Langtry had long worked with Jack in New York; he had assisted Morris and Eva whenever they were there, and she very much liked him. Fox explained that Langtry was unable to travel because he was recuperating from major surgery.

"Well, we can't afford to lose John," Eva said. "Now they're only five of us left. We were a very little team. But we pulled off quite a caper, didn't we?"

Some fifty relatives of Morris and Eva gathered in the chapel for the private service. Midway through the ritual, the rabbi paused and announced that Mr. James Fox, assistant director of the FBI, would speak. At mention of the FBI, some in the congregation gasped audibly; Boyle saw one woman, apparently unable to close her mouth, clasp her hand over it; another stared incredulously at Eva.

Fox, tall and dignified with gray hair, looked like a handsome, urbane diplomat as he stood behind the podium. "My name is Jim Fox. I am a friend of Morris Childs." More gasps. *Morris and Eva, friends of the FBI!*

> Most of you here today probably think you knew Morris Childs. I can tell you with certainty that outside the FBI no one here today knows of the enormous contributions Morris Childs made to the security of the United States.
>
> I am not at liberty to detail exactly what Morris accomplished over the years. I can assure you that his accomplishments were staggering. And I can say that whenever I hear people talking about a sensational James Bond movie or something from *Mission Impossible*, I think, "I know a better story, the story of Morris Childs."
>
> Morris was as kind and gentle as any man I have ever known. Yet for all his gentleness, leaders of both the free world and communist world repeatedly sought his advice.
>
> Once we told a very high White House official [Henry Kissinger, then national security advisor to the president] that we had reviewed the operation and decided to discontinue it for security reasons. This official replied that while he respected our judgment, he *had* to have the information Morris provided and that the operation *would* continue.
>
> I recall two occasions on which Morris perhaps sensed something of the enormity and importance of his achievements.
>
> On February 29, 1988, at our headquarters in Washington, Director William Sessions, in the presence of

Eva, presented Morris with the highest award the United States government can give a civilian. Morris, in failing health, struggled to his feet and for five or six minutes brilliantly told of what it means to serve freedom and the future of our children.

In late 1989, I stayed away from the office to work at home and by chance turned on the early CNN news showing the collapse of the Berlin Wall and communism in Eastern Europe. I put work aside and throughout the day watched history unfold before my eyes. That night I telephoned Morris and simultaneously we said the same thing, "Did you watch television today?" Together we marveled at the convulsions revolutionizing the communist world.

At Christmas, I received a card from Morris. With an unsteady hand, he wrote: "Our dreams of half a century are coming true in life—it is difficult to understand the speed and reality. We are glad we gave it a push."

Well, Jim Fox didn't give it much of a push. Morris and Eva Childs surely did. Few Americans have given our nation what they have given.

After the service, Fox and Boyle adjourned to a venerable Italian restaurant, settled into a booth, and over double martinis began reminiscing much like two generals reviewing an epic wartime campaign. Their conversation was disjointed, rambling from topic to topic. But in the anecdotes traded, they tried in one way or another to answer a basic question: How could we accomplish something so improbable for so long?

Of course, Morris himself was a large part of the answer. Boyle told a story about Morris, Angela Davis, and ten thousand dollars, a story whose climax he never reported to headquarters.

It began in 1970 during the trial of three convicts charged with murdering a guard at Soledad Prison in California. Someone smuggled weapons into the courtroom and a barrage of gunfire killed the presiding judge and three others. The FBI initiated a nationwide hunt for Angela Davis, a young communist and college instructor accused of plotting to slip the weapons into court. The search continued for nearly two months until Morris learned from a party official exactly where Davis was hiding in New York.

The FBI immediately arrested her and to protect Morris planted rumors attributing the capture to the acumen of field investigators and their supervisors. Headquarters felt guilty about crediting others for what Morris had done and proposed to compensate him with a cash bonus. To the Chicago office, it said: "Name any amount; we'll pay it." Boyle protested that Morris was not working for money and would resent being treated like a mercenary informant; he would most appreciate a brief letter from Director J. Edgar Hoover. Headquarters was adamant. By locating Angela Davis, Morris had saved the government millions of dollars that a continuing search would have cost, and he deserved a reward.[‡]

The Chicago SAC (special agent-in-charge), Boyle, Morris, and Eva sat around a big desk in the back room of the cover office the FBI maintained for the operation. After congratulatory remarks, the SAC started laying $100 bills, one by one, on the desk. Morris glowered at Boyle, elbowed the cash away, and inched his chair to the right, further distancing himself from the money. Barely speaking, he joined Boyle in escorting the SAC through the suite to the door. When they returned to the back room, the money, $10,000 in all, was gone; Eva had pocketed it.

Boyle and his wife had adopted six children, two of them black, through Catholic Charities of Chicago, and Morris knew that Boyle actively supported the charity. The next time Boyle came to the cover office, he saw on the desk in the back room an envelope addressed to him. Inside, he found a cashier's check payable to Catholic Charities of Chicago in the amount of $10,000.

The so-called CIA deal said still more about Morris' disdain for money and his motivation. While the FBI kept the CIA ignorant of the source, it necessarily shared some of the intelligence Morris

---

[†] A jury acquitted Davis of the charges against her. Testimony from Morris might have interested a jury. However, Morris could not testify nor could information he provided be introduced as evidence.

provided, blandly prefacing reports with the phrase, "A source who has provided reliable information in the past advised..." However, CIA evaluation and subsequent verification of the often spectacular reports made clear that they emanated from someone with extraordinary access to communist rulers or maybe even a ruler himself.

Ultimately, the CIA tried to buy the operation, or buy into it, without knowing exactly what it was buying. It offered the FBI *any* amount—"there is no limit"—in return for "some control" of the operation and promised to pay the principal source an annual, tax-free salary of $250,000 for starters.

The FBI had no intention of selling "the family jewels," as Boyle put it, but it felt obliged to relay the offer to Morris. The FBI paid him a small salary and he spent much of it on operational expenses. To earn a quarter of a million a year, he had only to keep on doing what he long had done.

It took Morris about thirty seconds to categorically and emphatically reject the offer. His loyalty resided with the FBI. "You have got to get people who devote themselves to this work because they believe in the Bureau and our country; not because they want money."

This idealism impelled Morris to jeopardize his health, risk his life, and submit to all sorts of indignities. Although he and Eva were people of means, they themselves had to scrub the floors and toilets of their apartment because Morris judged it unsafe to admit a maid or any outsider into the apartment. Once when Morris, sick and exhausted, reported to Gus Hall upon returning from Moscow, Hall dragged him to his Long Island home and put him to work digging in the garden. His small body was weak and frail; his will was not.

A waitress interrupted Fox and Boyle to inquire if they wanted to order lunch. Again, they instead ordered more martinis and continued their reminiscences.‡

---

‡ Later recapitulating their conversation, Fox said, "We were not drinking to get drunk. We kept delaying lunch because we did not want the moment to end. We doubted it ever would come again."

When Boyle first learned that Gus Hall referred to Morris as his "secretary of state," he thought it was some kind of joke. Morris assured him that Hall was quite serious. "To you, it sounds ridiculous. But if you think like they think, the title is quite logical. And you've got to learn to think like they think." Much of Morris' genius as a spy derived from a remarkable ability to think just as the Soviets thought and thereby exploit their delusions and myopia. For years he adroitly exploited Soviet delusions about the American Communist Party.

According to Soviet interpretation of Marx and Lenin, the laws of history ordained that the American party ultimately would be the ruling party of the United States. Hence, to the Soviets the party represented the bona fide government of the United States, "temporarily out of power" but predestined eventually to assume its rightful rule. These premises were fantasies, yet if the Soviets repudiated the dogma that spawned them, if they admitted that Marx and Lenin were fallible, then how could they justify continuation of their power? Because they clung to foolish dogma, they behaved foolishly by treating "that ignoramus" Gus as president and Morris as secretary of state, "temporarily out of power."

Morris understood that the Soviets also valued and sustained the American party because they vastly overestimated its influence, erroneously believing that in the 1960s and 1970s it could duplicate its successes of the 1930s. Because the party ardently supported the antiwar movement, the Soviets judged that the party was the primary instigator and manipulator of the movement. It was the same with any other movement or demonstration; if the party and noncommunists happened to agree on an issue and made common cause, in Moscow the party received the credit. Neither Hall nor Morris ever said to anyone in Moscow, "Yes, we were involved but our role was relatively minor." And the men in Moscow responsible for directing the party had every incentive to exaggerate its importance and the results of their labors.

Comprehending the Soviet view of him and the American party, Morris acted out the role of the secretary of state or foreign minister of a Soviet satellite nation. As such, he regularly dealt with Soviet rulers and addressed most of them by their first name.

Fox and Boyle agreed that even Morris probably could not have accomplished what he did had it not been for unorthodox actions by the FBI.

They never knew the identity of the executive responsible but someone at headquarters cast the basic mold of the operation well before they joined it.

Morris returned from Moscow and Peking in 1958 with stunning intelligence imparted to him by Nikita Khrushchev, Mao Tse Tung, and Chou En Lai, and the FBI recognized that the operation now had unprecedented potential. Thus far, the Chicago and New York field offices had made and executed all the operational decisions without seeking approval or advice from headquarters. A question arose in Washington. Given the suddenly apparent potential of the operation, shouldn't headquarters assume direct control of it?

According to FBI lore, the winning argument ran as follows: New York and Chicago created this operation. Chicago saw where it might go when none of us here dreamed it could go as high as it is going. New York and Chicago have brought us this far; they obviously know what they're doing; they have done everything right. Why should we substitute our judgment for theirs? If you have players who are scoring touchdowns, you keep giving the ball to them; you don't take it away from them. Let Chicago and New York run wild. We can always rein them in if necessary.

The decision not to change winning strategy and tactics had many enduring consequences. The FBI allowed New York Agent Alexander C. Burlinson to stay in the operation for twenty-four years. The FBI kept Walter Boyle in it for twenty years, John Langtry for fourteen years, and Carl Freyman for thirteen years. Never, before or since, has the FBI kept agents on the same case for so long.

The Chicago and New York offices as a result accrued a unique body of experience and expertise, and thus a capacity intuitively to make fine judgments and discern what was most significant. Boyle came to know more about Boris Ponomarev and Mikhail Suslov, two of the dominant Soviets with whom Morris most often dealt, than most people in Moscow; together with Morris, he could glean intelligence from their facial expressions. Langtry in New York came to know everything about the KGB officers who worked with Jack Childs, including which pasta their wives preferred.

Experience taught Morris and Jack they could count on their longtime FBI partners, with whom they could speak in "shorthand." And a uniting spirit grew among what Eva called "our little American team." Sometimes people on the periphery of the operation at headquarters accused Boyle and Langtry of "being too close to their assets." The few people who really knew, who were recipients of the hurrahs from the White House, CIA, and State and Defense Departments, did not care how close they were.

Until the last years when events beyond the control of the field offices created dangers with which only headquarters could cope, headquarters granted Chicago and New York the broadest of liberties, allowing them to do what Americans do best—adapt, invent, innovate, imagine. If Boyle wanted to recruit a physician who would take cryptic calls from Morris overseas at all hours, a pharmacist who would supply false labels on prescription medicine for Morris, a travel agent who would issue multiple airline tickets under fictitious names, he just did it. As Fox said over the fourth martini, "We always followed the rules. Of course, when we saw the rules weren't working, we made up new ones."

There evolved in Washington a mental set which held that the responsibility of headquarters was to *support* the men actually running the operation rather than tell them what to do. Consequently, headquarters and the special agents-in-charge of the Chicago and New York offices made available all that was needed—cover offices, special offices within the field offices, special stenographers, photographers, cipher and communications personnel, surveillants, money, and autonomy. Until nearly the end, headquarters let Chicago and New York "run wild" against the Soviet Union.

Also until nearly the end, headquarters kept the faith and the secret. It induced powerful men with powerful egos to undergo an implicitly humiliating ritual: You may read this report right now in my presence. You may not retain or copy the report. I must take it back to a special safe at headquarters. The few who knew never told their best colleagues—and this went on for almost thirty years.

When congressional meddling threatened to expose the operation, FBI Director Clarence Kelley and Assistant Director Raymond Wannall gambled as wildly as had Morris, Jack, Eva, and all the men in the field. Wannall told Senator Frank Church, chairman of a Senate committee investigating the FBI, that he was about to destroy the most important espionage operation the United States ever had sustained against the Soviet Union and that he was about to kill the most valuable American spy.

Visibly shocked, Senator Church asked, "Can you explain?"‡

"I can show you." Wannall thereupon displayed a photograph (see photo section) of Morris seated with Brezhnev and Politburo members in the Kremlin. He identified each Soviet in the photograph and explained how each helped rule the Soviet empire. He pointed to the image of Morris. "This is our man, the man you are about to kill." Wannall, with the concurrence of Director Kelly— but without that of Morris, Jack, Boyle, or Langtry—then outlined the history of Operation SOLO.

Church sank into his chair. "You have put a terrible burden on me."

Wannall said, "Yes. We are betting everything on your honor and patriotism."

Church thought for a while, then said, "I only wish the American people could know. This certainly would open their eyes. It has opened mine." Church pledged to keep Operation SOLO secret, and he kept his word.

Unbidden, the waitress brought a feast: antipasto, steaming pasta, *brusca* bread, and a bottle of superb red wine the proprietor reserved for real friends, such as FBI agents.

---

‡ Author's Note: Many former American intelligence officers, CIA and FBI, among them some of my best friends, to this day cannot speak of the late Senator Church except with contempt. They condemn him as a left-wing ideologue who, in their opinion, irreparably damaged American intelligence for partisan political purposes. His actions pertaining to SOLO speak for themselves.

Fox asked the waitress, "Who ordered this?"

"The gentlemen in the corner."

When Fox and Boyle had stepped out of the funeral home, two young FBI agents had greeted them, invited them to lunch, and offered to drive them to the airport or do anything else for them. One, the custodian of the Chicago SOLO files, looked them both in the eyes and said, "I know something about what you did. I am very proud to meet you."

Assistant FBI Director James Fox, Eva's "favorite Baptist Indian," had accomplished a lot but he had never learned how to lie and he didn't even try. "Thanks for coming out. I'll thank the SAC for sending you. Right now I just want to talk alone with Walt Boyle."

But the two agents followed.

"Our baby-sitters," Fox said.

"Our tribunes," Boyle said.

They buried Morris Childs, Agent 58, on June 5, 1991. On December 22, 1991, with the signing of the treaty of Alma Ata, the Soviet Union disintegrated itself, and Fox called Eva.

At first, Eva could not comprehend. "It doesn't exist anymore," Fox explained. "It's broken into pieces."

"Then, Jim, that means we have won."

"Yes, Eva, we have won."

two

MOSCOW'S MAN

MANY OF THE MOST FAMOUS figures of international communism personally knew Morris Childs and addressed him as "Morris."‡ To them, his credentials as a consecrated Bolshevik were impeccable, classical, ideal. His heritage and background show why they so thought, why they trusted him, and why he could do what he did.

Morris, whose original name was Moishe Chilovsky, was born June 10, 1902, outside Kiev, the first son of Josef and Nechame Chilovsky. As a child, he sometimes heard his mother call out,

---

‡ Among them were Nikita Khrushchev, Leonid Brezhnev, and Yuri Andropov, rulers of the Soviet Union; Mikhail Suslov, head of the Ideological Department of the Soviet Central Committee; Boris Ponomarev, head of the International Department of the Soviet Central Committee; Otto Kuusinen, a theorist and early member of the Communist International (Comintern); Mao Tse Tung and Chou En Lai, rulers of China; Ho Chi Minh, ruler of Vietnam; Walter Ulbricht and Erich Honecker, rulers of East Germany; Josip Tito, ruler of Yugoslavia; Fidel Castro, ruler of Cuba; and Palmiro Togliatti, head of the Italian Communist Party.

"Father, I see brass buttons." The brass buttons appeared on the uniforms of czarist police who came in the night to beat Jews. Morris and his younger brother Jack (aka Jakob) would run out the back door while their father and mother took blows from police truncheons in the hope that the police would not look for the children.

Josef Chilovsky reacted to the pogroms and other oppressions by engaging in sedition against the Russian czar, and one night Morris watched police drag his father off to prison and subsequent exile in Siberia. At age twenty-eight, Josef fled across Russia to the Black Sea and slipped aboard a freighter that, on March 15, 1910, landed him at Galveston, Texas. Josef made his way to New Orleans, then up the Mississippi River, and finally to Chicago, where he melded into the large community of east European emigrés.

Josef was an expert cobbler able to fashion leather into fine boots, and in less than two years he saved enough money to send for his wife and sons. They arrived on Ellis Island in New York December 11, 1911, and embarked by train for Chicago. Their coach was unheated, its wooden seats hard, and on the third day of the journey the mother told the boys they had no more money for food. A woman seated across the aisle overheard and said to them in Russian, "I have much food." From a basket, she gave them bread and sausages, and during the remainder of the trip other passengers shared food with them.

Parents and teachers at a demanding Jewish school constantly impressed upon Morris the importance of work and "self-elevation." Though at age fourteen he went to work as an apprentice in his father's small shop and as a messenger in the Chicago financial district, he continued to study. He read Russian classics, philosophy, and American history; took courses at the Chicago Institute of Art; and on Sundays attended free lectures delivered at the Hull House by notable speakers such as Clarence Darrow. He also explored the architecture and landmarks of Chicago, including the stockyards that promptly turned him to vegetarianism.

At the art institute, Morris fell under the influence of radical students who, despite their incoherence, disposed him toward radicalism. He and his father avidly followed reports of the Russian Revolution, and the more he learned of communism, the more its promises to humanity enthralled him. To obtain a job driving a horse-drawn milk wagon, he joined a union peopled with a few young communists and began to agitate with them. When various factions coalesced to form the United Communist Party of America, he formally joined at age nineteen and was considered a charter member.

Whatever the party asked, Morris did. He proselytized so energetically among union members and customers that they called him "the Red Milkman." Twice police arrested him during street demonstrations, and once they pummeled him with banana stalks. Now and then he questioned party tactics. Roused in the dead of night to stuff leaflets into residential mailboxes, he asked, "Why do we have to distribute these damn things at 2 A.M.? People might take us for burglars and shoot us."

He was told, "Because, this is the way the Bolsheviks did it." At the time, such an answer sufficed to silence any doubter.

The milk company paid deliverymen according to the number of customers served, and by adding new clients to his route, Morris earned relatively high pay. The births of two more brothers, Benjamin and Phillip, overcrowded the family house, and now that he could afford to do so he moved into a nearby apartment of his own. It became a kind of party social center and hostel for itinerant comrades who soon learned that he usually was good for a loan of a few dollars and he did not dun for repayment. Sharing was the essence of the communism he then understood.

Morris in the mid-1920s caught the attention of an important party functionary, Earl Russell Browder, who probably affected Morris' life more than any other man except Carl Freyman. A radical from Kansas who wore his prison term as a badge of honor, Browder served as the primary American agent of the Communist International (Comintern) established by the Soviets to control foreign communist parties. His wife, a Russian, still lived in Moscow; in the factional fights rending international communism, he ardently supported Josef Stalin; and the Soviets trusted him totally. Perhaps seeing in Morris something of his younger self, Browder favored him with enduring patronage and friendship.

The Comintern dispatched Browder to China on what amounted to espionage assignments. Other American party members who were sent had failed to return, and so before leaving Browder entrusted prized books and memorabilia to Morris. "If I don't come back, they're yours." On his return, Browder's accounts of adventures in China fascinated and excited Morris. He told of visiting a park in the former British extraterritorial zone near Shanghai and seeing signs that said "No Dogs Or Chinese." Browder told Morris that the Chinese liked Americans in part because the United States never exercised treaty rights to extraterritorial privileges and also because of the good works of missionaries.

Under the sway of Browder, Morris aligned himself with the Stalinists and against American party leader Jay Lovestone, who had made the mistake of propounding a thesis some dubbed "American Exceptionalism." It argued that because capitalism was flourishing in America, capitalism's demise would occur later than in European nations and consequently party tactics in the United States and Europe might have to differ. Lovestone compounded his mistake by traveling to Moscow to gain formal Soviet approval of his thesis, which Stalin regarded as rankest heresy.

Browder told Morris that Stalin ordered Lovestone detained in Moscow, but Trotskyites alerted him and with the connivance of foreign diplomats Lovestone escaped and was en route to the United States. At Browder's instructions, Morris led a group of Stalinists who physically seized national party headquarters in Chicago and stood guard to prevent Lovestone and his followers from reoccupying the building. After the party moved its headquarters to New York, the Comintern expelled Lovestone from the party and anointed Browder as the new leader of American communism.

Meanwhile, Morris helped unmask an industrial spy in Chicago, a private detective infiltrated into the party by a utility company, which blamed communists for strikes bedeviling it. Some comrade beat up the detective, who turned to police friends for revenge and apparently named Morris as one of those responsible for his undoing. Warned that the police were hunting Morris, the party hid him in a safe house and arranged to spirit him away to Moscow. At age twenty-six, Morris took all this melodrama seriously when, viewed only in the light of circumstances in Chicago, it was silly. Morris had committed no crime, and the police, upon questioning the oaf who hit the detective, released him. Real gangsters interested them more. Years later, Browder explained the theatrics. He deliberately exaggerated the gravity of the incident and the danger to Morris so the Soviets would grant his protégé sanctuary at the Lenin School, which trained future leaders of worldwide revolution.

The party equipped Morris with a false passport and identity papers, a ticket aboard the *Ile de France*, two hundred U.S. dollars, some French francs, and a new overcoat. Sewn on the lining was a small red patch that would tell any Comintern representative that he was bound for the Lenin School. He crossed Europe by train and reached Moscow in January 1929. A carriage mounted on a sled took him through caverns of snow to the school housed in the former palace of a Russian nobleman.

There he joined men drawn from all continents and from similar backgrounds. All were under thirty-five, came from the working class, had been a charter member of their national party or worked in it for five years without making a recorded mistake, and enjoyed the personal endorsement of their national party leader. The most illustrious communist theoreticians and politicians came from the Soviet Union and abroad to lecture or tutor them. In fact, in those days if you had not been invited to speak at the school, you probably had yet to make a mark in international communism. The standard course lasted two years, with summers given over to "practical studies" in factories or the countryside. Exceptional students were invited to remain a third year for specialized study under the direction of individual tutors.

Morris surrendered his passport, which indicated he had been born in Detroit, to the school administrator and in return received a card identifying him as Harry Summers, an auto worker from Detroit. Evidently not realizing that the passport was bogus, the school recorded his place of birth as U.S.A. After passing a physical examination, he underwent extensive oral and written examinations that enabled the Soviets to assess him politically and personally as well as gauge his general knowledge. Shortly thereafter, the administrator informed Morris that he would bypass the first year of the course and advance directly to the second, then spend another year in tutorials.

In addition to theoretical and political subjects, he studied the violent and clandestine techniques of making a revolution: rural and urban guerrilla warfare; sabotage; robbery; use of firearms; secret communications; and underground operations including maintenance of safe houses, courier and escape routes, and caches of money and explosives. He learned how to drive a train and blow up a train, how to ride a horse and wield a sword, and how to frustrate police by sticking hairpins into their horses. Sometimes he inwardly laughed at visions of himself, all five feet three inches of him, confronting mounted Irish cops back in Chicago with a sword and hairpins.

Except for the Chinese, who were consigned to segregated sleeping quarters, the students lived together in dormitories and dined at a cafeteria inside the palace where classes were conducted and there was little need to go outside into the cold. When they did venture out on the streets in springtime, Morris saw swarms of gaunt men with outstretched hands begging for bread or a few kopecks. Upon learning that they were former czarist officers or Orthodox priests who were prohibited from working, denied ration cards, and forbidden to enroll their children in school, he thought, *My God! What kind of society are we building?* An indefinable instinct caused him on the spot to make a decision which decades later would greatly benefit him and the United States.

He found that he still could understand Russian, which his family had spoken before emigrating, and his comprehension was rapidly increasing. He was able to keep this a secret because he did not have to use it at school; lectures simultaneously were translated into multiple languages and transmitted to students through earphones, so no one knew. Now he resolved never to let the Soviets know that he understood their language very well, just as he had decided not to let anyone know that he had studied art and music, lest he be considered an intellectual.

While a blizzard raged through Moscow in early 1930, an instructor at the end of the day's classes told Morris that there was a message for him in the administration office. The regular staff had left, and a lone, middle-aged man greeted him in passable English. The stranger, who smoked and coughed incessantly, began to chat amiably without troubling to introduce himself. He was happy to report that Morris' parents and three brothers, to whom he referred by first name, were all well. He also was happy to hear that the faculty rated Morris one of the most able and popular students. That did not surprise him, considering Morris' party record in Chicago. He especially was impressed by Morris' feat in ferreting out a capitalist spy. And he wondered: Had Morris ever considered that the imperialists might try to insinuate spies and "wreckers" into the Soviet Union in the guise of students? Had he considered that in the Lenin School itself there might be disguised Trotskyites or other "deviationists" who could infect students?

Morris acknowledged all possibilities.

Well, then, would Morris welcome an opportunity to help detect such subversives?

Momentarily, the question puzzled Morris because it connoted a request rather than an order. If the party wanted him to do something, it had only to tell him what to do. The maxim most drilled into him in Chicago and Moscow was obedience. The doctrine of "Democratic Centralism" in theory allowed free debate within party councils. But once the debate ended in the promulgation of a particular policy or order, the doctrine demanded absolute, unquestioning obedience from all. An instructor put it thus: "If the party says you're going to China, you'll be on the next train or boat to China. If the party tells you to climb a flagpole at midnight and hoist a banner saying 'Power to the Peasants,' you'll scrape your balls climbing that flagpole at midnight. If the party tells you to quit and go underground, at that instant you're underground."

Then Morris realized that it was not the party but the OGPU, the secret political police, that was importuning him to become an informant. The OGPU might be able to bribe, blackmail, or otherwise coerce almost any Soviet citizen into doing almost anything. As an American whose goodwill the Soviets coveted, Morris needed to be courted. The distinction did not matter to him. He was honored to serve communism by any means desired. Soon he was appointed a class secretary, a position that required visits to the administrative office where people could talk securely.

The OGPU encouraged him to make friends, and he made many. For administrative purposes, students were grouped into sections. Morris' included future party leaders from around the globe: two Chinese destined for senior positions in their party; two Mexicans; a Hindu; and an Australian. He got along well with them all, particularly the Chinese with whom he sympathized because they generally were shunned outside class. His best friend was a wiry little man who had immigrated from the Soviet Union to Canada and had anglicized his name to Sam Carr. A gifted orator and leader, Carr spoke six languages and could mesmerize equally well in English or Russian. Morris suspected that he also collaborated with the OGPU; regardless, they formed a significant friendship that lasted until Carr's death decades later.

During his second year, Morris also formed personal relationships with instructors who tutored him in more advanced subjects: manipulating unions and popular movements by creating secret communist cells or "nuclei" within them, establishing front organizations, exploiting temporary alliances of expediency with noncommunists, and inciting violence to provoke official repression. Kuusinen and Suslov were his closest mentors. Comintern member Kuusinen was a main architect of Soviet subversive methodology. His protégé, Andropov, ascended to the Central Committee of the party, ran the KGB for fifteen years, and ultimately ruled the whole Soviet Union. Suslov emerged as the premier party ideologue and long headed the Ideology Department. Suslov felt a special tie to his pupil. After arcane intrigues cast Suslov into disfavor and Stalin took away his ration card, Morris daily smuggled food to him from the school cafeteria. Suslov was a pariah for only a few weeks and doubtless could have survived with sustenance from others. Nevertheless, for the rest of his life, Suslov remained a benefactor of Morris.

Such was his worth that, even before Morris finished school, patrons in Moscow interceded to save his life. While he engaged in "practical" work in Stalingrad, a typhoid epidemic ravaged the city and thousands perished. One night as icy winds howled across the steppes, he collapsed in the snow outside his apartment. His housekeeper discovered him, notified the local party office, and got him to a hospital. When he regained consciousness, he lay on the filthy floor of a hospital corridor surrounded by dying men, women, and children; all beds were occupied and, besides, physicians gave him slight chance of living. During the next days, he drifted in and out of delirium until suddenly he felt himself being lifted from the floor and placed in a bed. Henceforth, a physician or nurse attended him almost continuously and administered medicine shipped from Moscow. After about a month, he walked out of the hospital, one of the few afflicted Americans to survive. He returned to Moscow regally in a private railway coach, staffed by a doctor, nurse, cook, and maid, all provided by the Comintern solely for him.

Clearly, by the time Morris departed for the United States in 1932 the Comintern regarded him as an important man—Moscow's man or, as the Russians would have put it, "nahsh," "ours."

While Morris was in the Soviet Union, his brother Jack at age twenty-four moved to New York to be with a paramour, and Browder, now ensconced in the new party headquarters, appointed Jack business manager of the Young Communist League. His primary job was to squeeze dues from members, and he performed well, probably because he received a percentage of all he collected. In 1932 Browder proposed that Jack go to Moscow for training in communications and underground tradecraft. The Comintern until recently had relied upon the German party to supply couriers and radiomen for communications within the international movement. As Nazis hounded German communists, it shifted responsibility to the U.S. party, believing that Americans were technically proficient and that the bearer of a U.S. passport could travel anywhere.

Morris had looked upon his journey to Moscow as a pilgrimage. Jack envisioned an adventure, a lark, a yearlong tryst with his lover paid for by somebody else. He consented to go provided that the Soviets allow him to bring his girlfriend and live with her.

Browder instructed him to procure a false passport because a valid one would show that he had been born in the Soviet Union and that might cause problems during passage through Germany.

"How do I do that?" he asked.

"You figure it out," Browder commanded.

Jack relished the challenge of fraud. Adopting the name John William Fox, he signed an affidavit averring that he was born in Gallaway, West Virginia, and mailed it to the town clerk there along with a request for a copy of his birth certificate. Unable to locate it, the clerk assumed that someone in the little town had misplaced the original and obligingly issued a new one. The State Department efficiently processed his application, and soon he had a passport in the name of John William Fox.

The Comintern put Jack and his girlfriend in a new hotel by the Moscow River, a short walk from the three-story stone mansion where field operatives, or "street men," trained. He studied theory and operation of radio, how to build a shortwave receiver, Morse code, invisible writing, disguises, the use of drops or hiding places for the exchange of messages, countersurveillance, security procedures, and methods by which Lenin eluded authorities before the revolution.

Unlike Morris, Jack was not an outstanding pupil but he did well enough for the Soviets to entrust him with a real mission. A Comintern official explained that the communist underground in Germany acutely needed money and that an American would have the best chance of delivering it. Would Jack be willing to try?

Jack somberly replied that hazardous as the job might be, he was willing to fulfill his party duty; actually he was eager for an escapade in Germany.

Wearing a money belt packed with U.S. dollars in large denominations, he traveled first class by train through Warsaw and Danzig to Berlin. In cafés and cabarets, galleries and museums, he acted as a young American tourist bent upon nothing except a good time. He lazily reconnoitered the rendezvous site, and the next evening during an encounter at a subway station passed the money to a German comrade who quickly disappeared into the night. To act out his cover, he lingered two more days enjoying German cuisine, wine, and old Berlin.

The Comintern congratulated him enthusiastically, and toward the end of his studies asked him to repeat the mission.

Jack registered at a middle-class Berlin hotel as John William Fox, 845 West 180th Street, New York, New York, U.S.A., and again stated that the purpose of his sojourn was pleasure. Again, he undertook to be the typical tourist with a little too much money. Dining in a restaurant off *Unter den Linden*, Jack kept stealing glances at a spectacularly configured blond seated at a nearby table with an older man. As he started to pay his bill, the man came to his table and politely introduced himself in English. He had overheard Jack speaking English to the waiter and guessed that he was an American. After Jack nodded, the German claimed to have relatives in St. Louis, professed admiration for the United States, and said that he and his wife liked to practice their English. Would Jack kindly join them for brandy and coffee?

The last time in Berlin Jack concluded that Germans tended to be formal and reserved with strangers. His new acquaintances seemed to be genuinely friendly and interested in him and the United States. The conversation turned out to be so convivial that they drank several brandies and agreed to meet for dinner two nights hence at a café near his hotel.

To Jack's delight, the wife undulated into the café alone and apologized that because unexpected difficulties had delayed her husband's return from a business trip, he would not be back until tomorrow. During dinner, she smiled often and impishly; her large, hazel eyes gazed at his frankly; and twice her leg brushed against his. Afterward he suggested they have champagne in his room, where they happily shared amorous hours.

The next day, after having handed over a package of dollars in another fleeting encounter in a subway station, Jack leaned back in a richly upholstered compartment of the train to Danzig. He was congratulating himself on his success and conquest when the door to the compartment slid open. There stood the cuckolded husband; his executioner, Jack thought.

The cheerfulness of the husband's greetings, however, kindled a little hope; maybe he didn't know after all. He did not mention his wife; instead he orated about the menace the bloody Bolshevik barbarians posed to civilization. In the end, he revealed himself to be a German intelligence officer who wanted to recruit Jack because his American passport would admit him to Russia.

Jack assured the officer that the offer flattered him. The Bolsheviks indeed were bastards. But as he had said the other night, he was about to begin a new job in New York crucial to his career and at least for a couple of years it would debar him from traveling abroad. Could he have a card or telephone number in case his circumstances changed? And by the way, "Thanks for the other night, and give my regards to your beautiful wife."

These exploits endowed Jack with a reputation of his own in the Comintern. Not only had he accomplished two hazardous missions into Nazi territory; he had parried the overtures of a professional intelligence officer while seducing his wife. Here was a young man with balls and a future; a man who could be counted upon and trusted; a worthy brother of Morris. When Jack got back to New York, Browder hired him at headquarters as his personal factotum, chauffeur, and bodyguard.

Morris meanwhile married a party member from a Ukrainian family and became the chief organizer in Wisconsin. At the Moscow school an instructor quoted Lenin as saying, "A good communist must have the ideas of a Bolshevik and the energy of an American." In Milwaukee, Morris displayed both by recruiting union members and intellectuals, addressing political rallies, leading street demonstrations, and running for mayor. The campaign netted him relatively few votes and several beatings, and he lamented, "Sometimes, I think it's not easy being an agitator."

He accepted the beatings, however, as a natural adjunct of his job. It never occurred to him that the popular hostility they manifested sprang from any deficiency in his political philosophy. He simply needed to master better means of delivering the liberating message to the masses. So he studied Coca-Cola advertising in quest of techniques that might be adapted to selling communism. He stood on street corners trying to analyze how Salvation Army missionaries effectively appealed to the downtrodden and derelict. He himself was so affected by their good intentions that sometimes he dropped a coin or two into their kettles. He really could not afford to give away any money. The party paid him twelve dollars a week, and though his wife earned a few more as a seamstress, they lived on the brink of destitution.

Visiting Milwaukee, Browder went home with Morris just as an ambulance drove from the house, and neighbors told Morris that his wife had given birth to a son. Browder asked, "How much money do you have?"

"I don't even have enough for a phone call."

"Well, I can give you enough for a call." From his watch pocket, Browder withdrew a tightly folded $50 bill and pressed it into Morris' hand.

By the mid-1930s, the Soviets concluded that Morris' talents were not being sufficiently utilized in Milwaukee. To them, Chicago was the most important city in America, the "heart of the beast," the "greatest concentration area"—that is, the largest center of heavy industry whose exploited workers in theory could most easily be mobilized for revolution. Through Comintern agent Gerhardt Eisler, they ordered the American party to put Morris in charge of Chicago and on the governing Central Committee. The appointments, added to his bond with Browder, made him one of the most influential American communists, exactly what the Kremlin intended.

Chicago also was the hub of an underground communist railway stretching from Wall Street to Hollywood, and Morris lodged many comrades on the run in safe houses. In a cryptic call from Canada, Sam Carr said that "a good friend" would be visiting Chicago and he hoped Morris would help him "rest." The fugitive who arrived was Tim Buck, a Comintern agent and head of the Canadian party. Morris subsequently gave him refuge several more times, and the two became intimate friends. Upon their friendship the FBI operation later turned.

Despite his party status, Morris still lived humbly, and when summoned to New York he had to hitchhike. Hobos introduced him to their own kind of communism by teaching him how to loiter in small towns and get himself jailed for vagrancy. Jails provided supper, a warm bed, and breakfast before release in the morning. Most of his clothes were castoffs donated by more affluent comrades who took turns treating him and his wife to Sunday dinner. The party finally did buy an old Model-T Ford for his official use but he had to pay for gas and maintenance.

Within the party, Morris was known as a "straitlaced, out-and-out Bolshevik." In public appearances, writings, and conversation with noncommunists, he seemed to many to be an urbane and reasonable idealist. He reviled the isolationist *Chicago Tribune*, yet he could argue amicably with journalists from that and other newspapers because he listened respectfully and never disparaged anyone personally. With perhaps more sincerity than he realized, he represented himself as a patriotic American actuated by the ideals of Thomas Jefferson, Abraham Lincoln, and Franklin Roosevelt, whose names he frequently invoked. He tried to depict communism as a democratic, mainstream political movement and the Soviet Union as a redoubtable foe of fascism. Typically, in recruiting three hundred men to fight alongside communists in the Spanish Civil War, he appealed for volunteers to fight against fascism rather than for communism. Still, in the underlying import of all he said, he never deviated from the prevailing Soviet position on any substantive issue.

The Comintern duly noted his fidelity and abilities in a dossier kept in Moscow. An example of its contents has been provided by Emory University Professor Harvey Klehr, an eminent authority on American communism. Allowed by the new Russian government to examine old Comintern files, Professor Klehr found and generously made available to the author the following report:

> File: 495–74
> SECRET
> 3 copies m.k.h.
> 31 January 1938
>
> Report
>
> Childs, Morris—CP USA Central Committee Member. Secretary of the state party organization in Chicago (Illinois).

Born in 1902 in the U.S.A., Jewish. His father was a boot maker. Childs himself is a footwear industry worker by training. He has a primary school education.

He was a member of the CP USA from 1919–1929, and a member of the Soviet Communist Party (Bolsheviks) from 1929–1931. He again became a member of the CP USA, and then a Central Committee member in 1934.

He began working in 1915. From 1929–1931 he studied at the M-L School. He has been a Party functionary since 1932.

Childs was arrested in 1928 and 1929 in Chicago in connection with meetings and demonstrations.

Childs' wife has been a member of the Communist Party since 1919. She works in the sewing industry and has relatives in Kiev who are workers, M. and J. Lerman.

His M-L School evaluations are favorable.

17 January 1938: Comrades Browder, Foster and Ryan give the following evaluation of comrade Childs: "He is politically stable and devoted. He is developing politically, and is a good party and mass organizer, capable of independent leadership."

Source: Material from the personal file.

/Belov/

Not long after this report was written, Browder relayed a Comintern directive instructing Morris to seek election to the United States Senate as the communist candidate from Illinois. Simply by conducting a dignified campaign, he could, at least in the eyes of some, coat the party with a veneer of respectability and insinuate Soviet themes into American political discourse.

Morris ran on a platform advocating "JOBS, SECURITY, DEMOCRACY, and PEACE" and United States intervention against Germany, Italy, and Japan. Echoing Soviet propaganda, his speeches inveighed against the evils and dangers of Nazism. The campaign against the Nazis earned plaudits from the Comintern and Browder, from his Canadian friends Carr and Buck, from rank-and-file party members, and even from some noncommunists.

Less than a year after the campaign ended, the Soviets mortified him by striking a deal with these very same Nazis. They pledged not to interfere with a German invasion of Poland; in return, the Nazis promised them a slice of the country they were about to devour.

Morris called Browder. How do we explain this sudden, perfidious collusion with the Nazis? What do we say? Equally dumbfounded and without instructions from Moscow, Browder had no answer. In public, Morris tried to mute or evade the issue. Privately, he tried, with only partial success, to dismiss it from his thoughts just as he tried to dismiss multiplying rumors of mass terror and murder in the Soviet Union.

The German invasion of the Soviet Union on June 22, 1941, restored his moral equilibrium. Once again the Nazis were bad, and he led cries for American action against them. To Jews who had quit the party in disgust, he offered a new Soviet rationale for the deal with Hitler. Far from being a pact with the devil, it was a brilliant ploy by Stalin to gain time to fortify Soviet defenses.

The German declaration of war on the United States after the Japanese attack on Pearl Harbor December 7, 1941, overnight made the United States and the Soviet Union allies, and transfigured communists throughout the land into seeming patri-ots. Having fomented labor strife for years, Morris now called for a ban on all strikes. They were unpatriotic. Desperate for U.S. arms and supplies, the Soviet Union cared more about increasing American war production than about the lot of American workers.

As a sop to the western allies, Stalin in 1943 ostensibly abol-ished the Comintern, which symbolized Soviet subversion world-wide. In reality, it continued to function as the International Department of the Central Committee, although wartime chaos diminished its ability to function as effectively as before.

Browder, however, thought the dissolution real and construed it as a signal that the Soviets meant what they said about friendship with their ally, the United States. In further wishful thinking, he concluded that the Soviets wanted communists to be a positive, progressive force in American society rather than subversives. Accordingly, he disbanded the American Communist Party as such and re-formed it as the Communist Political Association dedicated to supporting the war effort and political candidates who favored harmonious U.S.–Soviet relations, irrespective of their party affiliation.

The most important such candidate in 1944 was President Franklin D. Roosevelt, who sought reelection to an unheard-of fourth term. Morris organized a huge stadium rally in Chicago, and Morris and Browder spoke in behalf of the president. Morris directed communists infiltrated into the labor movement to exert all their influence to align their unions behind Roosevelt. And he personally appealed to John L. Lewis, president of the United Mine Workers, to put aside his personal hatred of Roosevelt in the interests of the country and labor in general.

Probably more favorable entries were recorded in the secret Moscow dossier on Morris, and anyone reviewing it in 1944 would have seen the profile of the quintessential Bolshevik. A worker himself, Morris was the son of an anti-czarist worker. He loyally and ably had served the American party from its inception and helped deliver control of it to Stalinists. In the Soviet Union, he had passed every test and distinguished himself both as a student and an informant of the secret political police. He had exhibited physical and moral courage. August leaders of international communism could and did vouch for him. Never had he deviated from the party line delineated by the Comintern. Repeatedly, he had proven himself to be in every sense Moscow's man.

Immersed in a righteous cause, able simultaneously to serve the United States and the Soviet Union, Morris in 1944 was a happy man until the wife of his youngest brother, Phillip, received a telegram that began: "The War Department regrets to inform you..." Phillip, an army lieutenant, had been killed in battle in France.

Morris, Jack, and their younger brother, Ben, sank into grief and depression.

three

FORSAKEN AND FOUND

MORRIS SUFFERED A HEART ATTACK in the summer of 1945 and consequently did not learn all the details of the coup until Eugene Dennis came from New York to see him in August.

Dennis also was Moscow's man. A graduate of the Lenin School, he demonstrated his allegiance to the Russians by leaving his small son Timothy in the Soviet Union for them to raise. He succeeded Morris in Milwaukee and the two long had been friends, or so Morris thought.

The account Dennis gave may be summed up thus: Browder, by disbanding the party, had angered the Soviets and forfeited their confidence. They wanted a vigorous, organized American Communist Party back in the business of spreading communism in the United States. At their behest, Dennis and William Z. Foster had engineered the expulsion of Browder and had reconstituted the party. Dennis was now its leader, and his most urgent task was to reconcile factions loyal to Browder with those loyal to Foster, who had become national chairman. He wanted Morris to help by serving as his deputy in New York.

Soon Dennis had another problem. Louis Budenz, editor of the *Daily Worker*, renounced communism and joined the Catholic Church, creating much mirth among anticommunists. Dennis needed someone with prestige, in and out of the party, to replace him as editor. Would Morris take the job? After Dennis dismissed his protests that he had no journalistic experience, Morris, the good soldier, agreed.

The ensuing correspondence evokes something of the atmosphere of the time. Party Treasurer Charles Krumbein on September 18, 1945, wrote Morris:

> Received word from Comrade Fine that the district paid you through September 20. We therefore are placing you on our payroll starting with the above date. We have set wage rates in the National Office that places [sic] you at $60.00 gross per week. From this is deducted $6.60 withholding tax (based upon two dependents, wife and child), 60¢ for social security tax and $5.30 for war bonds, which goes to your credit. On the basis of this and suggestions made to me, I am enclosing a check for $475 for ten weeks' wages which pays you up to December 1.

Dennis on October 5 wrote:

> We have been anxiously waiting to hear from you regarding the doctor's verdict. If you don't mind, I wish you would drop me a note and let me know what is what on the state of your health. Furthermore, I wish you would give us a tentative idea as to when you will be able to take up your new work.

However, some of the party leadership virulently opposed the appointment of Morris on grounds that he was a "Browderite."

Dennis on December 17, 1945, sent word that his opponents had been routed:

> We reached agreement on the following proposals which have been submitted to the DW [*Daily Worker*] staff and confirmed by an overwhelming consultative vote. Childs—Editor; Milton Howard—Associate Editor; Alan Max—Managing Editor; Rob Hall—Washington Editor; Claudia Jones—Negro Affairs Editor. The other two main editorial posts will remain as now, with either Jim Allen or Joe Starobin Foreign Editor and George Morris, Labor Editor.
>
> When you return I will inform you fully of the very prolonged and both lively and heated discussion which took place around these questions and around the broader issues of what must be done to affect [sic] drastic political and journalistic improvements in the paper. You should know that some of the comrades of the Staff were dubious at first regarding bringing in an editor who has had only a very limited acquaintance [sic] with the direct problems of editing and publishing a paper. It is well that these questions were raised because in the discussion most all the comrades acquired a more clear and correct Communist understanding and Communist character [sic] of our paper and the prime requisites which an editor must have. We asked for a consultative vote at the conclusion of the meeting and you received 26 votes for, 2 against and 2 abstentions.
>
> Warmest regards to you, Helen and Billie. Season's greetings to you all.
>
> Comradely,
> Gene Dennis

Morris moved to New York and began his duties as editor in early 1946. Shortly afterward, Sam Carr unexpectedly burst into his office in high alarm. Code clerk Igor Gouzenko had defected from the Soviet embassy in Ottawa and identified a number of people, including Carr, as Russian spies. "I can't go back," he said. "I need to get in touch with the Russians but I don't know how. What shall I do?"

While Jack sequestered Carr in the home of a wealthy party sympathizer, Morris telephoned Tim Buck in Canada. A week or so later Soviet agents spirited Carr off to Moscow. As far as United States and Canadian authorities were concerned, he simply vanished.

In 1947 Dennis asked the Soviets for permission to send a *Daily Worker* correspondent to cover a Moscow conference of foreign ministers beginning in March. They replied, "We want Morris." After Labor Editor George Morris applied for a visa, they sent another message: "We want Morris Childs."

Rumors that Stalin had renewed systematic persecution of Jews circulated in New York, and Paul Novick, editor of the Yiddish newspaper *Morning Freiheit*, urged Morris to appeal to the Soviets to cease the persecutions. He also gave Morris penicillin and other medicine to take to Jewish artists and intellectuals in Moscow.

Morris flew to Moscow in the company of thirty-four other American correspondents, among them such noted journalists as Walter Cronkite, Howard K. Smith, and Kingsbury Smith. Molly Perlman, a South African communist working in Moscow, came to the hotel where the press corps was lodged and announced that the Soviets had designated her to act as his secretary. She gave him a ticket to the ballet and told him he absolutely must attend.

The next evening two representatives of the International Department (aka Comintern) joined him in a box at the ballet. They pressed him for details of all that had transpired in the American party since 1943, an appraisal of its current condition, and evaluations of its principal leaders. They also asked for an appraisal of President Harry Truman. Morris characterized him as a "tough bird" and said he was not as sure as the American press seemed to be that Truman would be defeated in 1948.

During the day, Morris followed the routine of other correspondents, attending press conferences and briefings and filing stories. On most evenings he secretly conferred with the Soviets. When he raised the issue of persecution of Jews, they feigned shock that anyone but malicious imperialists could even imagine such a thing. It just wasn't so, and they would be glad to send Soviet Jews to New York to reassure the Jewish community. As for the artists and intellectuals, for whom he had medicine, they were in dachas or sanitoria receiving good medical treatment.

As gifts for old friends from his days at the Lenin School, Morris brought Kentucky bourbon, Camel cigarettes, medicine, perfume, nylon stockings, and Spam, a canned meat made popular in Moscow by American wartime aid. The presents won him invitations to Russian apartments where heavy drinking was customary. He ordinarily did not drink alcohol but among Russians he forced himself to drink to show that he was one of them and to be one of them.

During long drinking bouts, he heard appalling confidences. The Jewish artists and intellectuals were not in dachas or sanitoria; they were in prison awaiting almost certain execution. Other mutual friends had disappeared. Morris already knew that Carl Radek, Leo Kamenev, Grigori Zinoviev, and Nikolai Bukharin, all of whom lectured at the Lenin School, had been shot. So had countless other loyal party members, generals, scientists, intellectuals, and intelligence officers. Millions of peasants and their families had been deported to slave labor camps, and in Ukraine Stalin had deliberately starved hundreds of thousands, maybe millions, to death. Moreover, Stalin was no strategic genius who bought time to gird Soviet defenses by making a deal with Hitler. He was a fool who trusted Hitler and believed that through a union of German industry and Soviet natural resources, Communists and Nazis together could dominate the world. His trust had been so complete that he had unconscionably rejected warnings from both Soviet and British intelligence services of the impending German attack in 1941. When the predicted attack came, it rendered him literally speechless. He skulked in shock for days, and Foreign Minister Vyacheslav Molotov had to be the first to call the nation to arms.

Collectively, these revelations from unimpeachable confidants confirmed the vilest of anti-Soviet slanders and struck at the foundation of Morris' faith. And, Morris thought, I have been an apostle of all of this for almost twenty years.

The other American correspondents refused to accept Morris as a colleague. They regarded him as a Soviet apologist rather than a bona fide journalist, and they scorned the *Daily Worker* as a "commie rag." Howard K. Smith who, as a result of seating assignments, shared a table with him in the hotel dining room, was polite but avoided serious conversation. The rest spoke to him either curtly or not at all.

At a reception given for the press by the U.S. ambassador, General Walter Bedell Smith, Morris stood awkwardly and conspicuously alone until Mrs. Smith approached and asked why he was not joining in the festivities.

"I'm a communist," he said. "I'm a skunk. No one wants to have anything to do with me."

She smiled. "I do. Will you favor me with a dance?"

"I've never danced. I don't know how."

"Well, you should learn. Just follow me."

The sight of the ambassador's wife dancing with the leper attracted attention, and many watched as she afterward led Morris to her husband. "Bedell, this is Mr. Childs," she said. "His colleagues are ostracizing him because he's a communist."

An erect, imposing man, General Smith had been a wartime deputy to General Eisenhower; soon he would be director of the new Central Intelligence Agency. "Mr. Childs, as a citizen of the United States you are welcome at the embassy at any time," he said. "As a citizen, you are entitled to your political opinions and you may surmise that yours differ from mine. But when Americans leave their country, they leave their political differences behind and stick together."

"You should tell that to the other journalists," Mrs. Smith interjected. "Have a word with them, Beedle."

"I will."

Morris never knew what General Smith said to the correspondents. He obviously said something because the next day they began talking to him and exchanging notes and opinions, and some even became friendly.

Over breakfast Morris mentioned that someday he would like to visit his brother's grave in France, and Howard K. Smith suggested that he do so en route back to New York. Morris confided that though he was returning by way of Paris he did not have enough money for a side trip. At breakfast the day Morris departed Moscow, Smith handed him a sealed envelope and requested that he not open it until he boarded his plane. Airborne, Morris found inside the envelope a terse note: "We thought you should make that side trip so we took up a collection. Your fellow Americans." The envelope also contained three hundred U.S. dollars.

Above the grave in an immaculately maintained Normandy cemetery stood a white cross inscribed with the Star of David and the words: "Phillip Childs—First Lieutenant, United States Army—1918–1944." Morris knelt and offered an earnest prayer.

Flying homeward, he contrasted the spontaneous kindness of General and Mrs. Smith and the correspondents with the Stalinist terrors whose occurrence he no longer doubted, and he asked himself, have I perverted my whole life?

In New York, Morris returned to face more feuding and bickering. A clique headed by Foster caviled at Dennis and his followers, and Foster ridiculed Morris and his direction of the paper, accusing him of "Browderism." Dennis surprised Morris by not rising to his defense.

Unable to will away worsening chest pains, Morris consulted a physician who insisted that he temporarily stop working. Morris then asked Dennis for a short leave of absence from the paper. At a meeting of the National Committee in June 1947 Morris blanched in disbelief as Dennis formally proposed that Morris be granted an indefinite leave of absence and that John Gates replace him as editor of the *Daily Worker*. Foster seconded the motion, and it passed unanimously, every comrade in effect voting to fire him and purge him from the party leadership.

Earlier, Morris' wife had left him and taken away their son because she felt he neglected her for the party. Now the party, his deity, had forsaken him, as had everyone else except his brothers. He had no job, no income, no savings, no future, and no faith. Nor did he have recourse to protectors in Moscow because the party could tell them that he was incapacitated. Soon that was true. He rented a room in a Greenwich Village boarding house, and there a massive heart attack left him near death.

Jack, who had established a business selling electrical and painting supplies, took care of Morris as best he could and paid his medical bills. Ben also sent money. Still, except for visits by Jack, he was utterly alone until Sonny Schlossberg, a former party member in Chicago, heard of his plight. She had always admired and looked up to him, and she brought him from New York to her home in Chicago and acted as his nurse.

Had it not been for his ouster and illness, Morris doubtless would have been arrested. Congress in 1940 passed a law, the so-called Smith Act, which made it a crime to advocate violent overthrow of the United States government. After the Cold War began, the Truman administration applied the law to communists and the FBI arrested the top twelve active leaders of the party: Dennis, Foster, Gates, Gus Hall, Ben Davis, John Williams, Robert Thompson, Jack Satchel, Irving Potash, Gil Green, Henry Winston, and Carl Winter.

The government considered arresting Morris; the FBI subjected him to "spot" or periodic surveillance, and the watching agents saw that he was almost completely enfeebled. After walking only fifty steps or so he had to sit down on the street curb and rest for several minutes to regain strength enough to stand up again. Given his condition and the fact that he no longer was active in the party, the Justice Department decided not to bring charges against him.

The prosecution of Foster was delayed because he too had become very ill, but the other eleven leaders were convicted. The Supreme Court, by a 6-to-2 vote in June 1951, upheld the constitutionality of the Smith Act and the convictions. Hall, Gates, Thompson, and Green jumped bail and fled; the rest were imprisoned. Granted Supreme Court authorization and goaded by wartime passions, the FBI rounded up more than one hundred lesser communist functionaries around the country and virtually all were convicted. The remaining party officials, besieged and largely leaderless, then went underground.

In hope of catching the fugitive leaders and breaking into the underground, the FBI instituted a program titled "TOPLEV" and formed Underground Squads in New York and Chicago. The squads began the hunt by analyzing investigative and intelligence files to ascertain with whom Hall, Gates, Thompson, and Green most frequently associated. Then they undertook to identify former or inactive party members who had links to them. This search led to the file of Jack Childs, which indicated that he had not been active in the party since 1947 and hence might be disaffected.

On the night of September 4, 1951, Agents Edward Buckley and Herbert Larson stopped Jack as he walked near his home in Queens. Other party members they approached had profanely rebuffed them, and when Jack smiled sardonically they expected another rebuff. Instead, he said, "Where in the hell have you guys been all these years? I could have sired and raised a son during all the time you've been screwing around." He agreed to talk to them the next evening in a room at the Tudor Hotel. During that first interview, Jack withheld information about some aspects of his past and dissembled about others. But he honestly answered the most critical question put to him: Yes, he wanted to help the FBI.

The real debriefings took place in a spacious country home perched on a hillside in Westchester County. It belonged to Alexander C. Burlinson, a slender FBI agent with a granite face and searching gray eyes. A graduate of Fordham Preparatory School, Fordham College, and Fordham Law School, Burlinson was an accomplished writer, pianist, and linguist. He composed poetry in Latin and sometimes exasperated superiors by expressing his own exasperations in Latin. The front of his expensive shirts, which he changed daily, was usually soiled at the end of the day because he so often rubbed his stomach to assuage an ulcer. The ulcer and admonitions of his doctor notwithstanding, he smoked two packs of cigarettes a day and drank copious quantities of Scotch whisky in milk.

Some FBI agents prefer the excitement of street work and the gratification of arresting somebody who threatens everybody. Burlinson liked intellectual detective work, the quest for clues from old archives or new sources. He also enjoyed playing deception games with the communists and impudent games with bureaucrats. Traveling to Washington to attend a conference of assistant directors, he once told an apprehensive subordinate,

"Don't worry. They only know what we tell them." Although he had little personal ambition, his talents were such that colleagues thought he inevitably would wind up in an executive position at headquarters. As a result of events that began in 1951, he stayed in New York and for the next twenty-four years concentrated his career and life on one case.

The personalities of Burlinson and Jack Childs were quite dissimilar, yet the two were a good match. Burlinson was a great listener and Jack was a great talker, and they soon became friends and partners.

At the outset, Jack declared he "never really believed any of that communist bullshit." He joined and worked for the party for the sake of his brother. He now loathed the communists because they callously threw away his brother and when Morris was in terrible need they sent him not one dollar, not even a postcard. He was grateful to be an American. Until a few years ago, he had not perceived the Soviet Union as a dangerous enemy of the United States; now that he did, there was no question on whose side he stood. For these reasons, he would work for the FBI.

There was another reason at which he later hinted. "Look, I'm basically a con man. If I had a choice between entering a house by walking through the front door or crawling through a back window, I'd go through the window because that's more exciting." While his business was prospering, selling paint and light fixtures was not exciting. The prospect of taking on the Communist Party was.

In the next weeks, Jack recounted his training in Moscow, his two trips to Berlin, and the frolic there with the beautiful wife. He admitted supplying the party with birth and death certificates and illegally obtained passports. He also detailed party finances, named donors, and told of the secret Reserve Fund. Sure, he knew Sam Carr and many other communists about whom Burlinson asked, and he was willing to try to renew relations with them.

Burlinson did not expressly state that in addition to arresting the fugitives, the FBI needed to penetrate the leadership of the underground. Once Jack sensed this objective, he blurted out, "Look, Morris is your ticket to the top."

Jack was an apparatus man, never a party leader. Morris was a prominent leader. Jack knew a lot of people, and some liked him. Morris knew everybody who counted, and except for Foster and a few other snakes, everybody loved him, including the Soviets. Jack could seek people out; people would gravitate to Morris.

Would Morris cooperate? "He may if he's well enough," Jack answered. "But you can't deal with him like you did with me. He and I are different. When I screwed that Kraut knockout in Berlin, I at least took off my money belt. Morris, he wouldn't have taken off his money belt because he'd be afraid of losing commie money. Hell, Morris wouldn't even have screwed her. He's too strait-laced, too proper. You can't just walk up and proposition him cold. You've got to bring him along gently. You've got to send someone proper, a gentleman and someone who really understands all that communist crap."

They agreed that Jack would visit Morris and try to persuade him at least to listen to the FBI. Before seeing Morris, Jack conferred with Carl Freyman in a Chicago hotel room. Had he not known otherwise, Jack might have taken Freyman for a soft-spoken, pipe-smoking professor of communism. The knowledge he evinced of the party and Morris at first amazed, then reassured him. Freyman happened to be exactly the man he had described to Burlinson.

Strict Catholic elementary and high schools in Iowa afforded him a superb education as did an Evangelical Church college that required daily Bible study. After graduation from the University of Iowa Law School, he started his own law practice in his hometown of LeMars near Sioux City. He was doing well for a young attorney when the Japanese bombed Pearl Harbor. The next day he drove to Omaha to enlist in the navy only to be rejected because of deficient eyesight. The day after that he applied in Des Moines to the FBI, and in January 1942 it accepted him. At the end of his training in Quantico, Virginia, a supervisor said, "You're a farm boy, so we're going to send you to the big city and polish you up."

In New York, Freyman learned about counterintelligence, agent handling, and deception after the FBI arrested a German spy and converted him into a double agent. British intelligence had asked for American help in reinforcing Hitler's obsessive conviction that the Allies intended to invade Europe through Norway. One day Freyman took the German to a Brooklyn dock, and they watched as troops purposely clad in heavy arctic clothing filed aboard a transport. In a radio transmission to Berlin, the double agent detailed the embarkation and advised that the clothing obviously meant the troops were going "someplace very cold." When the Allies invaded Normandy, sixteen Wehrmacht divisions remained in Scandinavia guarding against an attack in Norway. The little play staged by the FBI was only part of an overall deception scheme implemented mostly by the British but it dramatized to Freyman the importance of recruiting double agents.

Transferred to Chicago in 1946, Freyman proved to be one of the FBI's best recruiters. He liked people, and his religious beliefs made him considerate and tolerant of others—some said too much so. Though he rarely discussed religion, he was at heart something of an evangelist. The FBI at the time had difficulty recruiting black agents. Freyman in short order recruited three, and became a friend of Olympic track star Jesse Owens.

Because of his counterintelligence experience in New York, the FBI assigned him to direct investigations of the party and its fronts in Chicago. He tried to qualify himself by reading Marx, Lenin, Soviet history, party publications, the writings of former communists, and voluminous FBI files. All the while, he taught himself how to think like a communist and how to talk to a man like Morris Childs.

Jack, coaching Freyman about how best to approach Morris, suggested that he not press for a prompt decision. He likened his brother to a chess player who deliberates before each move, thinking far ahead. Once Jack spoke with him, he would start thinking about the ramifications of collaboration; still, he would want more time.

When Freyman called and asked to see him, Morris said, "I'm not in the movement any more. I have no contacts. But if you want to talk to me, come on over."

Frail, bedridden, scarcely able to raise his head, Morris looked pitiful, and Freyman realized he mustn't stay long. He began by saying that through his work he had come to know Morris as a man of character and intellect who had sacrificed most of his life to a cause. Freyman wondered aloud whether the sacrifice was worthwhile, and he would be grateful if Morris considered a few questions. Had not Stalin betrayed all the ideals of Marxism? Had not communism exterminated millions of innocent men, women, and children? Was it not so that Soviet and Nazi persecution of Jews differed only in method and scope? Which did he think most benefited individual human beings and the world, Soviet communism or American democracy?

"We both know the answers," Morris said.

"How could a good and decent man serve such a cause?"

"When you're in the movement, you learn to close your mind to anything that might erode your faith. You cannot allow yourself to ask, is this right or wrong."

"You said you're not in the movement anymore."

"No, I'm not."

"Then you can ask."

"I suppose so."

Suddenly, Morris paled and took a dose of nitroglycerin. Freyman rose, apologized for overly imposing and asked if they could talk again.

"Come whenever you wish. I don't go anywhere these days."

Freyman knew that Morris was so attached to and dependent upon his benefactor Sonny Schlossberg that he would not cooperate without her assent. As she ushered him to the door, he paused to talk and casually asked her what she now thought about communism.

"I hate it. I hate it for what it's done to Morris, to Jews, to everybody."

"In that case, will you help us?"

"What do you want me to do?"

"Help us persuade Morris."

"All right."

Only two people from the party ever visited Morris after Sonny brought him back to Chicago. He occupied himself by reading— the Bible, the Torah, the Koran, John Locke, Thomas Jefferson, James Madison, and all the works of his favorite author, Thomas Mann. Pleasureful as reading was, he was lonely and increasingly he looked forward to visits by Freyman, whom he liked.

Morris said he knew nothing about where Hall, Thompson, Gates, and Green might be hiding, and he reiterated that he had no contacts in the party.

"You mean you have no current contacts," Freyman remarked. "You have many friends. With our help, you easily could renew contact with them."

"My God, man. I'm not physically able."

"The first thing we're going to do is improve your health. Later we'll set you up in a cover business so you can travel and have a visible source of income. But we're not going to do anything until we get you well."

Sonny again urged him to work with the FBI and pledged to stand by him if he did. Finally, Morris decided. "All right, I'll do as much for you as I can."

Freyman had no authorization to commit the FBI to pay for the expensive medical treatment of someone who had performed no services and might not live long enough to perform any. On the spot, he exercised his own judgment and initiative, hoping his superiors would agree. Once they did, through FBI friends in the medical profession he assembled a team of outstanding cardiologists to treat Morris as long as needed at the Mayo Clinic in Rochester, Minnesota.

A question arose: How could Morris explain where he got the money to pay for the costly treatment? In New York, Jack gave Burlinson the answer.

"I'll go to people all over town and tell them that doctors think they can cure Morris if he goes to the Mayo Clinic and stays there long enough. I'll say these famous doctors and this famous hospital cost a helluva lot of money, and Morris is dead broke, so we're asking our old comrades for donations to save his life. Almost none of those assholes will contribute a dime. But no one will ever say he didn't contribute." Jack noted that the solicitation also would provide a pretext to call on party people and begin restoring relations.

The treatment and new medications administered at the Mayo Clinic transfigured Morris. Color returned to his face, he gained weight, he spoke firmly and walked easily, and he could converse for hours without tiring. Doctors predicted that, if he adhered to the prescribed regimen of diet and exercise, and increased his exertions only gradually, he should be able to resume normal activities in six months or so.

To Freyman, the change in Morris' spirit was even more pronounced than in his body, and he understood why. The party had stripped his life of meaning and purpose, and thereby deprived him of incentive to recover. His decision to cooperate with the FBI restored purpose, and he left the hospital eager to start anew, to lose himself in a new cause.

In New York Jack threw out the bait little by little: Reports from the Mayo Clinic were encouraging. It looks like Morris is going to recover. Morris is up and about. I talked to him on the phone last night, and he sounded great. Morris is out of the hospital, and he's walking a mile a day. Morris wants to go back to work, and in a few months he'll be strong enough.

In 1954, the party underground bit.

Morris telephoned Freyman at a number reserved for him. "An anonymous caller just ordered me to be at a certain telephone booth on the North Side by 2:30 P.M. and to wait there for a call," he reported. "I don't know who it is or what it's about. I'll go and contact you as soon as I can."

Superiors demanded that Freyman at once put Morris under surveillance so they could identify anyone he might meet. Freyman absolutely refused. "Someone is using classic tradecraft, so he will be looking for surveillance," he said. "If he detects it, we lose the whole case. If Morris meets anybody, he'll tell us."

At about 2:35 P.M. the phone in the booth rang and the same anonymous caller instructed Morris to come to a room in the Sovereign Hotel.

The man awaiting him there was Phillip Bart, who had been organizational secretary and chief security officer of the party, and who now was a leader of the underground. He welcomed Morris as an old friend and began an interrogation to ascertain if what Jack said about his recovery was true and whether Morris was bitter about being deposed as editor.

Morris said that though he had not fully regained his strength and stamina, doctors assured him that he would and he felt good. He was also grateful for the donations that made possible his treatment at the Mayo Clinic. Certainly, he harbored no ill will toward the party. Because of his health, he could not possibly have continued working at the paper. Besides, there was no room in the party for pettiness.

Then was he willing to resume party work in the underground? What sort of work?

"The Reserve Fund is exhausted and we have to have money," Bart said. "To get money, we must reestablish contact with the Russians. You were always close to them. Could you put us in touch?"

Morris promised to try and asked, "How can I reach you?"

Bart said that because he always was on the run, he relayed and received messages through Betty Gannett, who had been office manager at party headquarters in New York. She was of insufficient rank to be prosecuted, and Morris could safely deal with her.

As if by afterthought, Morris mentioned that efforts to contact the Russians might entail travel, and he was not sure when the doctors would allow him to travel. If need be, could he use Jack?

Bart thought that an excellent idea.

Freyman, who had stayed at the office, heard from Morris about 2:30 A.M. "I had a very successful meeting. As soon as security permits, I'll tell you about it."

Once headquarters learned that a meeting had taken place, it teletyped an order to Freyman: "Get out there and interview him." Again, Freyman refused. If Morris judged it safe to meet immediately he would not have said "as soon as security permits."

When the two did confer, Morris said, "It was Phil Bart." Freyman smiled broadly. After Morris reconstructed the conversation, he smiled even more broadly, suddenly envisioning new and grand possibilities. The leader of the underground had invited Morris and Jack into the underground. If Morris could deliver Soviet funds, he would make himself indispensable and securely reposition himself in the highest councils of American communism. He probably would be the principal intermediary to the Soviets, who liked and trusted him. Should he establish clandestine relations with them, he could conceivably insinuate himself into their councils. An operation that began with relatively limited and modest objectives, it now held out the promise of vastly more.

The FBI initially code named the operation SASH. It gave Morris the code designation CG-5824S*; Jack was NY-694S*. Among themselves, FBI agents referred to Morris as "58" or "George"; they referred to Jack as "69." An asterisk at the end of a source designation denoted that the source could never testify in court or be otherwise identified. Usually that meant that the source was a telephone tap, a bug, or a burglary. Uninitiated analysts poring over reports from 58 and 69 for years thought that the FBI was running one hell of an eavesdropping operation.

At FBI headquarters on Pennsylvania Avenue, some supervisor, whose name cannot be retrieved from available records, bravely acted upon an intelligent insight. Freyman, during his FBI career, received seven formal letters of censure from J. Edgar Hoover (along with nineteen commendations). Unbeknownst to Hoover, however, Freyman refused to obey a direct order twice in twenty-four hours. Either refusal surely would have provoked Hoover to censure him or do worse. But Hoover never knew because the unknown supervisor reinforced an earlier headquarter decision: Burlinson and Freyman have brought the case along. Thus far, they've done everything right. They're on the spot; they know what they're doing. Why pester them? Let Chicago and New York run the case and work with each other directly.

That is pretty much what happened for many, many years.

four

THE
BREAKTHROUGH

MORRIS CONCEIVED AN OPERATIONAL plan
that Jack put into effect by calling upon Betty Gannett and suggesting that Jack ask Tim Buck in Canada to reopen lines of communication between Moscow and the underground American party. On
March 25, 1954, Gannett, probably having consulted Bart, emphatically instructed Jack to go to Toronto as soon as possible.

Although Jack knew Buck, at this meeting he represented himself as an emissary of Morris acting under the authority of Gannett, who presided over a skeletal staff at party headquarters in
New York. Buck was more than willing to help. He cautioned,
however, that in the aftermath of Stalin's death the year before,
chaos still reigned in the Soviet party and that the Canadians
themselves were having difficulty communicating. They agreed
that Jack should return to Canada periodically and that in an
emergency Buck would send his friend Elizabeth Mascola to New
York as a messenger.

The first results were discouraging. Throughout 1954 and 1955
no word came from Moscow. Morris and Jack did succeed,

however, in reestablishing themselves among the comrades. They demonstrated that the Soviets controlled the American party much more massively and minutely than even the FBI suspected, and that Soviet intentions sometimes could be divined from directives to the party. All that was useful, even important. Still, Freyman and Burlinson hoped for much more.

They got it in the spring of 1956 when Jack came back from Toronto with a document Buck characterized as "devastating." Buck attended the Twentieth Communist Party Congress in Moscow and afterward stayed a few days to tend to administrative business with the International Department. En route to Canada he stopped in Warsaw to see his friend, Wladyslaw Gomulka, chief of the Polish party and the puppet Polish government. Gomulka confided that on the night of February 25–26, 1956, there had been a secret session of the congress at which Nikita Khrushchev denounced Stalin and recited some of the atrocities Stalin visited upon the Soviet people. The Soviets did not intend for the speech to be made public, and foreigners were barred from the secret session. But they did send a copy to Gomulka, and he made one for Buck.

The FBI gave the State Department the copy Buck passed on to Jack and after a couple of weeks asked what the State Department proposed to do with it. The State Department denied having received the speech. Thereupon, an irate J. Edgar Hoover produced a letter in which the State Department had thanked the FBI for delivering it.[‡]

Publication of the speech by the State Department wrought moral havoc on communism. It had the same effect on many party members, sympathizers, and intellectuals that the revelations Morris had heard in 1947 in Moscow had had upon him. In the

---

[‡] The American intelligence community has long believed that the CIA obtained the speech from the Israelis. That well may be. But according to unequivocal statements made to the author by FBI Agents Donald E. Moore, Walter Boyle, William Brannigan, and John O'Toole, the FBI procured the first copy available to the U.S. government. Branigan and O'Toole are dead; Moore and Boyle are not.

minds of honest and informed people, Soviet communism never recovered as a spiritual force.‡

A tangled federal court ruling in 1956 in effect made further prosecutions of communists under the Smith Act impossible and allowed them to emerge from the underground. The party consequently in 1957 openly convened a national convention that

---

‡ Historian Bertam D. Wolfe, who Morris also knew in the party, summed up the import of the speech thusly:

> The speech is perhaps the most important document ever to have come from the communist movement... It is the most revealing indictment of communism ever to have been made by a communist, the most damning indictment of the Soviet system ever to have been made by a Soviet leader.
>
> There is about it a nightmare quality, felt alike by those who believe in communism and those who do not. To see one of the chief creators of the atmosphere of terror and of the monstrous cult of the living God calmly reporting to a Congress of those who were all terrorized agents of the terror and votaries of the cult; to hear the confidences as to what went on behind the scenes, torture, false confessions, judicial murder, perfidious destruction of the bodies and souls and very names of devoted comrades and intimates; to see the Reporter expects absolution and forgiveness and even continuance in absolute power because at long last he has revealed some of the guilty secrets in which he shared; to note the broad, self-satisfied smile which deprives the fearful avowals of any value of repentance; to catch in the flood of words only a sua culpa and not one syllable of mea culpa or a nostra culpa; to sense how much greater crimes have been committed against a helpless people by this little band whose deeds against each other are in part being recited; to think that men who are capable of doing such things to each other and tolerating, sanctioning, and applauding such actions, have managed to vest themselves of absolute power over belief and action, over manners and morals, over life and death and the good name of the dead, over industry and agriculture and politics and communication and expression and culture; and then to hear that the system which spawned these monstrous things is still the best in the world, and that the surviving members of this band are still in their collective wisdom infallible and in their collective power unlimited—who can read this recital without a sense of horror and revulsion?

degenerated into a near brawl as antagonistic factions clashed over the implications of the Khrushchev speech and the Soviet invasion of Hungary. At least, though, the party was again functioning. Released from prison, Dennis appointed Morris his deputy and designated him to deal with the Soviets, Chinese, and all other foreign parties. The Soviets finally resumed direct communications by inviting Morris to Moscow in late April 1958.

Morris rode from the airport in a curtained limousine to the party hotel, which he entered through a door reserved for foreigners. Having rested a few days at Soviet insistence, he began conferences with Boris Ponomarev, head of the International Department. Ponomarev was a hard-headed, dogmatic ideologue who in the 1930s compelled the American party to stop using a slogan, "Communism Is 20th Century Americanism," on the grounds that communism was an international movement. Now he very much wanted to revitalize the American party as an instrument of Soviet policy, and he professed to be delighted that Dennis had made such an able and trustworthy comrade as Morris its de facto foreign minister.

Ponomarev calculated that the Soviets could give the Americans $75,000 in 1958 and $200,000 in 1959. He solicited suggestions from Morris about how the cash might be delivered, saying he did not want to transmit it through the Soviet embassy in Washington and that a secure channel must be found lest discovery of the subsidies stigmatize the American party as a "paid whore." Morris noted that Tim Buck was willing to be a conduit and that, were the money passed through Canada, it would be more difficult to prove that the Soviet Union was the source.

Morris' old mentor and friend Suslov dined with him twice and shared the Soviet view of world affairs, which in the main was optimistic except with respect to China. Ponomarev had indicated that Soviet relations with China were not all they should be; Suslov said they were bad and worsening.

The Russians were considerate hosts. They spaced discussions so as not to tax Morris physically, and doctors examined him briefly each morning. He dutifully submitted although he had held Soviet medicine in low esteem since 1947 when a Russian physician treated Howard K. Smith for influenza by putting mustard seeds in his socks and prescribing vodka with garlic. A card admitted Morris to the International Department building and its buffet, which offered delicious fare—caviar, smoked salmon, herring, sturgeon, sardines, and a whitefish unfamiliar to him; lamb and veal cutlets, German wursts, and Hungarian sausages; cheese from Denmark and Holland; a kind of deviled eggs; pickled beets, marinated cabbage, and a variety of potatoes; and good, hearty bread and fresh butter. Usually, there was fresh fruit, then a rarity in Moscow. Always there was alcohol: vodka, Johnny Walker Black Label scotch; wines from the Soviet Republic of Georgia, Rumania, and Hungary; sparkling wines and brandy from Georgia. The Soviets knew Morris was Jewish and probably knew that he preferred to be a vegetarian. But he determined never to remind them that he was either and ate whatever Soviet hosts presented. He begged off alcohol during the day by truthfully citing doctors' strictures.

The card also admitted him to what he termed the "speakeasy." Past a plain, unmarked door and guards on the inside, he entered a cornucopia of Western food, drink, and merchandise available to almost no one in Moscow, and it was all free. He had only to point to what his whim fixed upon; all he specified was packaged and soon delivered to his hotel suite.

From the Soviet Union, he flew to Peking to renew relations of the American party with the Chinese, who accorded him an even more lavish reception than had the Russians. Mao Tse Tung conversed with him alone, except for the pretty young woman who interpreted, for nearly five hours. Mao declared that Khrushchev, by his 1956 denunciation of Stalin and subsequent policies, had betrayed the revolution, and the contempt he expressed for him in curdling terms astonished Morris. Other Chinese leaders with whom he spoke were less blunt but their comments persuaded him that the Chinese animus toward the Soviets was real and deeply rooted.‡ Wang Chia Hsiang, a member of the Secretariat of the

---

‡ Other Chinese leaders with whom Morris conferred included Hsuing Fu, Li Chi Hsin, Tang Ming-Chao, Lin Tang, Yu Chi-Ying, Li Shen Nin, Kang Sheng, Tent Hsia Ping, Hsu Bing, and Lili Ning Yi Ti.

Chinese party, took him aside and offered to give money to the American party on the sole condition that it not divulge the gifts to the Soviets. Clearly, the Chinese intended to compete with the Soviets for influence in the international communist movement.

Morris returned to the United States July 21, 1958, with the first hard, authentic intelligence that a breach was developing between the Soviet Union and China. The Sino–Soviet split long would preoccupy and torment the Soviets, and be the subject of many more reports by Morris.

Soviet cash began to flow from Canada on September 8, 1958, when Elizabeth Mascola came to New York with $12,000 for Jack; on September 19 he picked up $15,000 from her in Toronto. A few days later she brought $17,000 to Morris. Buck handed Morris $6,000 in Toronto, and Mascola gave Jack $25,000 in New York.

By forging relations with the Soviets and Chinese at the highest levels and by producing money, Morris made himself indispensable and securely positioned himself atop the hierarchy of the American party, just as Freyman had foreseen. He, Jack, and the FBI were now in business, business being espionage against the Soviet Union, China, and communism everywhere. The FBI retitled the operation "SOLO," because the operation centered on two spies, 58 and 69.

Dennis became terminally ill, and the International Department chose Gus Hall to assist and succeed him. The two selected Morris to lead the U.S. delegation to an international Party Congress in Moscow beginning in January 1959.

The party congress appointed Morris a recording secretary and assigned him a vault in the Kremlin to store documents. Late one night he accidentally closed the vault door on the little finger of his left hand, completely severing about a half inch. When doctors started to administer anesthesia before sewing up his finger he refused it out of fear of what he might say if anesthetized. Instead, he stoically stuck out the finger while the doctors did their work.

Word of the incident spread and after the congress reconvened in the morning Khrushchev took the podium and melodramatically described the heroism of a comrade who had endured terrible pain rather than risk spilling state secrets even to trusted Soviet physicians. "That comrade is among us today," he bellowed, motioning Morris to join him at the podium. There he embraced him, and holding up the injured hand, shouted, "I give you the last of the first Bolsheviks!" Khrushchev then announced that the remnant of the finger would be interred in the Kremlin wall.

Perhaps merely to test a new channel or perhaps because of temporary problems in Canada, the Soviets sent KGB officer Vladimir Barkovsky on April 23, 1959, to give $50,000 directly to Jack in New York. Payments through Canada resumed May 21, however, when Mascola delivered $41,000, and she returned with lesser sums throughout the year. After one delivery, she took back a letter from Dennis and Hall with a request that Buck forward it to Moscow. The letter certified that henceforth Morris Childs alone was authorized to represent the American party in dealings with the Soviets and Chinese.

After Morris had recovered from his heart attack, Freyman issued him an ultimatum: either marry Sonny or move out of her house. They married, and she, as promised, stood with him in all the intrigues. Doctors in the summer of 1959 discovered that she had inoperable cancer and had less than six months to live. Morris wanted to brighten the last of her life with a trip abroad, and the Chinese encouraged him to bring her along to ceremonies commemorating the tenth anniversary of communist assumption of power in China. They departed for Moscow September 23, 1959, and there Khrushchev incorporated them into his entourage to Peking.

The Chinese sought to detach the Americans from the Soviet delegation by placing them in palatial quarters remote from the Soviets, surrounding Sonny with a medical team led by an English-speaking doctor, and inviting them to remain as official guests for a couple of weeks after the ceremonies. They made it impossible for Morris to decline by adding that both Mao and Chou En Lai wanted to talk to him.

The Chinese soon provided compelling evidence that the deterioration in Sino–Soviet relations had accelerated. When Khrushchev concluded his speech on September 30, they condescendingly insulted him by folding their hands and withholding applause.

During a long audience granted Morris, Mao engaged in a disjointed, meandering diatribe against the Soviets and Khrushchev, whom he characterized as "uncouth, crude, and vulgar." The Soviet Union, he rambled, had become just as imperialistic as the United States, and Mao did not care if the two countries went to nuclear war. China would remain aloof "on the mountaintop and watch as two tigers clawed each other apart in the valley below." The Soviets had broken their word by abruptly stopping their assistance to the Chinese nuclear research and development program. China in turn had foiled Soviet tricks by rejecting a proposal to form a joint Soviet–Chinese naval fleet and refusing to allow emplacement of long-range Soviet radars on its territory. The unprincipled and opportunistic Soviets thought only in terms of five-year plans; the Chinese thought ahead a hundred years, nay, a thousand years. The world would not always remain as it was in 1959. Someday the United States would approach China and court its cooperation. But until the Soviets apologized for Khrushchev's denunciation of Stalin and repudiated policies adopted at the Twentieth Communist Party Congress (in 1956), there could be no reconciliation between China and the Soviet Union. China did not want one.

To Morris, Mao seemed to fluctuate from brilliant, logical analysis to illogical, almost incoherent ranting, to raw racism and chauvinism that exalted the inherent traits of the Chinese and their culture above those of all other peoples and societies. Thinking back, he wondered whether if upon visiting the lavatory Mao did not also consult an opium pipe.

Chou En Lai, without any of Mao's bombast, also tried to enlist Morris as a Chinese ally in ideological warfare against the Soviets. He said that the Soviets had proven themselves to be unpredictable and untrustworthy, and reiterated the offer of money for the American party. Chou also took an interest in Sonny, and at a reception he stroked her derriere several times, apparently indifferent to what Morris or anyone else thought. Toward the end of their stay, he said it would be a shame for her to come all the way to China and not see something of the country, and insisted that they avail themselves of a plane put at their disposal for sightseeing.

Accompanied by the medical team, they flew to Shanghai where, in a park, were the signs Browder had described in the 1920s: "No Dogs Or Chinese." The communists had retained them as symbols of colonialism.

On his way back to the United States with Sonny, Morris stopped in Moscow to report his conversations in Peking. The Soviets reacted somberly to his account and said that unfortunately it was consistent with their other intelligence. Ponomarev also advised that the International Department would raise the 1960 subsidy to the American party to $300,000 and that it was considering means of funneling the cash straight to Jack Childs in New York. To discuss this and other operational matters, they wanted Jack to come to Moscow in early 1960.

Upon landing in Chicago on November 5, 1959, Morris telephoned Freyman from the airport: "Sonny is dying." Barely conscious and unable to walk, she had to be carried from the airport. Soon she lapsed into a coma from which she never recovered.

To distract Morris from his grief and remind him that there was still much left to do in life, Freyman burdened him with work. One assignment required a detailed personal evaluation of Gus Hall (aka Arvo Holberg) who, with Dennis' incapacitation, had become general secretary, or boss, of the party. "He is a man without a friend in the world," Morris began.

Hall was a fair, handsome, jut-jawed man, born in Minnesota of Finnish parents who were communists. He joined the party in his early twenties, attended the Lenin School, and worked as an organizer among union members in Minnesota and Ohio. During the 1930s he openly advocated overthrow of the government and was implicated in bombings perpetrated by unionists against nonstrikers. He pled guilty to a misdemeanor charge of maliciously destroying property and paid a $500 fine. After his conviction under the Smith Act, he fled to Mexico, where authorities eventually arrested him and deported him to the United States and prison.

Morris portrayed him as a cold, humorless, robotic caricature of a bomb-throwing Bolshevik and an "ignoramus." Hall once asserted that "ballet is just an excuse for pornography" and that the Bolshoi Ballet should be more accurately named the "Bolshoi

Burlesque." The Hermitage in Leningrad exhibited some of the world's most prized paintings but Hall found it wanting. Returning from the men's room, he grumbled, "They've some nice paintings here. They ought to sell a few and buy some toilets so you don't have to use a hole in the floor." Most people disliked Hall; in fact, Morris knew of no one who actually liked him.

Hall had reaffirmed the status of Morris, assisted by Jack, as his principal deputy responsible for liaison with the Soviets and all other foreign parties. The primary reason, in Morris' judgment, was that they were producing what Hall craved most—money. He was by nature exploitive and avaricious, and the deprivations of prison intensified his greed. During his incarceration, neither the party nor anyone in it gave any help whatsoever to his wife and children, and he was determined that they would never again be impoverished.

And as long as the flow of Soviet cash continued through Morris and Jack, they would not be. After Burlinson or agents working with him counted and recorded the serial number of each bill, Jack would put the money in safety deposit boxes and subsequently disburse it as the general secretary dictated. Whenever Hall wanted money for the party or himself, he had only to call Jack.

Morris summed it up: The more money we can extract from the Soviets, the more Gus will be at liberty to pocket. The more he pockets, the more secure we and the operation will be.

The Soviet summons of Jack to Moscow heartened Freyman and Burlinson and made them laugh. Clearly, the Soviets intended to use Jack just as the FBI was using him—as a clandestine assistant to Morris. That was splendid.

Jack left February 3, 1960, for Prague, where he conferred with editors of the *World Marxist Review*, communists from different countries. One, Chao Yi-Min, slipped him $50,000, a present for the American party from the Chinese. In Moscow, he met Nikolai Mostovets, head of the North American section of the International Department, and his deputy Aleksandr Grechukhin. They discussed alternate ways of transferring money and asked if Jack would assist Soviet "representatives" secretly in New York. To the FBI, the most significant outcome of the conference was an order Mostovets told Jack to relay to Hall. He wanted the American party to establish direct communication lines with the Cuban and Mexican parties, which the Soviets could use if their own links frayed.

Timur Timofeyev (Timmy Timofeevich), the son of Eugene and Peggy Dennis, left in Moscow for the Russians to raise, treated Jack to a good dinner and an enlightening evening. Timmy had grown up with the privileged and pampered children of the Soviet oligarchy, had many friends among them, and circulated among their families.

According to Timmy, from the Soviet perspective the situation in Cuba had become "very good and happy" since Fidel Castro seized power. Castro's brother Raul and two other members of the new Cuban cabinet were steadfast communists loyal to the Soviet Union. The Soviets were gleefully confident that through Castro they could transform Cuba into their first outpost in the Western Hemisphere. They already enjoyed secret relations with him, and formal diplomatic relations would be announced after the forthcoming visit by President Eisenhower to the Soviet Union.

In compliance with Mostovets' order, Hall instructed Morris to arrange talks with the Cubans. Morris arrived in Havana on May 5, 1960. Anibal Escalante, executive secretary of the Cuban party, briefed him for the better part of four days, outlining the web of ties the communists had woven around Castro and inroads they had made into the regime. Escalante too was confident that they would prevail in Cuba.

With a false passport supplied by the FBI, Morris in July 1960 flew to Prague. Following procedures he would duplicate many times there and in other east European capitals, he showed an airport security officer a letter of instruction. The security officer promptly telephoned the International Department of the Czech party, and one of its representatives soon appeared. Morris stayed in a comfortable party apartment while the Czechs arranged a flight to Moscow and notified the Russians when he would arrive.

In Moscow, he met two KGB officers who treated him with deference rather than as a subordinate. They explained that they were to supervise transfers of money and clandestine communications with the American party on behalf of the International Department.

For several reasons, they wanted to start handing money directly to Jack instead of sending it in driblets through Canada. The fewer people involved in any operation, the better. Worthy as Comrade Mascola was, she, unlike Jack, had no professional training.

The sums of cash to be passed in the future, the KGB officer continued, were likely to be greater than an amateur could safely handle. Thus a KGB officer and an alternate in New York would be assigned to work with Jack, and he would know them both. One would meet him secretly outside the city in carefully planned rendezvous. To reduce the frequency of meetings, large sums would be delivered at each and messages could also be exchanged. In time, Jack would be informed of methods by which he and the International Department could communicate through the KGB without personal meetings. One of the officers gave Morris a list of code words to be used in future messages. Each word designated a person or nation. For example, Morris was "Mr. Good" (in later lists he became "Hub"); "Madison" meant the Soviet Union; China was "Hamilton"; and Castro was "Peach."

The FBI would prize all this information, but it paled in comparison to what Morris learned from the International Department. During a closed meeting with leaders of east European parties, Khrushchev venomously denounced China and Mao Tse Tung for "endangering world peace." He ridiculed the Chinese contention that nuclear war "is nothing" and poured scorn on Mao for claiming that the United States was "a paper tiger." Likening Mao to Stalin, Khrushchev accused him of subverting socialism by creating "a cult of personality" around himself and decreed that his writings no longer would be published in the Soviet Union. Heretofore, the Soviets had muted their reactions to Chinese calumny and tried to be conciliatory. Khrushchev's present denunciations amounted to a Soviet declaration of ideological war.

After Morris returned on July 30, 1960, the FBI sent the State Department a report of these statements, and it forthwith responded with an evaluation: "This is the most important single item the FBI has ever disseminated to the Department of State."

Morris had to leave immediately for Havana to represent the

American party at the Eighth National Assembly of the Partido Socialista Popular (the Cuban party). Mingling with communist delegates from all over the world, he gained new insights into developing alliances between their parties and the Cubans. From the Cubans themselves, he brought back more intelligence showing that communist influence on the island was growing.

As the war of insults between the Chinese and Soviets escalated, the Soviets convened a conference in October 1960 in hope of securing a truce and mediating differences, and Morris attended as the American representative. The Chinese, while making fleeting reference to the desirability of unity among all communists, remained intransigent and bellicose. They disdained the most reasonable and conciliatory appeals the Soviets could make without groveling, and refused the least compromise. Instead of improving relations, the failed conference further poisoned them.

When traveling to the Soviet Union, Morris rarely could be sure exactly how long he would need to stay. The men with whom he regularly dealt were important and busy. Unexpected demands upon their time and attention sometimes forced them to reschedule appointments; new subjects could arise necessitating lengthier discussions than planned; occasionally he had to wait until someone he had to see recovered from illness. If he was scheduled to be in Moscow only a couple of weeks or so, he was given a suite at the party hotel on a floor set aside for secret communists or national liberation foreign dignitaries. If he was to be around longer, he lived in an apartment. That was the case in the fall of 1960 when he was a delegate to a conference of eighty-one parties that did not end until December.

The well-heated apartment was situated on an upper floor of a centrally located building whose garbage chutes and stairwells did not reek of clogged refuse and stale urine. It had a parlor, a bedroom, a study alcove, a large safe for storage of secret documents he was allowed to study but not keep, and a decent bath and kitchen. A cook/housekeeper maintained an ample supply of food and drink, and replenished it daily. Before leaving for the day, she insisted on preparing a cold supper even if he was dining out. On such occasions, she took the supper home with her.

Morris soon discovered that members of the International Department liked to visit him in the evening. They may have been sincere in their professed desire to discuss "general problems" or "general intelligence." They undoubtedly were sincere in their enjoyment of the unlimited quantities of whisky and vodka they could imbibe for free. Morris welcomed them and all the inside information they imparted, wittingly or unwittingly. Now and then he did plead fatigue and suggest that prospective callers stop by later. On those evenings, he meant to copy documents by hand.

Ponomarev in late November or early December gave Morris two documents to study. One provided a chronology of events that culminated in the breach between the Soviets and Chinese; the other was a Soviet analysis of the gravity of the breach. Upon receiving the documents from the FBI in late December, the State Department declared them to be "of unique importance."‡

By the end of 1960, Freyman, Burlinson, and the few others in the FBI who knew about SOLO could be proud of its results.

At the time, some prestigious journalists, academicians, politicians, and foreign affairs analysts in the United States still believed Fidel Castro to be a crusading votary of liberty and independence for the Cuban people. To them, any suggestion that he might be willing to sell Cuba to the Soviet Union in return for personal status as an absolute dictator would have seemed nothing short of paranoid. The early intelligence emanating from SOLO, however, warned U.S. policymakers of what was likely to happen—and what in fact did happen—in Cuba, and thereby allowed them to plan accordingly.

To much, perhaps most, of the world, the Soviet empire and Peoples' Republic of China in 1960 appeared to be a fearsome monolith occupying a fourth of the earth's land surface and comprising more than a third of its population. Later, when little signs

---

‡ Over the years, Morris took many documents out of the Soviet Union. Some were originals entrusted to him for delivery to Hall. Others were illicitly made copies. Interviewed nearly a quarter of a century later, he could not remember with certainty whether those he brought out in December 1960 were originals or copies.

of trouble between them inevitably surfaced, they were widely dismissed as inconsequential. "Experts" could and did argue that far more united than divided the communist partners. For years, some influential U.S. intelligence officials even contended that the indicators were deceptions, part of a grand disinformation scheme.

Almost from the inception of the Sino–Soviet split, authentic SOLO intelligence gathered at the highest echelons in Peking and Moscow showed that the breach was real, widening, and perhaps irreparable.

Soviet leaders now welcomed Morris and Jack into their confidence; they relied on them to maintain the financial lifeline of American communism and trusted them to work with the KGB.

Freyman and Burlinson had every professional reason to believe that, if security and Morris' health held, there would be much more to come.

five

THE LUCK OF
THE FBI

NO ONE PROGRAMMED the events that made two new members available to the team. But Carl Freyman took full advantage of the good luck.

During the annual inspection of the Cryptanalysis Section at FBI headquarters in late 1960, Supervisor Walter Boyle stood accused of two transgressions.

The section chief, Churchill Downing, observed that some of his young civilian analysts and clerks voluntarily were staying after hours or coming in on weekends to do work they thought must be done. Their zeal impressed him all the more because they claimed neither overtime pay nor credit. "Walter, we ought to find some way to reward this extra effort," he said. "You're here all the time. I'd like you to start keeping a record of who's here in off hours so I can note it on their fitness reports." Someone found out about the informal log and filed a complaint that Boyle was attempting to coerce employees into working unpaid overtime.

Then there was the issue of the pretty girl, or "slut," as the inspector chose to call her. While her husband was away taking corporate training, the attractive clerk entertained a male FBI employee overnight at her home. Somehow the FBI learned about the tryst and at 4 P.M. on a Friday fired her for moral turpitude. The woman, who was twenty-three or twenty-four, reacted hysterically. She and her husband had just purchased a house, and they needed two incomes to meet mortgage payments. She did not know what to tell him and feared that dismissal from the FBI would so stigmatize her that she could not obtain another job.

Boyle telephoned his wife at their home in suburban Springfield, Virginia, and told her what had happened. "Friday afternoon is the worst possible time to fire anyone. She will brood all weekend, and she's suicidal. Could we invite her to dinner on Sunday night so she'll have something to look forward to?" A girlfriend dropped her off at Boyle's house; he consoled her by advising that in job hunting she could cite him as a reference, and after a pleasant dinner he drove her to her home in Maryland. Evidently the girlfriend told people in the office of the dinner; in any case, the inspector learned of it.

Leaning across a desk, he kept shaking his finger at Boyle while lecturing him about consorting with immoral former employees. "You stick that finger in my face one more time and I'll break it off," Boyle shouted. For that insubordination, the FBI demoted him from supervisor to street agent and banished him to Chicago through a "disciplinary" transfer.

A garbled account of the incident preceded him to Chicago, and he arrived there in early 1961 with the reputation of a piranha. No one asked him to lunch, for a beer after work, or to join a carpool, and no supervisor would accept him on his squad—until Freyman spoke up. "I'll take him. Let's give the man a chance and judge him by what he does." That was typical of Freyman. But he also had gone to the trouble of examining Boyle's background, which in ways paralleled his own.

Boyle was born April 6, 1929, in Jersey City, New Jersey, into an extended family that included three brothers, a sister, aunts, uncles, and grandparents. His father was a professional barefist boxer, then a stevedore, a dock foreman, and a salesman, and his mother had worked as a secretary in New York. Both parents read widely, quoted literature at the dinner table, and on Saturday afternoons gathered the children around the radio to listen to broadcasts of the Metropolitan Opera. Under a pseudonym, his mother, a member of the Third Order of Saint Frances, wrote book reviews for the Carmelite magazine published for priests.

Like Freyman, Boyle benefited from remarkable parochial schoolteachers who disciplined, stretched, and excited young minds. Sister Catherine Pierre was scarcely taller than her first-grade pupils at Saint Cecilia's Grammar School in Englewood, New Jersey, yet she did not hesitate to give their faces a sharp slap or an encouraging pat. She taught Boyle to read and to love reading. "It is a magic key that opens the door to the world." She so thoroughly ingrained in him the multiplication tables that by age seven he could multiply, add, subtract, and divide without pencil and paper. All his life he remembered her with gratitude. He also looked up to the football coach at adjacent Saint Cecilia's High School. His name was Vincent Lombardi.

Boyle's father taught his four sons to box, and they settled disputes by putting on the gloves in a makeshift ring he created by tying rope around four trees in the yard. At school, Boyle thought it only natural to resolve arguments with his fists, and the more prowess he demonstrated, the more challenges he provoked. Endowed with quick reflexes and body coordination, trained by an experienced boxer, and naturally pugnacious, he invariably won, and parents of his antagonists called his parents to denounce him as a hoodlum, menace, and disgrace. "You're acting like a mean, nasty kid and you're going to get us run out of town," his father warned. "If you get into one more fight, when you come home you're going to have to fight me." After the Saturday opera, his father gave him a basketball, took him to Saint Patrick's parochial schoolyard, and taught him to shoot baskets, and Boyle developed into an outstanding basketball player.

In the eighth grade at Saint Patrick's, a tall, bent, and frail sister, Maria Helena, ordered him to stay after class, and he wondered what he had done wrong. "I think there is something special about you," she began. "I want to talk to you about a special chance."

A wealthy Catholic laywoman dreamed of an academy that would mold brilliant boys into a cadre of Catholic intelligentsia with an education equal to the best in the world. To this end, she built a handsome four-story building on East 84th Street between Madison and Park Avenues in New York and there founded and endowed Regis High School. The Church staffed it with gifted Jesuits and scholastics and imposed an inflexible, classic curriculum: Latin, four years; Greek, two years; French or Spanish, two years; logic and ethics, four years; Shakespeare, two years; literature, two years; English composition, four years; ancient and modern history, four years; math (algebra, geometry, trigonometry, and calculus), four years; and religion, every day. The excellence of the school was so renowned that graduates were virtually guaranteed admission to any university, and it cost nothing to attend.

The problem was that thousands upon thousands of boys applied each year and only 140 were accepted. The sister told Boyle that she believed he could be one of them if he was willing to be tutored by her each day after school for the entrance exams.

Boyle entered Regis High School in September 1943, and from the first day it was tough. A Jesuit announced to the freshmen that the rules and standards of the school were unbending, and that probably only half of them would do well enough to be graduated. Boyle commuted by bus and subway from New Jersey, and had to get up at 5 A.M. to be on time for morning communion. Priests cheered the Regis basketball team that he captained but gave him no quarter the next morning, though they knew he could not have gotten home before 1 A.M. After a night game, he was sure to be called upon first. "Mr. Boyle, will you begin the reading?" Practices and games subtracted from his study time, and he struggled academically. But in 1947, he was one of 69 of the original 140 to be graduated.

Columbia University, being a proper Ivy League school, did not deign to offer athletic scholarships to buy professionals. A basketball coach put it to Boyle in a more sophisticated way: "You will receive a loan sufficient to pay all the costs of your tuition, books, clothes, and living expenses. At the end of four years, the loan will be forgiven. You will owe nothing."

Boyle was proud. He could attend a great university, study physics, play basketball, and make his family proud without burdening them. His father, who had quit his job at the docks as a result of an ethical dispute with Henry Ford, president of the Ford Motor Company, gazed upon him with a look that connoted both dismay and sadness. "Borrow thousands of dollars without any intention of repaying them! That's swindling or stealing. Don't you know right from wrong? No son of mine will be part of such a fraud."

Instead of an Ivy League university, Boyle enrolled in small Saint Peter's College, so close to home he could walk to it. He studied physics until the nuclear physics program was dropped for lack of students, then majored in mathematics. After Regis, college was easy; he starred in the classroom and at basketball, and looked forward to marrying a childhood sweetheart upon graduation in 1951. When the North Koreans invaded South Korea in 1950, he tried to join the Marine Corps only to be collared by his father. "An educated fighter is a better fighter. You get your degree first."‡

Upon graduation, he joined the Marine Corps which, after officer training, commissioned him a second lieutenant and sent him to the army artillery school at Fort Sill, Oklahoma. He liked Oklahoma—vast plains perfumed by sage and wildflowers, limitless skies, the purest of air and friendliest of people. At the Bachelor Officers' Quarters, he for the first time in his life had a room all to himself. Some evenings he browsed at the bookstore in nearby Lawton; it was usually crowded, and the interest people out on the prairie evinced in books impressed him. Later he realized that the popularity of the bookstore might owe something to the fact that the town bootlegger dispensed his wares from the floor above it.

Boyle had requested and received orders that directed him to proceed from Fort Sill to Korea in July 1952. Late in the afternoon, the lieutenant colonel in charge of his class proposed a change in the orders. In return for the army training its personnel, the Marine Corps obligated itself to provide instructors at Fort

---

‡ One of Boyle's brothers became a physician, another an architect, and the third a university professor. His sister became a nun and teacher, continuing the traditions of Sister Catherine Pierre.

Sill. "You are a mathematician and artillery fire is based on mathematics. Men respect you. You are first in the class, and you can
be an exceptional instructor. The army wants you to stay here, and
the Marines have agreed. If you agree, your orders will be changed
tomorrow and you will finish your tour of duty here."

"Sir, I did not enlist in the Marine Corps to serve in Oklahoma.
The war is in Korea."

"Lieutenant, I don't doubt that if you go to Korea you will be
one good artillery officer. If you do your duty here, there will be
many good artillery officers."

"Sir, I want to think about it."

"I need your answer by 0800 tomorrow."

That night Boyle walked around alone and aimlessly. He could
marry his fiancée, live with her in a neat bungalow on the base, and
take her to the Officers' Club on Saturday night and to church on
Sunday morning where patriotic families would contest for the
honor of taking them home to dinner. They could have children,
buy a car, take correspondence courses, and arrange for a job after
discharge. He would not be maimed or killed, and he would be
honorable. Logically, the colonel's rationale was faultless. He knew
he could be a good instructor and that it was the duty of any
Marine to do what the service wanted rather than what he wanted.

"What is your decision, lieutenant?"

"Sir, I thank you and the army for wanting me. I do not want
my orders changed."

Along with other marines and several navy nurses, Boyle flew
from California in a Mars Flying Boat equipped with comfortable
reclining seats and a full galley. Having ministered to torn and
dying bodies evacuated from Korea, the nurses knew what
awaited the young men in combat and they treated them affec-
tionately, acting of their own initiative as stewardesses. Boyle was
twenty-three, and the nurses looked to him to be about his age; he
guessed nobody in the cabin was much older than twenty-five. As
they parted upon landing at Barbers Point, Hawaii, the nurses
wished each marine good luck and some shamelessly bestowed
unmilitary hugs and kisses. Their spontaneous sweetness and
poorly masked sadness made Boyle feel like he was at his own

wake. Granted four hours liberty, he drank cold beer and, having recoiled at the native dish of poi, enjoyed a memorable steak, and he thought with admiration of the women, to him really girls only a few years away from their dolls, who had volunteered to try to ease the agony of the maimed and dying brought from battle.

In a spartan and noisy yet rugged and reliable DC-3, they flew from island to island, down the Japanese archipelago, and on July 7, 1952, landed in Korea. At the airport, he received his first command as a forward observer (FO). It consisted of a scout who was a corporal; three communications specialists, privates; and a sixteen-year-old Korean interpreter, "Junior." Contemporary technology lessens the need for human forward observers; in Korea they were essential. From a bunker on a barren hillside or snowy peak, they spotted enemy movements or positions and radioed to fire control centers behind the front line (main line of resistance, or MLR) mathematical coordinates of their location. As the American 155- or 105- or 75-millimeter artillery fired, the FOs watched where the shells exploded and redirected the fire (500 yards right or left, increase or decrease range 700 yards) until the shells hit the target. The Chinese and North Koreans understood that the observers spying from posts as much as a mile and a half forward of the MLR called down death upon them; they made the killing of FOs a priority. In Korea an FO's life expectancy was short.

Boyle and his little unit proceeded immediately to the front to support South Korean Marines and within three hours were engaged in fierce battle. He quickly learned from the juvenile interpreter a Korean phrase, *Papyon*, which roughly translated into English as "a shell is on its way." Through his battery commander's scope, he could see smoke that enemy artillery emitted upon firing and shouted to warn the Koreans to take cover. They in turn had learned to shout in English "corpsman, corpsman," which meant someone had been hit and desperately needed medical help. On that first night and succeeding nights Boyle often heard the call for medics and often shouted that shells were on their way.

Later in the summer they moved to an outpost overlooking Panmunjan, where truce talks were taking place while fighting raged unabated everywhere else. The United Nations and communist commands had agreed that neither side would fire into a demarcated zone around the negotiating site. But the Chinese sneaked artillery into the no-fire zone and each night lobbed shells at Boyle's bunker. Some rounds exploded on the mountainside in front of him, others on the slope behind him where troops were dug in. Hearing an anguished call for a corpsman, Boyle ran along a trench and came upon an American marine struggling to press his intestines back into his stomach, completely ripped open by shrapnel, and held him while he died.

Boyle had pinpointed exactly the location of the Chinese batteries in the no-fire zone, and back in the bunker he called for fire upon them. The fire direction center radioed back words to the effect of, "Sorry, those coordinates are in the no-fire zone." He waited and then called for fire on fictitious enemy forces not far outside the no-fire zone, and shells from marine howitzers soon struck quite near the positions he had specified. But Boyle told the fire direction center that they were off target and radioed a string of adjustments which marched the barrage right onto the Chinese guns inside the zone. Once the first howitzer and its ammunition erupted in flame, he radioed, "You're on target. Fire for effect." Spectacular fireworks from detonating Chinese artillery and munitions lit up the night sky until Boyle radioed, "Targets destroyed. Cease fire."

By morning, the marine command had figured out what happened; Boyle was ordered down from the mountain. A jeep screeched up, and an irate lieutenant colonel jumped out. "Did you order those rounds into the no-fire zone last night?"

"I did, sir."

"Did you know you were firing into the no-fire zone?"

"I did, sir."

"Do you realize you have created an international incident?"

"Sir, I don't know about that. I know that those particular batteries won't be killing any more marines, sir."

The Chinese could not protest without admitting their treachery in violating the truce zone, and Boyle heard nothing more about the incident.

Shortly before dusk on October 3, 1952, Boyle and his men

climbed into a bunker on Outpost 3 about a mile and a half forward to the front lines. The men they relieved left hastily, hoping to reach the MLR before darkness, and Boyle was trying to organize the outpost and find the maps when the Chinese initiated one of their fiercest offensives of the war. Boyle's service record told Freyman something of what transpired next and why he was decorated on the battlefield with a Bronze Star. The citation accompanying the medal said:

> For heroic achievement in connection with operations against the enemy while serving with a Marine division in Korea from 3 to 5 October 1952. Serving as a forward observer attached to a Korean Marine Corps battalion, Second Lieutenant Boyle displayed exceptional courage, initiative and professional skill in the performance of his duties. He was on an outpost 1,500 yards forward of the Main Line of Resistance when the enemy launched a heavy attack on the position. For a period of 30 hours he was subjected to intense enemy artillery and mortar fire but refused to leave his position until the enemy had been repulsed. During the action he called and directed friendly artillery fire on the enemy, and the accurate fire he adjusted inflicted approximately 400 casualties on the hostile troops. He expressed complete disregard for his personal safety, and repeatedly exposed himself to devastating enemy fire in order to make more accurate evaluations of the enemy dispositions and troop movements. Second Lieutenant Boyle's actions were in keeping with the highest traditions of the United States Naval Service.
>
> E.A. Pollack
> Major General, U.S. Marine Corps
> Commanding (1st Marine Division)

Boyle subsequently volunteered for even more dangerous duty as an aerial observer spotting over enemy territory from a light, slow, unarmed, and unarmored single-engine aircraft. Freyman noted that between January 3 and 17, 1953, he flew twenty low-level missions and received the Air Medal for "courage and devotion to duty," which the citation said were "an inspiration to all who served with him." He made more than 180 additional flights over Chinese and North Korean lines, each lasting about four hours. After ground fire incapacitated the pilot on one mission, he brought the plane back and landed it safely even though he never had any flight training. Before he left Korea in April 1953, the Marine Corps awarded him five more decorations.

Boyle's record in the FBI was also impressive up until his outburst at the inspector. He had worked as a street agent only eleven months when the FBI promoted him to headquarters and made him a supervisor at age twenty-six. In Freyman's experience, that was unheard of. Yet Boyle had justified the decision by excelling in the demanding, frustrating, and lonely work of cryptanalysis.

In sum, Freyman saw in Boyle a young man with great talent and promise. Of course, he would have to behave.

In part because Boyle still looked young enough to be a college student, Freyman assigned him to investigate youthful radicals. Following two suspected bomb throwers, he drove onto the University of Chicago campus. Students photographed his car, identified him as an FBI agent, and raised howls of protests against this "Gestapo-like" intrusion into academe. Freyman tried to conceal the incident from headquarters, then minimize it, then put it in the best light. As a result, both he and Boyle were reprimanded.

Still, he did not give up on Boyle. Two agents assisted Freyman in working with Morris, and when one was transferred, Freyman had an idea. Morris most respected people of high intellect; Boyle had that. SOLO required mastery of complex and arcane subjects; in cryptanalysis, Boyle demonstrated such mastery. The operation presented constant challenges; Boyle had responded more than well to challenges.

The senior agent-in-charge of the Chicago office at the time was James Gale, an old-time Bureau man who believed in delegating authority to subordinates, and he approved Freyman's proposal that Boyle be assigned to SOLO. Headquarters fairly raged and vetoed the assignment. "I'm running this office, and I'll use the men you send me as I think best. You sent me Boyle," Gale retorted, and he prevailed.

When they first met, Morris was almost sixty, Boyle only thirty-three. Initially, he treated Boyle formally, even brusquely, but his attitude changed as he discerned those qualities that Freyman had seen.

Boyle surprised him by his extensive knowledge of the operation and of him personally, knowledge acquired from intense study of all 134 volumes of the SASH/SOLO file. Morris was delighted that Boyle on his own started studying Russian at night school so that he could read Soviet publications and documents. And Boyle's willingness to take calls at all hours and listen to his analyses of new developments in the Soviet Union pleased him. As their relationship came to resemble that of a patient professor and an apt pupil, Morris began to teach Boyle about the Soviets and their mentality. "You must think like they do. Thoughts govern actions."

Just before Christmas 1961 Morris attended a dinner party in a Chicago suburb, and the hostess introduced him to a beguiling widow, Eva Lieb. To her, he seemed a dapper, cultured, and courtly man, and his stories of foreign travel interested her. There also seemed to be about him an air of mystery that further fascinated, and she found herself hoping he would invite her to a New Year's Eve dinner. Instead, he called in early January, and she suggested he visit her home in Evanston. They sat by a fire and talked happily for hours. Morris once got up, led her to a window, and pointed to a small red-breasted robin perched in the snow that obviously delighted him. Eva thought, *Anyone who would pay so much attention to a little bird must be a very nice person, kind and sympathetic.*

Morris and Eva started seeing each other often, and he decided he better let the FBI know. "I cannot live without a wife," he said to Freyman. "I need to find a noncommunist communist."

"How are you going to do that?"

"I think I've found one. She's a social worker who used to be on the fringes of the party. But she was just anti-Nazi, not really procommunist."

Verbal rockets rained down from headquarters. How could the

Chicago dunderheads allow the FBI's most prized asset to fool around personally with a damn commie, much less think of marrying her?

"We can't repeal the laws of human nature," Freyman replied. He did agree that Eva should be thoroughly investigated.

As Boyle put it, "Our orders were to find out everything about her down to the color of her toothpaste." They found that Eva came from a patrician family, had earned a degree in sociology from Northwestern University, and married a distinguished chemist who died in a laboratory explosion.[‡] She received substantial compensation from his employer, apparently invested it wisely following advice from a banker brother, and developed financial acumen of her own that enabled her to help others through social work. She had moved in communist circles, but there was no record of her having been a party member; and the results of the investigation of her political views tended to match those Morris gave. Friends characterized her variously as "loving," "witty," "gutsy," "learned," and "every bit the lady."

"I don't see how he or we could do better," Freyman remarked. "Of course, she will have to become an asset. We'll let 58 handle that."

While the FBI investigated, so did Morris, the party and, for all we know, the KGB. He took her on leisurely Sunday afternoon drives in the early spring into the countryside of Illinois, Wisconsin, and Michigan. "Look at how beautiful and healthy our country is and how much it is doing for most people," he said. "Do you love America and all it stands for?"

The question struck her as silly and she might have laughed had not his eyes so directly and seriously stared into hers. "Well, of course. Doesn't everybody?"

On another drive, she spoke up, "I'm about to marry you, but except for the fact that you are a wonderful man and I love you, I know almost nothing about you. What do you do?"

[‡] During the background investigation, Eva told a disguised investigator, "In the 1920s, most of us girls went to college to catch a good husband. I wanted a husband and a degree. In those days, degrees meant something."

"I'm in business. Don't worry. I have a good income from investments."

"What kind of business is it that takes you to China and Russia?"

She silently noted that his response was not an answer. "I'm thinking of starting a new business with my brother Ben. We think there's money to be made and good to be done by selling uniforms and other things nurses need by mail order at prices lower than they can get them retail. I'll take care of the finances, advertising, and marketing, but we'll have time for each other and we can travel."

"Will you take me to Rome? I've studied Italian. Ever since I was a little girl, I've wanted to throw coins into the fountain at Trevi, make a wish, and see if it comes true."

"I'll take you. But not until October."

Freyman, Morris, and Dick Hansen, to whom Boyle was a junior partner, held a council, and all agreed on the principles or strategy. It was absolutely essential that Gus Hall and the ID (as among themselves they now called the International Department of the Central Committee) approve the marriage as one made in communism and accept Eva just as they accepted Morris. As so often happened, Morris' concept of tactics ruled.

"I'll tell Gus I want to marry this lovely lady who is a woman of means and has a solid political background. I'll tell him that just to be sure, I'd like for him to take a look at her himself. Eva can charm snakes out of trees, and he'll like her, and more important he'll smell money. Then I'll tell him that I'd feel more comfortable if the party or maybe even the ID checked her out. Gus can't investigate his own fingernails, and the ID won't care whom I marry. It thinks women only exist to cook, clean, and serve men. Once Gus approves, he and they will be stuck with their decision, and no matter what happens everyone will always defend the decision."

Morris brought Hall to Eva's home, whose oriental carpets, tapestries, art works, leather-bound books, antique furniture, fine crystal, and china proclaimed to him that Eva was just what Morris had said—a cultured lady of means. Nothing so interested Hall as the "For Sale" sign Eva had planted in the front yard in anticipation of moving in with Morris after their marriage. He mused aloud. An elegant house like this surely would command a high price. Maybe Eva would consider donating a small part of her imminent largesse to his "club" which, like her, did all sorts of good works for the needy.

Afterward, Hall sent her three or four small "wedding" presents and cards encouraging her marriage. They married May 31, 1962. The newlyweds wrote a gracious note to Hall and accompanied it with a $10,000 check for his "club." Eva did not remember and available records do not disclose whether the FBI ever reimbursed them for the patriotic and, as it turned out, productive bribe.

Soon after the wedding Jack went to Moscow for operational consultations. During 1961 KGB officers had met him five times in Westchester County and given him a total of $370,000. In anticipation of larger transfers, the KGB wanted to plan with him more sophisticated means of scheduling and conducting meetings. Jack also gleaned prized intelligence from talks with members of the International Department: The Soviets intended to expand and fortify the Berlin Wall while avoiding actions that might provoke war, they regarded President Kennedy as inexperienced but "sagacious," they believed they could now "direct" Cuba, and they were about to instigate a worldwide "peace" campaign to depict the United States as a menace to everybody. Sino–Soviet relations continued to worsen.

Morris and Eva boarded a plane for Rome October 16, 1962, and she was surprised to find that he had purchased first-class tickets. (Later, she learned that Hall, the proletarian, insisted that he and his "secretary of state" always fly first class at party expense.) She dropped a coin in the fountain of Trevi, and Morris asked what she wished. "That we have a long, happy, and successful life together."

After a week or so Morris appeared nervous and restless, and she asked him what was wrong. "I have business in Moscow. I think we should go on."

The lavish and deferent reception accorded them in Moscow surprised and perplexed her. A man named Nikolai (Mostovets) who seemed to be a friend of Morris and to whom people obsequiously deferred, ushered them past customs into a limousine and finally into a three-room hotel suite. Shortly, a pretty woman knocked, introduced herself as Victoria, and in flawless English announced that she would be Eva's interpreter and escort for the duration of her visit. While Morris tended to unexplained business during the day, Victoria and a chauffeur took Eva to museums, galleries, special stores, and dining rooms in what she thought were private clubs. When she returned to the suite, brandy and chocolates were by the bed. Almost every evening, they were guests of Nikolai or Aleskei or other Russians, all of whom acted as if they were close friends of Morris. "Why are we being treated so royally?" Eva asked him.

"Because you are a queen."

Instead of proceeding directly through Europe to the United States as she expected, they stopped for four days in Prague, where Morris again had unexplained business. (He represented the American party at the Twelfth Congress of the Czech Communist Party.) Then he insisted on spending a few days in Zurich where he wrote a great deal, took solitary walks, and made cryptic telephone calls to the United States. The plane tickets Eva had seen listed flights from Zurich to New York to Chicago. Morris produced new tickets that took them to Los Angeles. There, as in Moscow and Prague, they walked straight past customs and immigration inspectors without submitting to baggage checks or questions. Morris told a porter to leave their luggage by the curbside and hailed a taxi. As they got in, Eva exclaimed, "We forgot our bags!"

"Don't worry. They'll be taken care of."

About an hour later in a spacious room at the Beverly Hilton Hotel, Morris said, "Eva, I want you to meet some special friends of mine. I know you will be surprised. I want you to know that I love and trust you and I am sure you'll always do what's right."

Instead of going into the corridor, he led her through a door of their room that opened into an adjacent room. Two of the handsomest young men she had ever seen rose; one was blond with blue eyes, the other had an abundance of perfectly trimmed coal-black hair, bushy, black eyebrows, and equally dark eyes which, Eva in her reminiscences said, "all at once, danced, flirted, reassured, and warned."

"Eva, this is Dick Hansen and this is Walt Boyle. They are with the FBI. And now I must tell you, so am I."

Boyle, who had investigated her and knew everything about her "down to the color of her toothpaste," addressed her as "Mrs. Childs." "You've joined what we hope and believe is the most exclusive club in the world. From now on, you're one of us; you're a member of a new family and a special team."

In that instant, Eva understood that her life had changed profoundly and irrevocably. Suddenly, the odd questions Morris had asked her, his unpredictable and inexplicable actions in Europe all made sense. Do you love America and all it stands for? From now on, she would share his secret life and all the stress and danger it entailed. She thought, *Well, if I'm going to be a spy, I will try to be a good one.*

The next day, the FBI listed her in top secret files as CG-6653S*.

six

INTO THE KREMLIN

BOYLE DROVE FROM THE airport hotel to the Los Angeles field office of the FBI, commandeered a crypto machine, and, alone in a cubicle, transmitted to Washington the first summary report of the mission. The Cuban Missile Crisis of 1962 had traumatized the Soviets. The resolve exhibited by President Kennedy and the United States astonished and dismayed them. Some were accusing Khrushchev of suicidal recklessness by emplacing missiles in Cuba in the first place.

Back in Chicago, during the next days, Morris briefed the FBI in detail about all he had learned, helped Boyle write reports, and, insofar as he could, answered questions posed to the FBI by the State Department, the CIA, the Defense Department, and other agencies. Then he went to New York to brief Gus Hall. When he returned, he had to answer more questions and start preparing for the next mission. Freyman and Boyle marveled at the stamina and energy displayed by a man in his sixties with a chronic heart condition. Clearly, Eva had brightened his life and given him still more reason to live.

The Soviets called the operation they were conducting through Morris and Jack "MORAT" (a Russian acronym for "Morris' apparatus"), and they wanted to safeguard it just as much as the FBI wanted to safeguard SOLO. Both sides took increasing security precautions.

At the Soviets' behest, Jack again detached himself from the party and dealt only with Hall and a few of his closest subordinates. Morris remained a secret member of the Central Committee of the American party and sometimes saw fellow members. But he engaged in no overt party activity in the United States and discussed real business only with Hall.

The operational necessity of constantly currying favor with Hall was for Jack irksome and for Morris odious. Jack did not mind carrying money and messages from the Soviets; that was his job. He did resent being suddenly summoned on weekends to bring cash or run personal errands or work around Hall's house. Hall believed that Jack and Morris were rich, and he asserted the right to partake of their presumed wealth, so they always had to pick up the check. Hall would propose a business dinner, and when Jack or Morris arrived at the restaurant, usually an expensive one, there he sat with his family. Walking along a New York avenue, he stopped, turned, and led Morris into a fancy haberdashery where he bought a suit. When the salesman asked how he wished to pay, he pointed to Morris and said, "He'll take care of it." Several times he required Jack to buy shoes and clothing for his children and once made him pay for his family's groceries. Yet submission to these petty extortions was a price that had to be paid.

The FBI worried that some thoughtful professional in the KGB or International Department might wonder about Morris' supposed wealth and ask questions. Where does his money come from? Is his wife really all that rich? If he is in business, how can he afford to leave at any time and travel abroad for weeks or months?

To answer such questions, Freyman, Hansen, and Boyle, with the support of SAC Marlin Johnson, established a mail-order firm for Morris. They rented presentable offices in downtown Chicago; embossed a sign on the door, "Women in White"; placed advertisements in medical and trade journals offering nurses' uniforms and accessories; and arranged to procure them if anyone ordered something. But who could be trusted to be in the office all the time, to fabricate records showing phantom shipments and profits, to fill orders and to know the purpose of the whole sham?

Morris nominated his younger brother Ben, who was a shoe salesman at Marshall Field's, then one of America's premier department stores. He had a good job and was good at it. Taught about footwear by his cobbler father, he could expertly advise customers. His bosses appreciated him, and he worked in elegant surroundings and had security. After Morris, Freyman, and Boyle talked to him, Ben at age fifty-two agreed to give it up and become manager of Women in White; his wife also gave up a secure job to be his assistant. When Hall next came to Chicago, Morris took him to the offices of Women in White, and Hansen and Boyle made sure the phones rang incessantly while he was there.

With the connivance of a friendly corporate executive, the FBI leased a three-room suite of offices in a high-rise building situated roughly midway between its offices and those of Women in White. The building had a large lobby and multiple street entrances, as well as an entrance through an underground arcade, heavily trafficked, that ran from the railway station. Its manager and maintenance and custodial staff understood that the offices were used by researchers, including a retired professor, employed by an eccentric multimillionaire investor. The FBI lined the walls with books and furnished the place to look like a research center. Whenever Morris came to the building, agents followed him to be sure he was not being followed; they also guarded against surveillance of themselves. Many of the most critical deliberations of SOLO took place in this suite, and over the years it proved to be an ideal sanctuary for conspiracy.

The FBI and KGB, as if partners rather than adversaries, both insisted that Morris travel to the Soviet bloc under a fictitious name. Both knew that the CIA and West European intelligence services tried to track Westerners venturing into the bloc. Unless the traveler was a diplomat, journalist, or someone with a conspicuously legitimate purpose in going there, he or she might fall under suspicion and, if repeated trips were detected, be investigated. The Soviets obviously did not want Morris investigated. The FBI did not want him or anything pertaining to SOLO to come to the attention of the CIA or other Western services. It was not a matter of distrust. The small coterie of FBI personnel involved in SOLO simply followed a fundamental rule of espionage: If someone does not have a clear need to know something, then don't let him or her know anything, and if you have to tell someone a little, tell only a little.

Freyman and the SAC applied this rule strictly to their own colleagues and subordinates in the Chicago field office. They isolated Boyle in a commodious office on the ninth floor of the federal building next to the room where wiretaps were monitored. It was a special, privileged redoubt—windowless and impenetrable. The walls were covered with soundproofing tile. No one except SOLO initiates could enter; only Boyle and his partner were allowed to answer the phone. The bookshelves were crammed with communist tracts and radical literature. Except during chance encounters in the corridors or garage, Boyle rarely talked to his fellow agents; he did not lunch, drink, or party with them; he could not ask for advice or help from them. Only one veteran stenographer possessing the highest security clearances took his dictation and typed his reports. Colleagues, most of them skilled investigators, regarded him as a man of mystery, a recluse who worked in "Sleepy Hollow." Some wondered whether he worked at all because he appeared in the federal building irregularly, sometimes not showing up for days, and no one ever saw any results from him. Perhaps because his envied office adjoined the wiretap room, others more kindly speculated that he was engaged in some extraordinary electronic eavesdropping operation.

To deny other government agencies as well as its own personnel the least clue about SOLO, the FBI granted those running it wide latitude to enlist civilians as unwitting conspirators in the operation. In New York, Burlinson and his men recorded the serial number of every dollar bill the KGB passed to Jack. The Federal Reserve Bank in New York detected in circulation $50 bills, which the arcane arts of money men determined at one time had been in Cuba, and suggested the FBI ascertain how and for what purpose the Cubans were getting dollars into the United States. The serial numbers of the $50 bills matched some of those provided by the Soviets. People at the Federal Reserve simply and very competently were doing their job—too competently. The FBI could not tell them to back off without telling them something about SOLO. Yet if the Federal Reserve persevered and traced more money from Cuba or the Soviet Union to the American party, a public hue and cry about foreign funding of American communism probably would ensue and end SOLO.

Burlinson took advantage of a standing invitation to lunch at the Yale Club with a lifelong friend, an eminent New York banker, and asked a peculiar favor. Could his bank accept from the FBI large sums of cash—hundreds of thousands, maybe more than a million dollars annually—and give back equal sums in different cash, and keep the transactions absolutely secret and make no profit from them? The banker thought a moment before saying, "I suppose this is important." Burlinson nodded. "All right, I will handle it myself." Imposing further, Burlinson asked if the FBI could rent safe deposit boxes under fictitious names and addresses. The banker laughed. "This is turning out to be a very expensive lunch. Maybe we should have gone to a Mafia restaurant; I feel like I'm talking to a don."

Boyle, after making a background investigation, recruited a travel agent who agreed to issue multiple plane tickets for the same journey under any name specified. These allowed Morris to shift his itinerary at will, enabled him to enter and leave the Soviet bloc by different routes, and gave him the option of pausing in Western Europe before proceeding home. Boyle did not have to present a passport or parry inquiries about why people for whom he picked up tickets so often went behind the Iron Curtain. In time, the travel agent taught Boyle how to write plane tickets and permitted him to issue them himself.

Morris always took along lots of medicine for himself and his Soviet friends. For their headaches and hangovers, the Soviets craved aspirin, which seemed hard to get, and Alka-Seltzer, which they did not have. They also prized decongestants such as Contac.

Ponomarev, one of the most privileged men in the Soviet Union, once spent several minutes extolling the wonders of Contac and he counted on Morris to keep him supplied. The labels on bottles of prescription medicine Morris needed had to match the name and background under which he was traveling. Again after a background investigation, Boyle recruited a pharmacist who provided the medications and appropriate labels. If Morris was about to travel as, say, Mr. Peter Schroeder of Cleveland, the labels showed that the medicine was prescribed for Mr. Peter Schroeder and had been purchased from a Cleveland pharmacy.

The FBI considered each reentry of Morris into the United States a time of potential trouble. He carried a false passport and often Soviet documents likely to arouse the curiosity of customs officials who were paid to be curious. Sometimes he also had unusual amounts of cash; not the huge sums such as the KGB delivered to Jack in New York but much more than a businessman or tourist normally would carry. Therefore, the FBI required that whenever he landed an agent be at the airport to persuade customs and immigration authorities to admit him without examination, to take care of trouble if it did arise, and to file a preliminary report of the mission as quickly as possible.

These receptions could not be scheduled in advance because Morris rarely knew in advance when he could leave the Soviet Union. So it was agreed that once he reached the West, usually Switzerland or Scandinavia, he would telephone Chicago. But whom to call? And what kind of number would be answered without fail twenty-four hours a day? Boyle thought, *a physician's number*.

After considerable searching and investigation, Boyle found a Chicago physician who agreed to relay from his home or office at any hour day or night cryptic messages from an unknown overseas caller to Boyle.

The travel agent, the pharmacist, and the physician never received any reward of any kind; they never knew just why they were asked to do what they did. They only knew that their services were important to the United States, and they were.

Morris was supposed to represent the American party at a

Moscow conference in May 1963, but a mild recurrence of his heart problem precluded travel and, as the Soviets had been asking to see Jack, Hall sent him instead.

The greeting at the airport, the limousine, the hotel suite, audiences with Suslov and Ponomarev, and dinners with members of the Central Committee and International Department collectively testified to Jack's new status. He still was an essential tool of the KGB; he also was, if not co-chairman, then vice president of MORAT and a personal emissary of Hall, the American head of state "temporarily out of power," and therefore above the KGB.

Fidel Castro was in Moscow at the time, and the Soviets said all might benefit in the future if Jack got to know him; delicately, they said Castro could be mercurial and that Jack should not reveal the extent of his "friendship" and that of the American party with the Soviet Union. The Soviets contrived to bring them together as if by chance at a dinner, and Castro talked to Jack affably and at length in English, insolently ignoring his hosts. Exaggerating the influence of the American party, Jack cited its efforts to generate popular support for Cuba. Castro thanked him and said he hoped they would meet again, perhaps in Havana.

Officially, the Soviets instructed Jack to inform Hall that border disputes with the Chinese might erupt into armed skirmishes. In hopes of averting conflict and reconciling other differences, they planned to try to negotiate with the Chinese in July.

Privately, some of the Soviets confided information neither Hall nor Jack had any business knowing: In the aftermath of the Cuban crisis, the Soviet Union was relocating its intercontinental ballistic missiles. Khrushchev's power was eroding, and Politburo members were competing to grab some of it. Repercussions from the case of Colonel Oleg Penkovsky, who had been unmasked as a British–American spy, continued; General Ivan Serov, head of Soviet military intelligence, the GRU, and several of his deputies had been fired.

Jack discussed operational matters with KGB officers who showed him a microfilm container that destroyed its own contents if improperly opened. They also trained him to use a new miniature transmitter–receiver for short-range communications in New

York; it recorded a dictated message lasting up to one minute. Having fitted it inconspicuously under his suit jacket and stringing the aerial inside his trouser leg, Jack was to appear in a specified department store or other public place and at the designated moment press a button that caused the device to transmit the message in a burst of a few seconds. A comparable device worn by a KGB officer loitering out of sight in the area would record the burst transmission, and when played back slowly it would become comprehensible. If Jack was to receive a message, he had to do nothing except show up at the appointed time.

The KGB advised Jack that it would leave both the microfilm container and transmitter for him at drops around New York. Ordinarily, KGB laboratories did not design esoteric equipment for just one operation—knowledge of new espionage instruments might help detect other KGB operations around the world. So the FBI looked forward to taking apart and duplicating those promised to Jack.

Analysts were still poring over reports from Jack's mission when Morris came back from Moscow and Prague in August 1963 with much more for them. The Soviets believed that North Korea was contemplating a military attack on South Korea to reunify the two countries forcibly, and the specter of another Korean War appalled them. They were not sure what the Chinese would do; they realized that the presence of American troops in South Korea would guarantee the United States' involvement; the uncertainties were nightmarish.

Castro was behaving like a Latin egotist and prima donna, alternately bellowing and pouting, and relations with Cuba were not entirely satisfactory. The Czechs intended to seek better relations with the United States. So did the Soviets, who still were feeling tremors from the Cuban Missile Crisis.

Most important, the July negotiations in Moscow between Chinese and Soviet delegations led by Teng Hsiao-Ping and Mikhail Suslov were a calamity. Suslov allowed his old friend and pupil, Morris, to read English translations of speeches by him and Teng, and to make copious notes. Morris made almost verbatim copies that documented a fact that many, maybe most, American analysts could not bring themselves to accept: China and the Soviet Union were becoming real, implacable, and emotional enemies.

Teng began the "negotiations" by extolling Stalin. He demanded that the Soviets recant their repudiations of Stalin, abandon the policy of "peaceful coexistence" with the West, renounce the doctrine that World War III was not inevitable, and admit that the war would not start until the United States had subjugated the Third World. In essence, he demanded that the Soviet Union, domestically and internationally, revert to Stalinism.

Suslov, who had attempted to be conciliatory and pleaded for civil, comradely discourse, replied, "Do you really expect to turn the world communist movement back to a situation in which one person rises like a god above the people?... How could you expect the Soviet people, who paid for the personality cult with the blood of millions upon millions of innocent victims, including their best communist sons, to support such a demand?... Why do you justify Stalin's errors and crimes? Why?"

The Chinese then accused the Soviets of cowardice for not looking forward to nuclear war. Some ten months before, during the Cuban Missile Crisis, Suslov sat with Khrushchev and Politburo members as officers of the Soviet General Staff gave their objective, professional judgment of the consequences of nuclear war. He echoed that judgment in his response to Teng: "It is clear that you do not recognize the possibility of preventing a world war. This means that you deny that war can be prevented... Scientific data on modern war and its consequences cannot be concealed from the people. It is estimated that between 700 million and 800 million people would die in the first nuclear blow." Suslov then accused the Chinese of treating the Soviets as enemies, of "intolerable rudeness," and of shouting "slander and lies."

Two days later, Teng countered with charges that the Soviet Union sought better relations with the United States and India than with China. "You are working wholeheartedly and cooperating with American imperialism... It is quite evident that our differences are of a very serious nature... Your great power chauvinism creates a serious threat of a split in the world communist movement... As the saying goes, 'Rein in your horses in the nick of time before you plunge into the abyss...' There is an old Chinese proverb: 'Good medicine is always bitter but beneficial.' We gave you much good advice. Take it."

Morris pointed out to Freyman and Boyle that these exchanges occurred over a span of ten days. After each exchange, Suslov and Teng had time to reflect and consult their respective governments or parties. So the import of the insulting words was graver than the words themselves because they represented the considered and calculated positions of the Soviet Union and China toward each other. Neither man had succumbed to a fit of personal pique and in anger said things he did not really mean.

Continuing his interpretations, Morris said that while Mao himself might be a little crazy, and the Chinese might sound crazy, and their Stalinist beliefs might be crazy, given their premises they were acting logically and there was some truth in their allegations. The Soviets indeed had renounced Stalin and policies resulting in the mass murder of their people. Soviet leaders were chauvinists: they put their personal interests first and perceived Soviet interests above those of international communism. They did behave toward foreign communist parties as Teng said—"like a father toward a small son"—and they did try to buy or control foreign parties for their own benefit.

At the same time, Soviet leaders, given their premises, were acting with equal logic. Since the 1920s they had been governed by a doctrine, the Correlation of Forces, which dictated that you never initiate a war or battle unless the balance of power so favors you that victory is certain or the enemy will realize the futility of even resisting. In a nuclear war with the United States, victory was far from certain; obliteration of all Soviet cities and basic industry was. Soviet strategists comprehended that whatever the other outcomes, nuclear war would leave them with a depopulated, primitive agrarian society vulnerable to hordes of Chinese. The Chinese professed not to fear nuclear war. They did not understand that it would return them to the Stone Age, and they believed they could afford to lose a few hundred million people, people being the one thing they had in abundance. Hence, the

Soviets, in defiance of what the Chinese considered fundamental rules of fraternal Marxism, refused to share nuclear weapons and withdrew technical assistance.

Morris taught Freyman and Boyle that the intentions of the Soviets often could be divined from what they said if you knew how to decipher the meaning of their words. The slogans "peaceful coexistence" and "peaceful competition" did not augur the end of efforts by the Soviet Union to expand its empire through espionage, subversion, propaganda, intrigue, and "wars of national liberation." They meant only that the Soviets would not wittingly risk provoking nuclear war with the United States, as Khrushchev very nearly did in Cuba.

In Morris' judgment, Sino–Soviet differences could not be reconciled; rather, they were destined to worsen because the Chinese would not moderate their ideological demands and the Soviets could not possibly accede to them. Events had proven Morris' past analyses so correct and insightful that Boyle thought he would be derelict if he did not allow headquarters and policymakers to consider this one. So after Sunday morning Mass, he devoted most of the day to incorporating it into a report. Neither Freyman nor Boyle ever uttered profanity, not so much as a "damn"; to them use of obscenities reflected ignorance of the richness of the English language and disrespect for others. But Boyle came close upon reading the headquarters response to his report: "We are an investigative organization; not a think tank. We are interested in facts; not opinions. Take note."

ON NOVEMBER 1, 1963, Morris began what is recorded in an informal FBI history of SOLO as the "Fourteenth Mission." By now the Soviets had established a routine that required him to come to Moscow each autumn to receive instructions for the American party, to submit a budget detailing what the American party proposed to spend in the forthcoming year, to answer questions and offer opinions about conditions and personalities in the United States, and generally to survey the world and discuss strategy. Almost always during these

annual consultations, he spent many hours with Suslov, Ponomarev, and Politburo members; usually he also saw Khrushchev
and, later, Leonid Brezhnev as well as senior KGB officers. That
November he thought he discerned among those with whom he
drank, dined, and conferred collective gloom and individual
uncertainty.

The Soviets were more exasperated, even enraged, by the Chinese than they had been in the summer. They claimed that China
with premeditated malice was arming wild revolutionary bands
around the world with Soviet weapons so that the Soviets would
be blamed for the mayhem and murder committed with them. It
appeared they deliberately had set out to incite enmity toward the
Soviet Union both in the West and Third World. Their strident
insults and calumny made it difficult even to talk to them, and
Suslov despaired, "The more reasonable and conciliatory we try
to be, the more unreasonable and bellicose they become." The
KGB colonel, who liked to drop by Morris' apartment in the
evening for "general intelligence," lots of bourbon, and Camel or
Chesterfield cigarettes, expressed Soviet frustrations more grimly.
"They don't understand what nuclear bombs can do. If they keep
on, someday we may have to give them demonstrations."

The Chinese were competing with the Soviets for ideological
influence in the Third World and were courting Castro, who by
himself was vexing enough. He had started smuggling arms to
guerrillas in Venezuela and promising arms to revolutionary or
ragtag gangs elsewhere in Latin America without, Morris inferred,
first securing Soviet concurrence. The Soviets did not object in
principle to arming insurgents and terrorists; they did that themselves, directly and indirectly. But you had to know what you were
doing, what you reasonably could expect to gain, and what you
might lose. The Soviets were not sure Castro knew what he was
doing and worried that he was becoming more intent upon
mythologizing himself as a world leader than in advancing the
global interests of the "socialist camp." As he was being sustained
by their economic largess and military protection, they considered
him obligated to consult them and abstain from impulsive theatrics that might drag them into another nuclear confrontation

with the United States. Still, to retain their base in Cuba, they were willing to put up with a lot and indulge him as one would a temperamental child—up to a point.

The Politburo still hoped to use the American party as a means of influencing Castro and communicating discreetly with the Cuban party. Ponomarev observed that when Jack and Castro met in Moscow, each seemed to like the flamboyance of the other and Jack successfully flattered Castro with his inflated accounts of all the American party was doing to help him in the United States. The Soviets hoped to transform this embryonic personal relationship into an auxiliary tool for spying on and influencing Castro, and they proposed that Jack go to Havana under the pretext of delivering a formal communication from Gus Hall. They would make the necessary arrangements, pretending to be acting only as an intermediary of Hall and at his initiative. And they would explain that, to circumvent restrictions prohibiting U.S. citizens from traveling to Cuba, Jack would fly to Havana from Moscow. Thus, they could brief him before the trip and debrief him after his visit to Havana. Ponomarev or maybe his deputy suggested that Jack bring along his wife because her presence might enhance social entrée in Cuba.

Both Morris and Ponomarev understood that the annual review of the next American party budget was largely a charade. Morris laboriously wrote down how much the party needed to maintain headquarters activities in New York; to sustain front groups and publications; to travel, demonstrate, and proselytize; and to pay the salaries and expenses of party leaders. (Much of this was fiction written by him and Boyle.) On the other side of the ledger, he put down how much the party expected to receive from Hollywood and Manhattan donors and from others of the monied radical chic who thought it cute or deliciously daring to contribute. Always there was a deficit, which amounted to what Hall wanted the KGB to slip to Jack at night around New York.

MORRIS WAS IN MOSCOW on November 22, 1963, when President John Kennedy was assassinated. As Soviet rulers hastened to ask him about the possible causes and import of the assassination, he witnessed firsthand the consternation it produced among them. They first of all feared what the assassination might portend for them, but some also seemed personally to regret the murder of the charismatic young president, even though he was an enemy. Having survived the many murders ordered by Stalin, they had tacitly agreed among themselves that after future power struggles in the Soviet Union, the victors would not kill the vanquished, and the specter of political assassination in America mystified and frightened them because in their minds it denoted unpredictability and instability.

The initial confusion produced many questions. Did not well-qualified bodyguards protect the president when he traveled? How could their protection fail unless some of them had been co-opted into a plot? Could the assassination be part of a right-wing or fascist coup? How was it likely to affect the United States' foreign policy and more particularly policy toward the Soviet Union? What kind of a man was the new president, Lyndon B. Johnson? How would he differ from Kennedy?

To these and numerous other queries posed during the day, Morris could offer few factual answers because about the events in Dallas he knew only what the Soviets had told him and he had no special knowledge of Johnson. He did understand the political history and processes of the United States, and, drawing upon this understanding, he offered Soviet leaders analyses that later enhanced his reputation among them as a remarkable seer. In essence, he told them:

> He could not say whether the security men in Dallas had been derelict; considering the dangers to which American presidents exposed themselves by riding around in open cars and mingling with crowds, they might not have been at fault. Pending more details, it was too early to tell.
>
> Many attempts on the lives of presidents had been made; only one, the assassination of Abraham Lincoln by John Wilkes Booth, was politically or ideologically

motivated. The rest were perpetrated by deranged individuals. Virtually any U.S. citizen could buy and keep a gun; arguably, one percent, or more than a million American adults, were certifiably insane and there was no accounting for what madmen might do, alone or in concert with others.

A covert political coup in the United States, however, was impossible, and rational people of all political persuasions recognized this reality. The U.S. armed forces were obedient to civilian authority and loyal to the office of the presidency, whoever occupied it. Abetted by the FBI, they would crush any incipient coup, violently if necessary.

In the near term, there would be no basic change in American foreign policy. Johnson, having inherited the presidency by chance, would concentrate upon earning it in the 1964 elections. He probably would retain, at least until after the elections, Kennedy's principal foreign policy advisors, heed their counsel, and risk no new initiatives. Additionally, Congress exercised considerable control over foreign policy and Congress' composition remained the same.

Matters would have to be reevaluated after the next presidential and congressional elections.

Ponomarev was talking to Morris in his office about Johnson when subordinates burst in, their faces ashen. Unaware that Morris understood Russian, they ignored him and at once informed Ponomarev that Dallas police had arrested Lee Harvey Oswald for the murder of President Kennedy. Other ostensible facts they rapidly reported explained their alarm, which bordered on panic.

Oswald, a former U.S. Marine, had defected to the Soviet Union and lived there with his Russian wife. Soviet psychiatrists who examined him after he attempted suicide in Moscow concluded that he was very abnormal and unbalanced, if not insane. When he asked to return to the United States, the Soviets were glad to be rid of him and they had no contact with him until a few weeks ago. Then he appeared unbidden at the Soviet embassy in Mexico City and requested a visa to go back to the Soviet Union, saying he intended to travel via Cuba. The embassy, following standard procedures, routinely asked Moscow for guidance. KGB headquarters reviewed his record, adjudged him a useless misfit, and ordered the embassy to brush him off. Accordingly, the Soviets in Mexico City advised Oswald that they could not issue a visa until he obtained a visa to enter Cuba. Forewarned, the Cuban embassy told him it could not issue a visa until he obtained a visa to enter the Soviet Union. This contrived runaround succeeded in turning Oswald away, and the Soviets heard nothing more from or about him until just now.

The KGB swore to the Politburo and International Department that before, during, and after the time Oswald lived in the Soviet Union it never utilized him as an agent or informant. The Politburo had confiscated his KGB file, and the copy that aides gave Ponomarev apparently contained nothing to contradict this claim.

Throughout the excited exchanges, Morris sat mute and phlegmatic, trying to transcribe into memory every word he heard. One of the Soviets finally took note of him and asked, "What are we going to tell this American here?" Ponomarev certified that Morris was completely trustworthy and declared he should be told the truth. Through an interpreter, Morris thereupon heard basically the same account given Ponomarev. Almost pleading, the Soviets beseeched him to believe they had nothing to do with the assassination.

Logic and professional training inclined him to believe them. While the Soviets had not foresworn assassination as an instrument of state policy, even low-level murders had to be approved in advance by the Politburo, and Ponomarev surely would have known of any plan to kill the president. Neither Ponomarev nor other ranking Soviets with whom Morris spoke could have faked the kind of shock he personally observed. If Oswald was as unbalanced as the Soviets alleged, Morris doubted that they would entrust Oswald with a mission tantamount to an act of war. If Oswald was a Soviet assassin, why would he openly present himself at the Soviet and Cuban embassies where CIA or Mexican surveillants were likely to spot him? And what did the Soviet Union conceivably have to gain from the assassination?

However, Morris realized that among many angry Americans logic might not prevail and that the conspicuous Soviet trepidation was justified. The FBI or CIA quickly would ascertain that Oswald had fled to the Soviet Union and probably that he had visited the Soviet embassy in Mexico, and the findings would spawn reasonable questions. The Soviet Union was not known as a champion of human rights nor a haven for foreigners escaping economic or political repression. Why did Oswald want to live there, and why did the Soviets admit him, unless they expected to exploit him? Hundreds of thousands of KGB border guards patrolled Soviet frontiers not so much to keep aliens out as to keep Soviet citizens in! Why did the Soviets let Oswald go? Why did Soviet diplomats talk to him in Mexico?

Ponomarev and Morris had just heard plausible explanations and could see for themselves that they were offered earnestly. But how many Americans would believe whatever the Soviet government said? And what might the supposedly crazy Oswald say? If the U.S. government or a majority of Americans were persuaded that the Soviets had arranged or abetted the murder of the president, the United States would probably retaliate. Lesser provocations had started wars.

The bizarre murder of Oswald in the basement of the Dallas police headquarters after his arrest compounded Soviet fears. Now those prone to blame the Soviets could argue that the assassin had been assassinated to bury evidence of Soviet complicity. Some in the International Department proposed that Morris be sent home forthwith to convince the U.S. government of Soviet innocence.

The absurdity of the proposal was a gauge of the desperation of Soviet officialdom. As Morris diplomatically pointed out, he was among the last persons the American government or public was likely to believe. Although he had not been openly affiliated with the party since 1947, he had been a prominent communist and Soviet advocate. Any protestations by him of Soviet innocence would be construed as evidence of Soviet guilt and, besides, how was he supposed to know what he was talking about? The same held true for the American party, and he urged that it be instructed to limit its statements regarding the assassination to expressions of regret and abhorrence of political violence. He also argued that the Soviet government should officially convey to the U.S. government, secretly or publicly, the complete truth about its dealings with Oswald, down to the last detail.

Ponomarev and Suslov ultimately agreed, and Morris flew back with instructions for Hall, landing in New York December 2. In a motel room near Idlewild Airport (now JFK Airport), he told to Boyle all he had heard and seen in Moscow pertaining to the assassination. Scribbling notes, anxious to be accurate, Boyle grasped the magnitude of the intelligence Morris was imparting and the urgency of transmitting it to Washington. They agreed to dispense with the customary summary report briefly outlining all the information the mission had yielded, and Boyle left for the FBI field office in Manhattan. En route he mentally composed an aseptic report that clinically stated facts and omitted any interpretation or comment. However, the raw facts he personally encrypted and dispatched to headquarters collectively communicated an unmistakable message: The Soviet Union had nothing to do with the assassination of President Kennedy, and its leaders were as stunned by the tragedy as was anyone else.

Without revealing the source of information, agents personally briefed President Johnson; Attorney General Robert F. Kennedy, brother of the slain president; and a few other administration leaders. The Warren Commission investigating the assassination received a secret summary of what Morris learned. Thus, within two weeks of the assassination, at a time when public passions and political emotions ran high, U.S. policymakers had compelling evidence that they did not have to act against the Soviet Union.

Nevertheless, Oswald indisputably was a communist sympathizer, a subscriber to communist publications, an adherent of Fidel Castro, and a former resident of the Soviet Union who had wanted to return to the Soviet Union. And the government could not reveal to the public what Morris personally saw and heard in Ponomarev's office. So the communists embarked upon a systematic campaign to persuade the American people and the world that ultra-rightists, rather than a communist sympathizer, killed President Kennedy.

On November 25, 1963, Jack Childs (NY-694S*) called for a "crash" meeting with Burlinson in New York. At 2:26 P.M. that day, the New York office flashed to Director J. Edgar Hoover in Washington a coded dispatch labeled "URGENT" and sent copies to SACs in Chicago, Dallas, and New Orleans. It said:

On instant date NY-694S* advised as follows:

He contacted Arnold Johnson, CPUSA Legislative Secretary, who advised the informant that Gus Hall had instructed that the informant transmit to the Soviets an important message, which message was to be given to CG-5824S* [Morris] who in turn would give it to the Central Committee in the Soviet Union. The message was to the effect that the Soviets were to notify at once all world communist parties on our behalf to continue public campaign which directs fire against the ultra-right elements and provocateurs in the United States who are the real perpetrators of the assassination of President Kennedy and also to strike against those commentators and others including public officials especially in the South who are falsely accusing the CPUSA and the USA working class. Your statements and articles which have already appeared are most effective and correct and need to be continued.

Johnson also stated that Gus Hall wants NY-694S* to immediately get in touch with his Russian contact in the United States and advise that he assumes that the Russians are still interested in Lee Oswald's wife since she is a Russian and possibly will go back to Russia. The informant is to request that the Russians, in the event they interview her, determine if her husband had any connections with the ultra-right... Informant will attempt to initiate contact November 26...

For information [of] New Orleans and Dallas,

NY-694S* is an extremely sensitive source and information containing instant teletype should not be reported but used for lead purposes only.

Soviet President Boris Yeltsin in his book *The Struggle for Russia* (Random House, New York, 1994) on page 307 quotes a memorandum KGB Chairman Vladimir Semichastny sent on December 10, 1963, to the International Department. It is based mainly on a report from "Brooks," whom Yeltsin characterizes as "a well-known American communist and KGB agent." "Brooks" at the time probably was the Soviet code name for Jack. Excerpts quoted by Yeltsin state:

In the opinion of Gus Hall, *the official representative of the Soviet Embassy in the USA* [emphasis added], we would find it expedient to visit the widow of Oswald, since interesting information about events in Dallas can be obtained from her, as a Russian and citizen of the USSR... in the opinion of the Rezident of the Committee for State Security [KGB], a trip from a Soviet Embassy officer to Oswald's wife was not expedient.

Thus Yeltsin and KGB files confirm that Jack did what Hall dictated. So did Morris.

seven

ALMOST CAUGHT

THE SOLO TEAM JUDGED that Eva could be a rejuvenating and sustaining confidant of Morris, and in the beginning that is all the FBI expected her to be. However, through the tutelage of Morris as well as her own intelligence and daring, she transfigured herself from a sweet, caring social worker into perhaps the most effective female spy the FBI has ever had. In Moscow, she gathered from Kremlin wives insights into their husbands' private thoughts and emotions, the kind of intimate personal details no male could obtain. She gradually formed some of the wives into a sort of feminist movement and encouraged them to assert themselves in a male chauvinist world. Eva empowered the women by announcing that she would not attend a banquet or reception unless wives were invited, and her female friends knew that they owed their entrée into high male society to her.

When Boyle warned that interpreters reported every word she spoke to the ID and KGB, Eva said, "So much the better. We'll just be speaking to a larger audience, won't we?" Eva was not only stealing Soviet secrets and smuggling out important documents, she was also becoming an agent of influence—someone who not only reported enemy behavior but also helped affect it.

If Eva could do so much as a female spy, how much could Jack's wife, Rosslyn, do? Surely Roz would be welcome in Moscow. She had gone there in the 1930s to work as a secretary for the Comintern, and her subsequent party record in the United States was unstained. Although she had not been politically active for years, she remained on good terms with Gus and Elizabeth Hall.

While Roz used the excuse that motherhood left her no time for party work, in fact, she had lost all faith in communism and the Soviet Union. She nonetheless supported Jack and Morris when they chose to resume party activity, for reasons she did not understand. She was courteous to the Halls and the few other party members who occasionally visited their home.

Toward the end of a brief vacation in Florida, Jack suggested that on the way back they stop in Washington, D.C. Roz assented, drawing up a detailed list of all the sights they should visit. But the trip did not turn out the way she had planned. When they presented their tickets at the Miami airport, the attendant said that because the coach section of their flight was overbooked, they were being upgraded to first class. Once on the plane, Roz noticed empty seats in coach. At Washington National Airport, two young men, who looked like linebackers for the Washington Redskins, introduced themselves as "friends of Mr. Sullivan" and announced that they had a car for them outside. Roz asked about their luggage. "It will be in the car," Jack said. As soon as they stepped outside the terminal, a limousine with police escort stopped in front of them. Roz had reserved an inexpensive room in Alexandria. Instead, the limousine took them to one of the most elegant hotels in downtown Washington. Without pausing at the registration desk, the young men carried their bags to a lavish suite. Awaiting them in the room were flowers, chocolates, canapés, champagne, and a man Roz had never met—William C. Sullivan, then the FBI assistant director responsible for SOLO. He told her about the operation and Jack's role in it;

then he, in effect, said: Your country needs you. Your husband
needs you. Will you join us?

Roz first spoke to Jack rather than to Sullivan, "I'm proud of
you."

The Soviets wanted Jack to come to Moscow for consultations
with the KGB, and they hoped that afterward he could fly to
Havana, see Castro, and then report back to them. Before he and
Roz departed in April 1964, Morris composed birthday greetings
for Jack to deliver to Khrushchev in the name of Hall and the
American party. Boyle thought the letter Morris wrote was outra-
geously saccharine and obsequious. "This isn't meant for the commanding general of the Marine Corps," Morris said. "You've got
to think like they do."

Khrushchev long had been a sycophant. While presiding over
the extermination of millions of Ukrainians in the 1930s, he variously characterized himself as "Friend and comrade in arms of
Stalin... Closest pupil and comrade in arms of Stalin... Stalinist
leader of Ukrainians and Bolsheviks... Closest companion in arms
of the great Stalin." In 1944, Khrushchev compelled thirteen poets
to write a collective poem to the Great Stalin from the Ukrainian
People, and made 9,316,972 people sign the poem before sending
it to Stalin. Morris reasoned that Khrushchev, as a former sycophant, was vulnerable to sycophancy.

Morris was right. The letter so delighted Khrushchev that he
ordered copies circulated among the Politburo and Central Committee, and he invited Jack to a state dinner honoring Algerian
Premier Ben Bella on May Day. Famous marshals, four cosmo-
nauts, and the entire Presidium were present. With much fanfare,
Jack was introduced to all as the representative of the American
party, and many drank fulsome toasts to him. As Morris had
instructed, Jack responded with a treacly toast to Khrushchev, and
Khrushchev in turn said to him: "Now this great day is complete.
It is truly international and here stands a representative from the
country in which this great day gave birth. When I hug you I hug
your great Secretary [Hall]. Good health to him. He indeed is a
staunch leader of your brave Party. Ah, he is my son! Enjoy
yourself on this occasion. Sit with us. You are more than

welcome." (The quotations of Khrushchev are extracted from a report Jack submitted to Hall.)

While Ponomarev escorted Ben Bella, Jack dealt with Mostovets and his assistants, Aleksei Grechukhin and Oleg Korianov. At his request, they provided him with an American typewriter so he could write to comrades back home. In plain-language code, he wrote to "Vivian," an FBI mail drop in New York. Decoded, the letter said: "Mostovets and Grechukhin are even more anxious that I go to Cuba than I am myself. It seems that even patrons of the arts are kept waiting at the door while Castro looks at the mirror and admires himself... Things are even worse with the Chinese than one can imagine—much worse."

On May 4, Jack was summoned to meet "a special comrade," the KGB officer overseeing support operations from Moscow. Partially out of his natural insolence but also for calculated operational reasons, Jack treated KGB personnel as his subordinates. Jack made it clear that he was working for Khrushchev, Suslov, Ponomarev, Mostovets, and the august general secretary of the American party, and nobody else. If something went wrong, he loudly and brazenly accused the KGB of incompetence. So the KGB, perhaps at times contrary to its best professional judgment, humored him or left him alone, which is just what he and the FBI wanted.

The support officer looked like a young Abe Lincoln. Speaking perfect English, he addressed Jack by his first name without identifying himself. He exhibited thorough knowledge of operations in New York and several times insinuated he was acting under the direct authority of the Central Committee.

"Look, Mr. X, if that's what you want to be called, I do business with the Politburo and Central Committee personally," Jack said. "If anyone there wants to tell me something, he will do it, face to face. So let's come to the point. Why am I sitting in this hotel room?"

As if unveiling some great technological marvel, the officer produced a microfilm container that would destroy its contents if improperly opened. He began a lecture about its value and functions.

"You guys showed me this thing last year," Jack interrupted. "I know how it works. You said you would give me some at a drop or meet. Is this a museum piece, or do you want me to use it? If you do, get it to me."

The Soviet told him that cryptologists had devised a new code for MORAT communications that Jack would soon be trained to use.

"That's good," Jack said. "Thirty years ago when you were a boy and I was studying intelligence in Moscow, I learned that codes should be changed often. As for the lesson, you'll have to check with the people at ID. They control my time."

Playing his trump card, Mr. X proudly stated that the Soviets had decided to deliver $300,000 to Jack upon his return to New York. He acted as if the money came from his own pocket and clearly expected expressions of gratitude.

"Mostovets already told me that," Jack replied. "It's not as much as my secretary expected, but it will help. By the way, send it in $50 bills; mostly gangsters go around with $100 bills, and they attract attention."

Meekly, the officer agreed that $50 bills would be better.

They parted affably, having agreed to meet later to discuss new cipher systems with a KGB expert.

While Jack awaited a visa to Cuba, Korianov counseled him about how to deal with Castro. "We are very familiar with Comrade Castro. We know him very well. You know that Khrushchev spoke to him twice. He talked to him very precisely, accurately but tenderly, as one to a child... Comrade Castro is a very sensitive comrade. Our experience has been to talk to him most carefully. We even have learned that there are times not to speak to him, since he is a man of many moods. If his mood is good, he will listen, he will agree with you; but should it be bad, he will shout and pout." Korianov stressed that the Soviets did not want the Cubans to know of their interest in his trip and they could not contact Jack in Havana. All they could do was help him obtain a visa and make him comfortable on their plane.

The day Jack was scheduled to meet the KGB cipher expert, a KGB officer greeted him coldly.

"There will be no expert present today, and you will receive no instructions in codes," he began. "I have come to tell you that a very serious situation has arisen in New York, and we are gravely disturbed. The New York *Journal American* on May 14 published an article by columnist Victor Riesel. It said that the head of the FBI knows how the Communist Party is getting its money from Moscow and that he could name names and places and furnish proof in detail of his allegations. There will be no delivery of the money we discussed."

For a moment, Jack could not speak. He felt nauseous with fear. The KGB obviously suspected him; both he and his wife were in mortal peril. Not knowing what else to do, Jack did what he did best. He started playing the big con, trying to bluff his way out of trouble.

"This doesn't make sense!" he shouted. "How could you people make a decision to cripple my party at a time like this? The *Worker* is depending on the National Office for money. The presidential elections are coming up, and we are preparing for a National Convention. This is a rash and hasty decision on the part of your New York comrades. I'm not going to let a faker like Riesel harm my secretary Gus Hall and my party. I'm going to appeal to the highest authority in the Central Committee against this decision."

"I am sorry," said the KGB officer. "There is nothing I can do. The New York comrades have the right to make decisions where security is concerned and such decisions are always final."

"It's not that simple," declared Jack. "I will not go home until this decision is changed. That is what my secretary would expect."

The telephone rang, interrupting the conversation. The Cubans had granted a visa, and Jack needed to be at the airport in two hours.

He now dreaded the trip to Cuba, and he dreaded having to return to Moscow after he was done there. He could not back out without making himself more suspect. But he could try to spare his wife. As he packed for Cuba, he told Roz what had happened and ordered her to take the next available flight out of the Soviet Union. When they parted, Jack wondered if he would ever see her again.

Back in the States, the FBI traced the leak to a senior assistant to J. Edgar Hoover, who was trying to curry favor with the press and Congress. The assistant knew almost nothing about SOLO but had seen reports to Hoover about the cash smuggled into New

York. Since he could not be prosecuted or fired without compromising the operation, the aide was warned to keep quiet and get lost for a while. The FBI made sure that those who fielded any queries from the press, Congress, or other government agencies were totally ignorant of SOLO. To anticommunists in Congress, the FBI said: "It would be wonderful if this were true. But we can't produce a single source who can verify any of that." The Bureau did not say there were no such sources; it said they could not *produce* any. Finally, the FBI managed to convey this message indirectly to a few members of Congress and aides who had contacts with the Soviets in Washington.

After the initial story, no other newspaper paid attention. The storm had passed, though Jack, stuck in Havana, had no idea that he and his wife were safe.

The Cubans placed him in a comfortable little villa. On the second day of his stay, Ramon Calcines, a young member of the Presidium responsible for relations with foreign communist parties, paid a courtesy visit. He said Castro knew Jack had arrived and looked forward to seeing him as soon as his demanding schedule permitted. Calcines added that as Castro kept very irregular hours, he might call at any time, day or night, so Jack should stay in the villa until he heard from him.

Some eight months earlier Hall had stationed Beatrice Johnson, a veteran communist, in Havana to provide liaison between the American and Cuban parties. She came to Jack's villa the third day, looking worn and disheveled, and recounted a tale of endless adversity. The Cubans had consigned her and her small daughter to a slum unequipped with either a refrigerator or fan, and she was forced to keep perishable food in the icebox of a comrade six blocks away. Her savings and the money the party gave her before she left were exhausted; she subsisted on a pittance earned from a menial job with the Cuban party. Ultra-leftist Americans sympathetic to the Chinese continuously deceived the Cubans with malicious lies about the American party, and she had been unable to see Castro or anyone else of importance. She had been "pushed around, beaten up, and isolated."

Just confiding her travails to Jack, whom she had known in

New York, seemed to raise her spirits and energize her. After recounting her woes she gave him a comprehensive briefing about Cuba. They dined together at the villa every evening, and he came to rely on her advice. After a week without any word from Castro, Johnson told him that some people waited for months. She recommended that Jack compose a melodramatic letter to Castro announcing an urgent need to confer. He did so and sent it to Dr. Rene Vallejo, a close friend and confidant of Castro.

A few nights later, both Castro and Vallejo came to the villa. As in Moscow, Castro was quite cordial, and the flattering personal greetings Jack relayed from Hall made him more so. After Jack handed him a letter from Hall, Castro asked, "Should I read it now or take it with me?"

"It might raise some questions, so perhaps it would be better to read it now," Jack answered.

Castro read and studied the letter, then said emotionally, "This is one of the most beautiful documents I have ever read, and I speak from the heart. I will always remember and keep it."

Jack began his presentation by asking, on behalf of Hall, what the American Party could do to help Cuba. "What can we do as a party to build a closer relationship? I also wonder if you would mind meeting our representative. She has been in Havana eight months and still has not been able to meet you."

Castro jumped from his chair and exclaimed, "You mean she has been here eight months! Why? How is this possible?"

"Well, it's possible because many people keep people from seeing you. She has tried and tried hard."

Within fifteen minutes, men marched Beatrice, half-dressed and holding her child in her arms, into the room. Castro courteously introduced himself and invited her to sit and join the discussion.

Jack reviewed efforts of pro-Chinese radicals in both Cuba and the United States to keep the American and Cuban parties apart and lamented that to some extent they had succeeded. He noted that his party could not send literature into Cuba whereas large volumes of Trotskyite, ultra-leftist literature circulated in Havana.

Castro again jumped up, startling everybody. "I never heard of such a situation!" he yelled, with real anger. "I never heard of people who are spreading rumors against us and you. Where are they? Let me know."

Jack replied, "Comrade Castro, I have had a long and hard path to reach you. Our party is very much concerned that this be a successful mission. I feel wonderful to be here in your presence. Everyone in our party has great respect and esteem for you. Let's not spoil this meeting. Let this be a meeting of love.

"Yes, I will tell you who these people are, exactly who they are. They will be listed in a letter formally signed by General Secretary Hall. It will be handed to you in a few days by our comrade here, Beatrice Johnson. The important question is how best to make contact."

"I will give you the best contact I can," Castro said. "That contact will be myself together with your Beatrice Johnson. My companion here, Rene Vallejo, will act as go-between. They should never hesitate to get in touch with each other immediately. This is how we're going to do it." He then directed Vallejo to give Beatrice his address and telephone number and to take down hers. As for literature, he said that the American party could send whatever it wanted through the Cuban Mission at the United Nations.

Having calmed down, Castro asked Jack, "Do you think Oswald killed President Kennedy?" Before Jack could answer, Castro continued speaking. "He could not have been in it alone. I'm sure of that. It was at least two or three men who did it; most likely three."

Castro explained that he and a sharpshooter, using rifles with telescopic sights similar to that found in Dallas, tried to replicate the assassination, firing under the same conditions and from the same height and distance as Oswald had. They concluded that one man could not have fired three shots from the same rifle within the time available.

"Oswald was involved," Castro insisted. "Our people in Mexico gave us the details in a full report of how he acted when he came to our embassy. He stormed into the embassy, demanded a visa, and when it was refused him, he headed out saying 'I'm going to kill Kennedy for this.' What is your government doing to catch the other assassins? Yes, it took about three people."

Beatrice made a suggestion that pleased Castro. She recalled that, during the Russian Revolution when Bolsheviks were under siege from all sides, Lenin wrote his famous letter to the American people. As Cuba was besieged by American imperialism, was this not an appropriate time for Castro to write a letter to the American people?

"Brilliant! Fantastic!" Castro shouted. He proposed to compare in the letter what the Cuban government was doing for students, workers, and farmers with what the U.S. government was not doing. "This is an example of how one party helps another party. This is what is called a closer relationship."

Jack had accomplished every one of his objectives. The party now had a direct link and easy access to Castro personally, which would give the Soviets the hidden link they wanted. Castro had opened Cuba to American party propaganda, which would say whatever the Soviets dictated. He had implicitly promised to confront pro-Chinese radicals and the ultra-left. And he appeared utterly sincere in desiring to keep close ties.

Jack was content to listen as Castro rambled on in English about sugar crops, genetic research, nuclear war, industrialization, chicken breeding, and ways to circumvent the U.S. trade embargo, until he exhausted himself. At the end of the evening, he thanked Jack for coming and Hall for sending him. "You have covered the longest 90 miles in the world. Let this be the beginning of new, closer and better relations between our parties."

Throughout the stay in Havana Jack lived under a shadow of fear cast by "Mr. X" in Moscow. He struggled to conceive ideas of how to persuade the Soviets to disbelieve the Riesel column. Again and again he shuddered because it was so accurate, and he felt helpless. When he returned to Moscow May 30, he was not sure he would ever leave it alive.

Accompanied by Mostovets, he called upon Ponomarev at the International Department and, just before entering the conference, said, "I'm going to fight like hell against their decision [to cease contacts in New York]."

"Look, Jack, let me tell you something," Mostovets said in a warning tone. "Your New York contact [KGB officer Aleksey Kolobashkin] is in Moscow. He arrived yesterday."

"Is he here on vacation?"

"He's in Moscow because of an article of May 14 by Victor Riesel concerning Soviet connections with the CPUSA and also because of Nosenko, who defected in Geneva.‡ The article has created a very serious situation, and there has been talk about it

---

‡ Mostovets referred to KGB officer Yuri Ivanovich Nosenko who, without ever knowing it, indirectly affected SOLO.

Soon after Nosenko arrived in the United States, influential CIA officers decided that he was a false defector purposely sent to spread disinformation, just as they decided that multiple reports of Sino–Soviet enmity were manifestations of a great disinformation scheme. The CIA, without any legal authority, built a little jail at one of its Virginia installations and locked him there in solitary confinement. For nearly twenty months, the CIA psychologically tortured him while trying to extract a confession, which it completely failed to do. Ultimately, the CIA exonerated Nosenko, made such restitution as it could, and for many years employed him as a consultant.

The FBI from the first judged Nosenko to be a bona fide defector and so told the CIA. There were several reasons. The leads he provided enabled the FBI and other Western counterintelligence services to unearth spies. Nosenko worked in the North American section of the KGB Second Chief Directorate charged with counterintelligence and recruitment of foreigners inside the Soviet Union. He reported that through homosexual entrapment the KGB had recruited a Canadian ambassador in Moscow. During interrogation by the Royal Canadian Mounted Police, the ambassador confessed and died of a heart attack.

In Moscow, Nosenko had reviewed the KGB file on Oswald and observed the panic at KGB headquarters caused by Oswald's arrest. His accounts of Oswald's stay in the Soviet Union and of Soviet reaction to the Kennedy's assassination coincided with what Morris had reported months earlier. So the FBI knew that Nosenko told the truth about perhaps the most important subject of which he had knowledge. Because of the secrecy shrouding SOLO, the FBI did not share these details with the CIA. It simply said he was legitimate.

Released from captivity and officially rehabilitated, Nosenko married a beautiful woman whom he met while she played the organ at a Washington restaurant. She became the organist of the Methodist church in a lovely Southern town, and he became chairman of its board of stewards. Townspeople asked him to run for mayor, which he declined to do because the Soviets had sentenced him to death in absentia. In 1974, he received American citizenship. Before the naturalization ceremony, the presiding judge, in a departure from custom, announced that no photographs of the ceremony would be permitted. Afterward Nosenko, stood on the courthouse steps with his wife, removed a tiny American flag from under his coat lapel, and pinned it on the front.

in Washington. I advise you to be quite careful in your comments to Comrade Ponomarev."

Instead of the inquisition he feared, Jack received enthusiastic congratulations from Ponomarev, who considered the Cuban trip, which he helped engineer, a brilliant coup. In an ebullient mood, he declared that Jack had "performed an important service" for the parties of both the Soviet Union and the United States.

After answering a few questions about his experiences in Cuba, Jack, despite Mostovets' admonishment, decided to gamble. "With all respect, I must request that you try to use your influence as secretary of the Central Committee to change the decision of the New York comrades," he began. "It will cripple our party, our efforts in the coming presidential election, and all other operations."

"This is a very serious situation which puts both our parties in a most difficult position," Ponomarev replied. "Under the circumstances, I think the New York comrades are the best judges about what should be done."

Jack said that in Cuba he had thought a lot about the Riesel article and concluded that it had to be a fabrication either by Riesel himself or the FBI. First of all, unless one of the New York comrades was leaking information, there was no way the FBI could know about the money transfers, and he was sure all the people in New York were loyal comrades. During the past five years, he received money on many occasions, and if the FBI had known about the deliveries it could have arrested him and the New York comrade with him on any one of those deliveries. The arrests would have caused great embarrassment to the American party and the Soviet Union while enhancing the prestige of the FBI. Why had there been no arrests? If Congress and the Treasury Department ever discovered that the FBI knowingly was allowing the Soviet Union to smuggle large amounts of money into the United States, there would be hell to pay. And if the FBI possessed such secret information, why would it want to publicize it and why through a newspaper that did not enjoy all that much standing?

Ponomarev had no answers, and Jack elected to gamble further. "Has any other newspaper published these allegations?" he asked. Ponomarev knew of none.

Finally, Jack emphasized the contributions that Hall, Morris, and he had made by aligning the American party firmly with the Soviet Union and against the Chinese, by supplying a wealth of political intelligence, and by supporting Soviet causes. Ponomarev acknowledged that these contributions were important and appreciated. "Well," Jack threatened, "if the decision of the New York comrades stands, they can't continue."

Ponomarev rose to shake hands and said, "I will see what can be done to ease the tensions created by this unfortunate situation."

Back in the United States Gus Hall, who disliked Riesel, was disposed to disbelieve the column, and Morris persuaded him that it either was made up out of the whole cloth or that it was an FBI publicity stunt to increase its appropriations. But for the moment, there was nothing he, Morris, or Jack could do.

Jack and the FBI listened, as the radio schedule required, for messages from Moscow. All they heard was "SK," which meant "nothing to transmit." The fate of the operation was still being debated in Moscow.

Then in late June a transmission said that the "300 pairs of shoes" ($300,000) would be delivered as previously planned. A political decision to overrule the professional judgment of the KGB had been made, and in the future it would be difficult for those who had made it—Ponomarev, Suslov, and others—to admit they were wrong.

eight

THE SENSATIONAL
BECOMES ROUTINE

THE INDISCRETION IN WASHINGTON that endangered Jack in Moscow infuriated Burlinson, Freyman, and Boyle, and without ranting they vented their wrath in messages to headquarters.

Morris and Jack always feared for their lives when in the Soviet Union. By the early 1960s, Soviet rulers had stopped killing each other but they still sanctioned murder of lesser beings. As Morris said to the FBI, "If ever they find out that we have duped all their leaders and the KGB for all these years, hundreds would vie for the honor of destroying us." Everyone knew that Morris suffered from chronic heart disease and that Jack's health was no better. The Soviets easily could liquidate them: an incapacitating injection, then a lethal injection, then an announcement that Comrade Childs had died of cardiac arrest. Who could prove otherwise?

Neither Morris nor Jack risked their lives for money. Both had enough to retire to the hospitable climates of Southern California, Arizona, or Florida and live in financial security. They asked only that the FBI keep the faith, the secret, and not betray them. Now they felt betrayed, and they were frightened.

"How can we ask these sick old men to go on?" Boyle said to Freyman. "How can we ask them to keep risking their lives, how can we look them in the face if headquarters can't keep a secret? How can I send 58 off on another mission? What will happen to 69 at his next meeting in New York?"

Freyman replied, "When you were over North Korea in that little plane and your pilot was shot up and you didn't know how to fly, did you wail and moan about your problem? Or did you land the plane and save the pilot and live to keep fighting?"

Headquarters did not try to minimize the gravity of the leak to the newspaper columnist. Instead, it implemented new security measures in hopes of preventing future leaks. It further restricted the number of people outside the FBI to whom SOLO reports were shown and the number of people inside the FBI who could have knowledge of SOLO. It established a new system of accountability that would make everyone with knowledge of SOLO suspect if another leak occurred. Heretofore, if Morris at the end of a mission had landed in Los Angeles, San Francisco, Seattle, or Boston, Boyle had gone to the local FBI field office and transmitted the initial mission report. Now headquarters decreed that, except for an extreme emergency, SOLO reports could be filed only from the Chicago and New York offices. And it authorized Chicago and New York to inform Morris and Jack of these and other new precautions.

Mollified, if not completely reassured, they elected to go on. So did the Soviets, having seen no repercussions from the Riesel column nor any evidence to corroborate it.

A cataclysm rocked the communist world in October 1964 when the Soviet oligarchy suddenly deposed Khrushchev. Hall instantly dispatched Morris on a crash mission to Moscow to ascertain what had happened and what the coup might mean for the American party. Although they had not expected him, the new Soviet rulers, including Brezhnev, took time to brief Morris fully and frankly. They considered Khrushchev guilty of many "harebrained" and destructive acts. One was his impulsive pledge to finance construction of the Aswan dam in Egypt. "He carried the national treasury around in his pocket," Brezhnev said. His quixotic agricultural policies, among them costly attempts to grow corn on untillable Siberian soil as if it were Iowa farmland, had produced only disaster. His industrial policies had wrecked the economy. And his mad venture in Cuba very nearly had precipitated nuclear war and gotten everyone blown up.

The new "collective leadership" that had succeeded Khrushchev intended to revitalize the Soviet economy, particularly agriculture. Morris, however, saw no indications that they contemplated major departures in foreign policy. Suslov remained entrenched as head of the Ideological Department of the Central Committee, and Ponomarev was secure at the ID. They told Morris that Hall and the American party could continue to rely on the Soviets for financial and political support.

Morris returned to Moscow in December 1964 and again in the spring of 1965, this time with Eva. On both trips they copied or made extensive notes from secret documents entrusted to Morris for study. One provided a detailed account of discussions between the Soviets and Chinese in Moscow during November 1964.

Chou En Lai at the outset declared, "We are talking to you as victors because we believe that Khrushchev's removal was due to the pressure of genuine Marxist–Leninists."

Premier Alexei Kosygin, Brezhnev, and Suslov successively responded that the ouster of Khrushchev had not changed Soviet policy.

"Will you change your program which emphasizes peaceful coexistence?" Chou asked.

"No," answered Brezhnev.

"In that case, there is nothing to discuss," Chou said. "We thought that after the removal of Khrushchev, you at least would abandon the erroneous decisions of the Twentieth and Twenty-second Congresses."

"Comrades of the Chinese Party, suppose we forget the past," Brezhnev replied. "Let us imagine we are starting with a blank sheet. Our task is to find ways and means to end our split and restore unity to the socialist camp."

"Well, since it is obvious that nothing has changed in the Soviet Union, we cannot discuss anything; to put it bluntly, there is no point to this discussion," Chou said. To further conciliatory proposals by Brezhnev, he responded, "If you persist, your fate will be the same as that of Khrushchev. It is obvious that no agreement between the Communist Party of China and the Communist Party of the Soviet Union is possible. You are the willing tool of U.S. imperialism."

Brezhnev interrupted him, "Why make such an irresponsible charge? You are slandering not only our party, but our government and people."

Chou continued, unfazed, "Is it not a fact that Comrade Kosygin shook the hand of the American ambassador who is a representative of U.S. imperialism? You, the leadership of the Communist Party of the Soviet Union, are not fighting U.S. imperialism. You are running in the same harness and along the same path with U.S. imperialism."

Everyone fell silent, embarrassed by the acrimonious atmosphere. As the talks ended, the Soviets could not elicit from the Chinese even an agreement to talk again. To Morris, Suslov described the meeting as "horrible."

The Soviets did persuade the Chinese to receive Kosygin in Peking after he visited North Vietnam and North Korea in February 1965. Extracts from other documents showed that, from the Soviet perspective, the Peking conference with Mao and the rest of the Chinese leadership was even more "horrible" than the meeting in Moscow.

According to one of the extracts, "Mao Tse Tung made cohesion between the Communist Party of the Soviet Union and the Communist Party of China directly contingent upon the aggravation of international tensions and the outbreak of war." Mao said that until then "the split has to go on." As for Soviet pleas to put an end to the war of polemics between China and the Soviet Union, Mao declared, "There is nothing to fear from them. They will continue for another ten thousand years." He dismissed Kosygin's pleas for "comradely, business-like" discussions of Sino–Soviet differences as "unsavory." The Chinese, again according to the Soviet account, intransigently and insultingly rejected every gesture of friendship Kosygin offered—cooperation in foreign policy; increased trade; more cultural, scientific, and technical exchanges. To each, they said, "The time is not ripe." The Soviet specialist who compiled the document from which this particular extract came, added, "Vietnam is the most graphic example. The Chinese refuse cooperation. Mao said, 'The people of North Vietnam are doing a fine job fighting without us.' Regarding U.S. bombings in Vietnam, Mao said, 'They are American stupidities. Their bombings have caused only a small loss of life. There is nothing terrible in the death of a small number of people.'"

In this single extract that Eva had wrapped in plastic around her waist before leaving Moscow on April 25, 1965, there was more chilling intelligence submitted by the best Soviet analysts to the highest Soviet leaders:

> The Chinese are discouraging transit shipments by land to Vietnam. [Morris thought the linguist who translated the document into English may have meant *obstructing* or *blocking* rather than *discouraging*; the Soviets had already told him that the Chinese refused to allow Soviet aircraft to fly over their territory to Vietnam.] They want to encourage the conflict and worsen both the military and economic position of Vietnam. They want to embroil the Soviet Union in a military conflict with the United States and, to further this overall policy, want to force Soviet ships with supplies to Vietnam into direct confrontation with U.S. military forces.
>
> Recently, they have started to foist on the European socialist countries their thesis that to render effective aid to the Vietnamese people and the struggle against U.S. imperialism, they must create war in Europe...
>
> On maps issued in China in 1965, a number of sections of the Soviet–Chinese border were designated as "unestablished borderline" and the Chinese names of the cities of Khabarovsk, Blagoveshchensk, and Vladivostok were given in brackets... Chinese authorities are

engineering the seizure of sections of Soviet territory, organizing unauthorized farming and other work on these lands...

The population in China is being systematically brainwashed in an anti-Soviet spirit. The Chinese people are being conditioned for the possibility of a full break and even armed conflict with the Soviet Union, which is the "chief enemy." The Communist Party of the China press and radio are frantic about the "threat from the North." The Chinese are now holding anti-Soviet mass meetings. On March 6, 1965, for the first time in the history of socialist countries, such a demonstration was held in front of the Soviet embassy in Peking. The Chinese are making anti-Soviet broadcasts in Russian urging Soviet citizens to rise up against the Central Committee of the Communist Party of the Soviet Union and against the Soviet government.

The Chinese declared that the Soviet Union and China "have what divides them and lack what unites them; have what sets them apart and lack anything in common."

Other documents Morris saw sounded similar themes. The Soviets appreciated the geopolitical importance of maintaining China as an ally and the danger China would pose as an enemy. They had made every conceivable, reasonable effort to placate the Chinese. The Chinese had rebuffed, often arrogantly and rudely, their every overture.

From his private conversations in Moscow during March and April, Morris garnered more secrets. The "collective leadership" of the Soviet Union was falling apart, and each of its members was scheming to gain undisputed power for himself. The winner of this hidden power struggle almost certainly would be Brezhnev. Under his rule, the Soviet Union would probably seek a stable, nonconfrontational relationship with the United States while engaging in unremitting subversion and ideological warfare against the United States. It would do all it could to undermine the United States in Vietnam without risking war.

Not long after Morris and Eva came home in late April, the CIA termed the report embodying this information "the most significant piece of intelligence data ever supplied concerning the Soviet Union."

As important as it was to know who was likely to rule the Soviet Union and what he was likely to do, to Freyman, the copious data about the Sino–Soviet split was in the long term more important, and he wondered whether its importance was being made clear to policymakers.

Headquarters had enjoined him, Boyle, and Morris from putting opinion or analysis into reports. "We are an investigative organization," it said. That was true and, in Freyman's mind, therein lay a potential problem. As an investigative organization, the FBI at the time had no analytical unit tasked with measuring and collating facts to deduce their underlying or overall meaning. And he was not sure who had seen what.

So Freyman asked Boyle to assemble copies of all SOLO reports pertaining to China dating back to 1958. From them and notes Boyle turned over, he wrote a history of the Sino–Soviet split which delineated a clear pattern of a progressively worsening relationship that had turned allies into enemies. Collectively, the authoritative, consistent reports Freyman cited showed why relations between the Soviet Union and China would not improve; why instead they would only become more envenomed.

Freyman submitted the history to Washington as a report rather than as an analysis and noted he had compiled it on his own time. Headquarters forthwith had an agent take a copy to the White House, which soon said, in effect: Now this is real intelligence; this is as outstanding as you can get; this is what we want.

Subsequently the FBI started asking Boyle, in consultation with Morris, to analyze or comment upon certain reports, developments, or issues. Jim Fox, on becoming Boyle's supervisor, instructed him and Morris to analyze and comment whenever they wished without waiting for nods from headquarters. Thus, to the end Morris was simultaneously an analyst both for the FBI and the Politburo.

Shortly after, Freyman—out of his own initiative and sense of duty—did something original that yielded important, enduring benefits, he did something everyone thought was wrong. He retired from the FBI.

He was at the height of his powers; no one in the Chicago office was more esteemed or respected; and he loved his work. The operation he and Burlinson gave birth to more than a decade ago was generating such spectacular intelligence that the White House, State Department, and CIA clamored for more and more; as Boyle said, "the sensational became routine." If Morris and Jack stayed alive, there was every reason to expect that future results would be even more spectacular. Morris was developing a close personal relationship with Brezhnev, who delighted in direct dealings with a fascinating man the Soviets had come to regard as one of their greatest agents. Morris also retained his longtime friendship with Suslov and Ponomarev, still two of the most knowledgeable and powerful men in the Soviet Union. If need be, he probably could speak directly to his old acquaintance, Yuri Andropov, chairman of the KGB. And he was the chief lieutenant and confidant of Gus Hall, who depended upon him and Jack for what he valued most—money.

After the fifteenth SOLO mission, Freyman and Boyle glimpsed a dazzling possibility that reached beyond collection of information. Jack had influenced the thinking of Ponomarev, persuading him to overrule the KGB; he had influenced Castro, inducing him to establish direct communications with the American party. If Jack could affect the decisions and actions of communist chieftains whom he did not know all that well, what might Morris do with Soviet leaders who were his friends?

Yet Freyman thought like a professional athlete who elects to stop playing before his abilities wane. It was not unusual for him and Boyle to work seventy hours a week, during which they sometimes had to make immediate decisions that were, literally, a matter of life and death. He feared that as he aged, he might not be able to constantly maintain the mental acuity and vigor SOLO demanded.

Then there was Boyle. Partially to put his adopted children in a happy environment, partially to be relatively near O'Hare Airport,

Boyle bought a house not far from Freyman's suburban home. The two often rode the commuter train together, and Freyman, ever the astute judge of people, came to understand Boyle probably better than anyone did other than Morris. Boyle could be unconventional, wild, ferocious. How many politically conservative Caucasians adopt black children and integrate them into an all-white neighborhood? How many FBI agents go to church to pray during their lunch hour? How many men volunteer to fly more than two hundred aerial combat missions, how many earn six decorations in ten months of unceasing combat? How many risk their careers by threatening superiors with fisticuffs? But SOLO itself was unconventional and wild, and it required ferocity. It was, after all, aimed at some of the most murderous thugs and despots in history. Boyle had won the intellectual respect of Morris, who treated him increasingly as a son; Eva doted on him; and he was completely consecrated to SOLO.

Certain that he was leaving Morris and Eva in caring and gifted hands, Freyman bade a cheerful farewell to all and never again involved himself in the operation that represented his greatest achievement. Boyle became, and for the duration of SOLO remained, the principal handler of Morris and Eva. Although he always answered to a supervisor, the Chicago SAC, and headquarters, he made most of the day-to-day operational decisions pertaining to Morris and Eva and drafted all of the reports incorporating the intelligence they supplied.

The secrets Morris gleaned from Brezhnev, Suslov, Ponomarev, and Politburo members during his next three missions to Moscow made Freyman look like a prophet. In October and November 1965, the Soviets convinced Morris with facts and figures that they were doing all they could to assist North Vietnam militarily and politically. Then they gave him a translation of a formal communication from the Chinese party and government to deliver to Hall:

> Frankly speaking, we cannot trust you. We and other
> fraternal countries learned bitter lessons in the past
> from Khrushchev's evil practice of control under the
> cover of aid. The tricks you are now playing on the

Vietnam question are even less likely to work. China is not one of your provinces. We cannot accept your control. Nor will we help you to control others.

We have carefully observed your activities on the Vietnam question during the past few months. A series of facts compel us to conclude that you are pursuing a policy of appeasement toward the United States, attempting to strike a political bargain with U.S. imperialism and betray the Vietnamese people's cause of liberation, and that you are practicing great-power chauvinism toward fraternal countries, attempting to gain military control over them and hitch them to your chariot of Soviet–U.S. collaboration for domination of the world. Your proposal for a summit meeting of Vietnam, China, and the Soviet Union was an important step in your line of appeasement and great-power chauvinism. You intended to lure us into your trap through such a meeting so that you could obtain qualification to speak on behalf of Vietnam and China in your international maneuvers, strengthen your position for doing a political deal with U.S. imperialism, and build up your capital for deceiving the revolutionary people throughout the world...

You should immediately cease your overt and covert complicity with U.S. imperialism and stop your political dealings with the United States for a sell-out of the Vietnamese people; you should cease to coordinate with U.S. imperialism in plotting the swindle of "peace negotiations" and cease to undermine the revolutionary struggle of the Vietnamese people.

As Suslov pointed out, after railing on and accusing the Soviets of all sorts of treachery and perfidy, the Chinese in a sly gesture of contempt offered "Fraternal Greetings!" With a shrug of despair, he remarked, "It's hopeless."

In addition to documents, Morris brought back intelligence confided to him orally. The competition for supreme power continued among the "collective" leaders, and Brezhnev was still the probable winner. The Soviet economy was in shambles, a condition conveniently blamed on Khrushchev. Because of a shortage of hard currency, the Soviets could afford to give the American party only about $700,000 in 1966, whereas they had forked over more than $1,000,000 in 1965.

During the Twenty-third Party Congress in March and April of 1966, the Soviets briefed Morris in detail about the extent and nature of their military and material aid to North Vietnam, and their plans to enlist Western intellectuals in a propaganda campaign to force U.S. withdrawal from Vietnam. They also gave him another baleful appraisal of their relations with China, which seemed to worsen by the month.

Together with Gus Hall, from August 7 to October 15, 1966, Morris toured Eastern Europe and the Soviet Union, conferring with Anton Novotny, president of Czechoslovakia; Walter Ulbricht, boss of East Germany; and Brezhnev.

Brezhnev had triumphed in the competition to become the supreme ruler of the Soviet Union and was now unchallenged. The new leader also happened to like Morris very much and would be an important, though unwitting, source for SOLO intelligence in the future.

In his first meeting with Hall, Brezhnev was much more formal and reticent than when alone with Morris, and while he paid lavish tributes to the American party and Hall, he said little that could not have been read in *Pravda*. Suslov and Ponomarev did. They advised Morris that Brezhnev had triumphed in the competition to become the supreme ruler of the Soviet Union and that he now was unchallenged. Both appeared confident of their futures under his reign, and Suslov said Morris should be happy too because Brezhnev very much liked him.

In the judgment of Suslov and Ponomarev and, Morris gathered, the entire Soviet leadership, China constituted the most urgent and dangerous international problem confronting the Soviet Union. They believed more than ever that China was trying to drag the Soviet Union, Western Europe, and the United States into a nuclear holocaust from which it could stand aloof and after which it would emerge as the dominant power in the world. From Brezhnev on down, everyone in the Soviet oligarchy was truly fed up with the Chinese, or the "yellows," in general and Mao in particular. Passages from Soviet reports and analyses Morris copied or noted suggested why:

> The anti-Soviet campaign in China, which already was widespread, has flared up with new force. On August 20, 1966 the street on which the Soviet embassy is located was renamed "Struggle Against Revisionism." Buildings, fences and roads all around were covered with anti-Soviet slogans in the most extreme language such as "Sweep out the revisionist dogs and devils" or "Revenge for everything when the time comes." Posters hung near the embassy read, "When the time comes, we shall skin you, pull your guts out, burn your corpses, and scatter your ashes to the wind."
>
> Monuments manifesting friendship between the Soviet and Chinese people have been defaced or smashed (for example, the monument to Aleksandr Pushkin in Shanghai, the Soviet–Chinese friendship monument in Shanghai, the summer house of Soviet–Chinese friendship in Hangchow, and others). Soviet citizens permanently residing in China have been subjected to bandit attacks, searches, beatings and humiliation...
>
> The Soviet embassy was subjected to constant anti-Soviet demonstrations for over a fortnight. The loudspeakers blared around the clock, torturing Soviet citizens. The [Chinese] service staff quit the embassy, declaring they had gone on "strike." Anti-Soviet demonstrations in Peking with their outrages continue until this day. This is why the USSR decided to recall families of Soviet representatives in the embassy, the trade representatives, the staff of economic advisers and the Tass office.
>
> The Chinese did not ensure normal conditions for

the departure of Soviet people. Acts of violence, humiliation and mockery were perpetrated against women and children. The most elementary norms of international law and human relations were violated...

[Chinese] Radio propaganda beamed to the USSR is becoming more intense. Almost every broadcast appeals to the "overthrow" of the Soviet leadership. Anti-Soviet literature is mailed to Soviet institutions and private persons. All sorts of ruses are used by the Chinese to avoid state organs of the USSR [the KGB]. Anti-Soviet brochures are placed between the pages or inside the covers of books, including books for children.

The Chinese embassy in Moscow has become a fount of anti-Soviet literature and rumors spread among Soviet people. The Soviet Foreign Ministry protests this illegal activity but the Chinese diplomats continue their provocative activities. Chinese students studying in the USSR and the citizens of the Chinese People's Republic residing in our country, public figures and tourists are made vehicles of anti-Soviet propaganda.

In the foreign arena, the Chinese are conducting an unbridled anti-Soviet campaign aimed in one way or another at discrediting Soviet foreign policy. The Peking leadership endeavors to smear the Soviet support of the heroic Vietnamese people...

There are constant provocations on the Soviet–Chinese border. More than 450 violations of the border from the Chinese side were registered in 1966.

The most revealing and definitive document the Soviets allowed Morris to study, in this case for just one night, was a "Stenogram" filed by the KGB or Ministry of Foreign Affairs from Peking. Written in a professional and objective style, it reproduced the February 1966 conversation between Premier Kosygin and Chairman Mao. Reading it, Morris could imagine listening to what they said and see in their words the enormity of the chasm between the Soviets and Chinese. He knew that everyone on the little SOLO team, as Eva referred to their closest FBI conspirators, trusted and believed him. But he doubted that others would give credence to his version of the "Stenogram" unless they saw it verbatim. He had no camera, so he labored through the night copying it by hand. Nearly three decades later, some passages leap out from the copy he made for the FBI:

> In Mao's view, war strengthens people and tempers them and therefore war is nothing of which to be afraid... Mao said that although it was true that the raids [U.S. bombing of North Vietnam] were killing some people, he nevertheless feels that this experience strengthens the Vietnamese people... Kosygin then asked Mao if the People's Republic of China would join the USSR in a coordinated plan of action to assist the Democratic Republic of Vietnam. Mao replied that the Chinese did not have to worry about this. The people of North Vietnam can get their revolutionary experience by themselves. They need this experience... Mao then stated in a sarcastic manner that the USSR could deal with the West while the Chinese handled the East... Mao continued in a very crude and offensive manner showing none of the usual Oriental politeness. Mao stated that the Communist Party of China does not favor settlement of these problems [between China and the Soviet Union]... In Mao's opinion, the Chinese Communist Party and the Soviet Communist Party have opposing viewpoints and the Chinese want to state these differences sharply... Mao said sarcastically, "We are dogmatists. We are war-like. We do not believe in disarmament. You get together and discuss general and total disarmament. Discuss your big illusions."... Kosygin then asked Mao if he would agree to a meeting of Communist Parties to reduce frictions among them. Mao responded, "Maybe in a thousand years."... Mao then began to talk in a very strange way. He expounded on how tough the Chinese are. He

rambled on about how the Chinese walk around in zero weather without coats because they are tough. He explained this in a way indicating that he believes the Chinese are a "super race." He went on like this in a very childish manner.

Brezhnev on September 26, 1966, gathered Hall, Morris, Suslov, and Ponomarev around a table in the Kremlin and spoke with relative candor about the Soviet economy before turning to the even more dolorous subject of China.

He began with agriculture:

> You know about the differences and complexities of our agriculture [just as Morris secretly understood the Russian language, he understood Soviet jargon, in which the words *complex* or *complicated* often meant a *real mess*]. Our assets are that the rural areas are socialist. We have a broad variety of climates and soils in our country. We forced the growth of industry but did not take proportionate action in our agriculture. This is why we are now looking for solutions in agriculture. In an economic sense we need to make farming profitable and then introduce material incentives for our people engaged in agriculture. The problem of raising productivity is in part also related to the use of chemicals, insecticides, etc.... It is necessary to tell the full truth that for three years we had difficulties in agriculture. This was not only due to bad weather but also because of some mistakes. Today, there have been noticeable changes. There is stability and guarantees for the future of those engaged in agriculture... Maybe these things are not important to you in the United States but we have had real difficulties for three years. But in two years now we have made great changes. This change is reflected in a different attitude on the part of agricultural workers toward labor... There has been continuous democratization of collective farms. There

has been an introduction of pensions for age and disability. Privileges are now given to the farmers that the workers already have. This has improved the mood of the peasantry, and we are getting millions of letters of thanks from the peasantry.

As to industry, just some brief comments on some major problems. Because of rapid growth we have achieved a tremendous level of capital investment in industry. We need to supply all this new industry, and this is why the smallest lagging behind even in one industry, for example, the electrical, has its effects. Because of this tremendous growth, we always have problems. This growth means we need new scientific centers, cadre, etc. We have to be alert to science and technology in other countries. At the same time, we must train engineers and skilled workers for these new industries...

To build our industry, the idea came up to place new plants near the raw materials. As a result, there are new cities where the raw materials are located. This has created problems because it was necessary to build apartments, schools, airports, trollies, railways, stadiums, etc.; this is just another of our problems.

One of the most important problems is creating incentives for greater production and quality. Gradually, we have started to shift work to a five-day week. This again creates its own problems as to how to use equipment, which is idle on these [off] days, in the interest of society, and yet at the same time provide the worker with two days of rest.

In surveying the economy, Brezhnev was dispassionate; when he talked of China, his voice hardened with anger:

We have not lost [any of] our friends in the world except in China... China's policy hinders our common effort and helps the U.S. aggressive position. The recent policy of China has been to try to influence Indonesia, other countries of Asia, events in Africa and even to interfere in Cuba. These policies as uttered by Chen Yi and Liu Shao-Chi ended in failure. In Indonesia, they resulted in the destruction of the Communist Party... The economic policies of China are a complete failure. All their leaps and communes accomplished was to throw their economy back to the year 1958. These are their figures.

We have no contact with the Central Committee of the Chinese Communist Party. We have only a sketchy picture. In 1960, the Chinese were actively putting forward four points, 20 points, 40 points about banning nuclear weapons and other world issues. Now they are silent. During the past period, there was the impression held by some that if the Communist Party of the Soviet Union reached agreement with the Chinese Communist Party, everything would be all right. Some also felt that the situation between the Chinese Communist Party and Communist Party of the Soviet Union was from bad things done by the Soviet Communist Party. Now, everyone sees that is not merely a question between us and China. How they used to shout about "great power chauvinism." But today things are much clearer and people understand. The Chinese would not mind unleashing a war provided others do the fighting. The Chinese work day and night to stir up conflicts between Parties. They are crude and vulgar.

In a laudatory evaluation of SOLO intelligence, the CIA wrote, "Whoever this source is, he obviously has back-room access." While anything Brezhnev confided to Morris was interesting or important to American analysts, Morris' private conversations with Suslov, Ponomarev, Mostovets, and others in "back rooms" frequently revealed more. Ponomarev two days later gave Morris an even better understanding of Soviet attitudes and intentions toward China:

We foresee no reconciliation with the Chinese... We are against a split in the communist movement; at the same time fear of a split will not cause us to give in on any matter of principle. We will continue to fight for our line... The Chinese Communist Party has its strategic plan to split all the communist parties and establish communist parties under its leadership. They seek to split off from five to ten people and then call them a Party. Already, we have examples of this in Brazil, Chile, Belgium, Switzerland and other countries. This action is worse than anything the Trotskyites ever did. That is why it is very important to expose them... There are some Parties that now agree with the Chinese. Some of these same Parties could not be bought or influenced by the bourgeoisie. Obviously, the Chinese succeeded where the bourgeoisie failed...

One argument of the enemy is that there are no national Parties. The Chinese Communist Party says that the Communist Party of the U.S.A. is an agent of Moscow. So if Moscow asks that polemics subside or stop and your Party automatically stops such polemics without consideration of principles, this would indicate to them that you were following the baton of Moscow. Besides, the Chinese Communist Party is acting in such a way that we may have to intensify our polemics...

The Chinese haven't the slightest understanding as to what is happening in capitalist countries today but they are establishing closer relations with the capitalist countries and class. This is happening in Japan, England, France and West Germany. I want to point out to your Party that some U.S. monopolies are also establishing closer ties with the Chinese. They are doing this through establishments in Japan and other places...

George Picheau (phonetic), a representative of French business, was recently received by Premiere Chou En Lai and he was very attentive to the representative of French business. He told him France should not be worried about their recognition of Formosa. He then suggested perhaps the French not only might be interested in opening a trade mission in Peking but also possibly an embassy. If France was not ready for diplomatic relations, Chou En Lai noted that the trade mission could act with ambassadorial powers.

Now let me give you a little detail or story. As you know, information from China is not always complete or reliable.

Top Soviet leaders personally briefed Morris and allowed him to study top-secret documents for several reasons. They wanted to explain their problems, positions, and objectives; they wanted him to understand the rationale behind their orders to the American party so that he more effectively could implement them; and they sometimes wanted his advice. It was a given that he could make notes to aid his memory; he was not supposed to copy a document or reproduce a briefing verbatim in writing. Normally, he and Eva had a fallback or cover story, if by mischance the handwritten copies and overly voluminous notes were discovered: The writings were intended for Hall; they were concealed on their persons to avoid detection by Western customs inspectors; and, oh, he really did not realize there was a limit to how much he should write. On this mission (the twenty-first), such excuses would not be plausible because Hall was along, and as the contraband of Soviet secrets he put on paper grew, so did his apprehensions.

After writing until almost 4 A.M., he lay down exhausted, but anxiety and tension deprived him of sleep. In the morning his frail and ghostly appearance caused Ponomarev to propose that before flying home he rest at a Kremlin resort. Ponomarev even offered to go with him. "You know, we always worry about your health and we both work too much." Morris thought that Ponomarev was sincere, that he was speaking as a real and considerate friend. However, the gesture left him utterly unmoved.

While outwardly accepting the friendship of Ponomarev, Suslov, Mostovets, Andropov, and Brezhnev, Morris regarded none of the Soviet oligarchs as a friend. In myriad conversations with the FBI, he made it a point of honor never to refer to any of them as a friend or comrade or by any other appellation connoting respect or goodwill. He once said to Boyle, "God may forgive them for what they have done; I can't." Eva recalls only one occasion during their long and loving marriage when Morris angrily lashed out at her. He was trying to decompress in Geneva, and they were walking along the lakeshore on a clear, cool evening. She remarked that a Politburo member who invited them to dinner at his *dacha* doted on his grandchildren. "Anyone who cares so much about children must be a nice man," she said innocently.

"Never talk like that!" he shouted. "That man has the blood of hundreds of thousands of people on his hands and he never can wash it off. How do you think he got where he is? Never forget. We are dealing with mass murderers."

Still, under other circumstances he would have gone off with Ponomarev, because during a few days with him on the Black Sea he could have learned a lot. However, two months in the Soviet Union and Eastern Europe, the stress of stealing secrets while feigning indifference to them, and the burden of toadying to the insufferable Hall had drained him physically and mentally. Besides, he already was surfeited with information he believed the U.S. government needed to know. So he told Ponomarev that he previously had booked reservations for a vacation in Florida and that Eva would be sorely disappointed if they had to cancel their plans and forfeit deposits.

Because the Soviets did not want Morris to be seen in public with Hall, who was listed on customs and immigration records throughout the West as an ex-felon and prominent communist, Morris was able to make the trip back to the United States alone. Hall always flew first class and insisted that Morris, his "Secretary of State," and Eva do the same. Morris felt a little guilty whenever he settled into the spacious forward cabin of a Boeing 707 or 747. Considering his age, his physical condition, how often he flew, the distances he traveled, and the fact that Soviet money usually paid for his tickets, such feelings were unwarranted. Yet, he thought, *Here is a country that can't afford to give most of its children an orange or banana, and it's spending money on first-class tickets.*

In Switzerland, he sorted through all he had learned and formulated for the FBI an analysis of Soviet–Chinese relations.

By the mid-1960s, public demonstrations, published articles, and border clashes provided visible evidence of Chinese animus toward the Soviet Union. But there remained in the American intelligence community those who argued that these indicators were superficial shams devilishly concocted to dupe the West. Other analysts held that despite the obvious differences between China and the Soviet Union, there still was much more to unite them than divide them and that in their mutual interests the most powerful communist nations eventually would negotiate an end to their disputes.

This long had been the Soviet view and hope. The documents Morris saw and the statements Soviet leaders made to him revealed that it no longer was. Ponomarev unequivocally declared that there was no possibility of reconciliation. The Soviets were resolved not to modify their basic positions even if adherence to them meant widening the breach with the Chinese. They were contemplating intensifying their ideological counterattack on China and were urging foreign parties to do likewise.

Mao rudely had told the Soviets to their face that the Chinese had no desire to settle their differences, that they were determined to maintain the split, and that Chinese ideological assaults would continue for a hundred or a thousand years. The Chinese aspired to shatter the worldwide communist movement dominated by the Soviet Union and out of the shambles build a movement dominated by them. They were making subtle, covert diplomatic and trade overtures to the West, and they consciously were accepting clandestine commercial ties with the United States through third countries.

In the Chicago cover office, Morris undertook to explain to Boyle the thinking of both the Soviets and Chinese. The Soviets envied the economic and technological prowess of the United States and feared its military might. They would continue to be its enemy, to try to equal or surpass it militarily, and to outmaneuver it internationally. In the internal lexicon of the International Department, the KGB, and the Ministry of Foreign Affairs, the

United States for years had been referred to as the "Main Enemy" (*Glavny Vrag*), and the lesser informed still used that term. But the Soviets believed that the United States would act rationally and that when necessary they could have logical talks with the American government. On the other hand, the Soviets now hated the Chinese and did not count upon them to behave rationally. Americans were not clawing at the Soviets' borders or laying preposterous claims to large swaths of their territory, and anti-Soviet statements emanating from the United States sounded positively decorous compared to the vitriol spewing out of Peking and out of Chinese embassies around the world. If the Soviets launched a nuclear strike against any country, it would be China.

As for the Chinese, ideology and dogma committed them to public enmity toward the United States, and for the time being they would oppose American interests on many fronts, including Vietnam. But their assistance to North Vietnam would be measured and limited and would entail no action that might precipitate military conflict with the United States; hence their refusal to coordinate aid with the Soviets, allow Soviet aircraft to fly over Chinese territory, or permit Soviet ships to unload supplies for Vietnam in Chinese ports. The Chinese did not believe that the United States threatened their territory or sovereignty. Morris recalled that in 1958 or 1959 Chou En Lai said to him that, if political philosophies were set aside, China and the United States as nations were not natural enemies. The Chinese did feel threatened by the Soviets, and they looked upon Soviet rulers as traitors to communism, as naked imperialists who were greedier than the Europeans or Americans because they were needier. Daily, the Chinese party tried to indoctrinate the entire Chinese population with the conviction that the Soviet Union was the "Main Enemy."

There was in the data and analysis Morris supplied an implicit and instructive message for American policymakers: When playing poker with the Soviets, play the China card; when dealing with the Chinese, play the Soviet card. Ultimately, the message was heard, comprehended, and acted upon.

After filing all the reports of a mission and answering consequent questions from Washington, Boyle and Morris customarily sat down and reviewed the mission again, dwelling upon incidents and details not incorporated into the reports. These reviews sometimes stimulated insights more enlightening than many of the specifics reported to headquarters, and, in going over the statements Brezhnev made to him and Hall, Morris articulated one of them: Ideology could blind the Kremlin to reality.

Brezhnev cited as a major advantage of Soviet agriculture the fact that it was "socialized"; however, this was the root cause of the chronic agricultural problems. That should have been obvious to Brezhnev and everybody else. Peasants were allowed to till tiny private plots as they judged best and sell for their own profit whatever they grew. While these plots constituted less than 1.5 percent of the land under cultivation in the Soviet Union, they yielded more than half the potatoes and eggs and a third of the vegetables produced in the entire country. The clear reality was that, left to their own devices and given incentives, Soviet farmers could produce prodigiously; the heavily regulated and bureaucratized collective and state farms could not, as they annually demonstrated. No amount of tinkering with this congenitally inefficient and irredeemable system could change this reality. Brezhnev really seemed to believe that by throwing out a few little sops he had brightened overnight the mood of peasants across the land. Indeed, he depicted them as being so overjoyed that by the millions they had taken to their desks, pen in hand, to compose letters of gratitude. The reality was that nothing had changed. The peasants still were enserfed in mean huts on primitive and frequently isolated collectives where almost nobody gave a damn about what was produced or whether machinery ever was repaired or whether crops rotted in open fields. However, ideology decreed that the system of state and collective farms was the best; ergo, it was the best and Brezhnev boasted of it as an "asset."

"Some day that kind of thinking could be dangerous," Boyle remarked.

"Yes, it could be," Morris said. "Look at what it's cost them already."

nine

PLAYING WITH
THE KGB

NIKOLAI TALANOV STOPPED HIS car at the edge of a deserted lane that wound through the woods and estates of Westchester County, raised the hood, and focused a flashlight on the engine as if trying to ascertain what was wrong. Another car approached and its headlights blinked a message. He is coming. As far as we can determine, you have not been followed. It was a given that the driver of the second car and his female companion would be watching and guarding from down the lane.

Jack parked behind Talanov, got out, and asked, "Do you need help?"

The FBI had difficulty making Jack pay attention to details he considered mundane or inconsequential. But if Jack sensed that he was to be a central actor in a grand scheme or scam, he acted out his role enthusiastically, and that night he followed the FBI script flawlessly. The script was written to minimize potential threats to SOLO.

Because of atmospheric vagaries, the KGB in Manhattan

sometimes could not hear radio transmissions from Moscow. The FBI, with the best equipment in the world, always received them and passed the decrypted contents to Jack. Why could Jack always hear the transmissions when the KGB could not? The KGB, the International Department in Moscow, and Gus Hall collectively were levying upon Jack more tasks than one man reasonably could be expected to perform. How could Jack do so much and do everything unerringly? How could he, upon doctors' orders, periodically retreat to Florida in the winter and still get back to New York whenever something needed to be done? The FBI feared that sooner or later the KGB would ask such questions.

Having identified the problems, the FBI proposed a solution in the form of NY-4309S*, code named "Clip." An American of Russian descent, Clip was an accomplished radioman and photographer. During the 1930s he served as a Comintern agent and throughout Western Europe taught members of the communist underground how to set up and use clandestine radio transmitters and receivers. After the United States entered World War II, he volunteered for the Marine Corps and served honorably. Morris once said of Walt Boyle, "You can take the boy out of the Marine Corps, but you can't take the Marine Corps out of the boy," and that was also true of Clip. After the war, Clip approached the FBI, reported his communist past, offered his services to the United States, and became a reliable, productive FBI asset.

If the KGB could be swindled into enlisting Clip as an assistant to Jack, his presence would largely answer the questions the FBI feared. He lived a considerable distance outside New York, and atmospheric conditions there well might differ from those around the KGB radio room in midtown Manhattan. If the Soviets asked Jack why he heard transmissions they could not hear, he could say that Clip picked them up. Soviet files would portray Clip as an experienced, skilled conspirator; the Comintern had trusted him with knowledge of much of the European underground before the war, and he had vindicated that trust; surely he now could be trusted to relay radio messages and service drops.

The furtive meetings in the countryside were brief, so the FBI script was economical with words. Jack re-created a fictitious encounter that supposedly occurred on the street outside his office (a well-furnished cover office the FBI leased for him at 3 Battery Place). He chanced to run into an old friend and comrade from the 1930s (Clip), whose true name he gave. Clip asked if Jack still was active in the party, and after Jack assured him that he was, Clip requested a favor. Could Jack ascertain what happened to Clip's father in Russia? The request suggested to Jack that Clip retained sentimental ties to the "Mother Country," and it suggested to him an idea. Jack was worried about his capacity to continue by himself to do all that was being asked of him; he needed help and it seemed to him that someone as proven and reliable as Clip could be an ideal assistant, especially with the radio. The comrades knew best; Jack hoped they would think about the possibility.

Talanov a few weeks later gave Jack a photograph of the grave of Clip's father and a sympathetically worded account of his father's last year. He also gave an order to Gus Hall: Investigate Clip. Hall assigned Jack to oversee the investigation; Jack reported that Clip seemed ideologically sound but that both he and Morris wanted the comrades to make the final decision. The KGB then asked if Clip was willing to come to Moscow for talks. In Moscow, Clip passed the ideological examinations; the technical tests by the KGB of his communications skills ended abruptly after only about thirty minutes. The KGB examiner said, "There is no point in going on. You know more than I do. Why don't we have a good lunch?"

To protect both Clip and SOLO, the FBI for many years let Clip think that, in dealings with Jack and Hall, in recording the radio messages—in all he did—he was spying on a Soviet spy ring. Clip, the Comintern agent turned U.S. Marine, did not learn the truth until toward the end. His contributions always were valuable; toward the end they were invaluable.

THE SOLO TEAM ACQUIRED a new and main member in 1966 when the FBI assigned John Langtry to be Al Burlinson's deputy. Langtry soon became a principal handler of Jack and one of the best friends of Burlinson, Boyle, Morris, and

Eva. In selecting him the FBI, whether by sagacity or luck, once again picked exactly the right man.

Langtry was born May 10, 1924, on Long Island, the son of a striking Scottish mother and an American father of Scottish–Irish descent. His father was doing well, managing the family construction business until 1929 when he was killed in an accident. The crash of the stock market that same year wiped out the family assets, and his mother was left a widow without any money. While millions were jobless during the ensuing Depression, she was fortunate enough to obtain employment by a wealthy New York family as a governess. However, alone and working full time, she felt unable to provide the kind of family environment she wanted for her son, so she packed him off to his grandparents in Yarmouth, Nova Scotia.

There, discipline reigned. One morning at breakfast Langtry refused to eat his oatmeal. "You must eat it, wee laddie," said his grandmother.

"I will not."

Because the public school was only three blocks away, Langtry walked home for lunch. That noon, the only food on the table was the breakfast oatmeal. Again, he spurned it. At dinner he once again faced the cold and now repulsive oatmeal. His grandmother said, "You'll have no other food until you finish your oatmeal." Famished, Langtry forced it down—and learned not to disobey.

He made his own bed, washed dishes, and helped with the laundry. In the winter he stoked the furnace and stacked firewood; in the summer he mowed the lawn and tended the garden. Until he completed his chores and homework, he could not listen to the radio, and he could not look at the newspaper before his grandparents read it. If he complained about being punished at school, his grandparents said, "You deserved it."

At the same time, his grandparents enveloped him with affection; his mother wrote often and sent presents, particularly books; and he was happy. On winter evenings by the fire, his grandfather enthralled and excited him with tales of the Victorian era, of Scottish brigades in India, and of Kitchener at Khartoum. The works of Rudyard Kipling and Alfred Tennyson further fired his imagination, and he dreamed of charging with the Light Brigade and marching behind the bagpipes of a Highland regiment.

The Canadian Maple Leaf flew daily from a tall flagpole in the front yard, but on Langtry's birthday and the Fourth of July his grandfather raised the Stars and Stripes, and the phonograph blared out "The Star Spangled Banner." And throughout Langtry's childhood and adolescence, his grandfather imbued him with an ethos embodied in three words—"God, Flag, Truth."

His grandfather taught other enduring lessons. Once Langtry asked, "Will God punish me if I play with Catholic boys?"

"Laddie, why do you ask such a question?"

"Father LeBlanc says that if Catholic boys play with Protestant boys, they will go straight to hell."

The grandfather said, "No, it doesn't matter to God where you worship. He cares only that you do worship and try to live by His word."

With Canada at war, students underwent mandatory military training during their last two years of high school, and in 1942 Langtry wrote his mother that he intended to enlist in the Canadian army after graduation. She immediately replied, "You will do no such thing. You will join the armed forces of the United States."

In Langtry's mind, the fighter pilot had displaced the cavalry officer as the most romantic and heroic of figures, so he applied for admission to the U.S. navy aviation cadet program. The competition was intense, but the navy accepted him and called him to active duty in January 1943. He was not far away from a commission and, he hoped, aerial combat in the Pacific when the navy in 1944 abruptly reduced the number of aviation cadets, and he finished the war as a meteorologist at Alameda, California.

Discharged in 1946, he applied to several colleges he could afford to attend on the GI Bill stipend and entered the first that accepted him, Drake University in Iowa. The trauma of the Depression had instilled in him as a child a visceral fear of unemployment. An officer at Alameda, an accountant in civilian life, had told him that a competent, honest accountant probably always could find a job. Without much enthusiasm, he earned a degree in accounting and went on to graduate school on a scholarship.

While playing handball at the YMCA, Langtry fell in with the local police chief, who urged him to think about a career in the FBI and extended a special invitation. The chief moonlighted as a security guard in an after-hours hotel nightclub that illegally sold liquor. The FBI watched the establishment because it attracted, among others, criminals and fugitives, and one night the chief introduced Langtry to two agents. They spoke glowingly of the FBI as an elite organization offering adventure, camaraderie, and good pay; more important, it offered a man the opportunity to help protect the public and the nation, to do something of which he could be proud. The prospect of hunting down gangsters and spies seemed very romantic, like being a cavalry officer or fighter pilot, and more romantic than being an accountant.

Langtry most remembered two strictures given to his class at Quantico where he began FBI training in April 1951. One instructor emphasized that, if endangered, an agent must never hesitate to use his weapon: "Better to be judged by twelve than carried by six." Another said, "Sometimes you are going to have to be the 'Director' and make decisions on your own. There will be no manual, no supervisor, no telephone."

The first arrest he made at his first duty office in Savannah, Georgia, entailed none of the glamour he had envisioned. With search warrant in hand, he entered a room where a baby slept on a bed. From under the bed he dragged a frightened fugitive, the baby's father. Within the year, though, the FBI posted him to Chicago and challenging duty on the Underground Squad tasked with finding communists who had gone into hiding after being convicted under the Smith Act. Now Langtry began really to learn about the Communist Party as well as how to work the streets of a huge city. He met and admired Freyman, and heard that Freyman was involved in some important, mysterious operation, but he knew nothing more.

Each FBI agent annually lists his "office of first preference"— the city in which, given the choice, he most would like to work. Langtry put down New York, and in 1955 the FBI transferred him to the domestic intelligence section there. For a decade, he studied and infiltrated informants into the American Communist Party. By the time he was introduced to SOLO he knew as much about the party as any field agent in the FBI, and he knew a lot about the KGB. And his knowledge had been gradually amassed from first-hand experience and the personal tutelage of veterans rather than from manuals and lectures.

Langtry also possessed another body of knowledge hard to acquire from books or lectures. He knew New York: its subways, traffic patterns, and byways, and its bars, ethnic cafés, parks, and museums. And he was almost as familiar with its suburban counties—Suffolk, Nassau, and Westchester. He was at home on the streets, in the subway, and in neighborhood bars, and he moved about the city easily and confidently. Burlinson, while waiting for Jack, was once nearly arrested by a transit officer for smoking on a subway platform. That would never happen to Langtry.

Langtry needed his ability to navigate the city and suburbs because he had to do or involve himself in most of what the Soviets thought Jack was doing.

The KGB radioed transmissions from Moscow three days a week, each day at a different time and on a different frequency. The FBI in Washington recorded and deciphered each transmission, using a copy of the cipher pad the KGB annually issued to Jack, and flashed the plain-language text to New York. (Sometimes a transmission consisted only of the letters *SK* which meant, "We have no message today; as far as we know, all is well.") Clip also recorded transmissions composed of groups of five numerals. Because neither the KGB nor the FBI in the early years entrusted Soviet ciphers to him, he did not know what the transmissions said. All he could do was photograph the recorded numerals, pass one photograph to the FBI, and leave another in a drop for Jack. Thus, every time a message arrived, Langtry had to take the deciphered text from the FBI offices in Manhattan to Jack somewhere in Queens, then pick up the still-enciphered version from a drop Clip had filled.

Next, someone had to park a few blocks from the Soviet Mission to the United Nations and signal by means of a walkie talkie that the message had or had not been received. Signals were effected through a small rubber doll that emitted a squeak when squeezed. Three squeaks said yes; five said no. Jack could also call for an emergency meeting, to be held the next day, by making the doll emit seven squeaks. The KGB acknowledged receipt of a signal by sending back from its doll the same number of squeaks heard in the Mission.

Before 8 A.M. five days a week, Langtry had to check a signal site for chalk marks signifying that the KGB desired contact with Jack that day. A chalked *V* summoned him to a brief personal meeting at 4:05 P.M., and an *O* to a lengthier meeting at 7:05 P.M. An *X* announced that the KGB would deposit a message in a drop by 4:05 P.M. (In appealing to the KGB to allow him an assistant, Jack cited the frequent necessity to locate and photograph for Soviet approval new meeting, drop, and signal sites. Actually, the FBI and particularly Langtry did most of the scouting for them.)

The KGB would hand over money directly only to Jack or, in his absence, Morris. Even so, each delivery required much preparation and work by Langtry and the FBI.

The Soviets recognized that if they were caught slipping hundreds of thousands of dollars to Jack, the operation would end, and they strictly followed set procedures to minimize that possibility. Because the KGB believed that the FBI was understaffed and less vigilant on weekends, the transfers almost invariably took place on a Saturday night. The previous Friday afternoon, the KGB officer chosen to pass the money would drive with his family from the city to the Glen Cove estate the Soviets maintained as a weekend retreat, or collective *dacha*. He was trying to persuade any surveillants that he was taking a respite with his wife and children, and wouldn't be working that weekend. But on Saturday afternoon he would drive out of the compound and meander circuitously through the countryside toward the rendezvous point, followed at some distance by another KGB officer. About half an hour before the meeting with Jack, the two would stop at a service station or shopping center to talk briefly and then drive on, the officer behind looking out for the one in front. At the meeting site, Jack's handler would park, raise the hood of his car, and peer at the engine. Jack would stop, get out of the car, and ask if he could be of help. From the trunk of his car, the KGB officer would hand him one to three large packages and a slip of paper with a telephone number and time written on it. Jack in return would give him a cigarette package concealing the microfilm container and a note cryptically listing what was on the film—intelligence reports, messages from Hall or Morris to the Kremlin, answers to Soviet questions, Morris' travel plans. Ordinarily, the exchanges took less than a minute. After Jack drove away, his handler again would meet the colleague who followed him to detect any surveillance. If they were truthful, such KGB countersurveillants always must have reported that they saw no signs of surveillance. For at these furtive encounters among American estates, Jack was the only surveillant.

Meanwhile, Langtry would wait outside a roadside diner, tavern, or all-night pharmacy that he had selected in a previous survey of the area and, at a comparable place he had picked a mile or so away, his supervisor or other agents also would wait. Shortly, Jack would drive up and turn over the packages and slip of paper with the telephone number. "Be damn sure you call it on time," he would say. Precisely on time, Langtry would dial the number, let the phone ring three times and hang up. The telephone numbers were in public booths around the Soviet Mission, and the three rings assured a KGB officer listening outside that Jack and the cash were safe. Langtry then relayed the money to colleagues awaiting him nearby, and they took it straight to a safe in the New York office.

Once, because of impossible weather, the transfer money from Jack was delayed, and it was agreed that he would hand it over at a motel near La Guardia Airport. The FBI rented adjacent rooms and picked the lock of the interior door that joined them. Burlinson and Langtry waited in one room for Jack and Morris, who happened to be in town, to come to the other with the cash. Morris knocked on their door, then silently and urgently motioned for Burlinson and Langtry to follow him. In the elevator he whispered, "Jack's had a heart attack."

While Jack stood by his car in the motel parking lot clutching his chest, Morris opened the trunk to remove the packages of cash. One of the packages had broken, and the trunk was littered with

$50 bills. As Burlinson and Langtry rushed to stuff the bills into a suitcase, Morris rose and banged his head sharply against the lid of the trunk. The spectacle of two old men staggering around and moaning and two younger men frantically scooping up cash entertained onlookers standing on an embankment above the lot.

Having gathered the loose money, Langtry started off with it toward his car while Burlinson helped Morris and Jack into the motel. In the chaos, Langtry had forgotten where he parked, and he paced the lanes of the lot looking for his car. A pickup truck followed him, slowly and closely, turning wherever he did. Langtry stopped and, hand in jacket, confronted the driver, "Just what do you want?"

"Your parking space."

Cardiograms persuaded physicians that Jack had not suffered a heart attack, and they attributed his indisposition to acute indigestion. Morris, except for a cut on the head, was fine, and in his reports to Washington and New York made no mention of the incident.

A few weeks later at a Washington conference, Burlinson, Langtry, and Boyle were rebuked for not sharing more operational details with headquarters. Everyone was on the same side; lessons learned from SOLO could be applied to other operations; and wise Washington elders now and then might lend useful advice. Members of the SOLO team had no intention of telling headquarters or anybody else any more than absolutely necessary, and Burlinson did not want to be saddled with any new reporting guidelines or operational restrictions, so he tried to make everyone forget the issue. "I admit there are some things we do not tell you. I'll give you one example." Burlinson then recounted, perhaps with some embellishment, the events at the motel. Amid much laughter, Burlinson asked, "Do you really want us to put such things on paper?"

"No, we would rather you tell the story when you think it should be told," said the assistant director presiding. "To quote Shakespeare, 'If it ain't broke, don't fix it.'" As the meeting adjourned he invited Burlinson, Langtry, and Boyle to be his guests at lunch.

His words and the conspicuous absence of a luncheon invitation to any of the other assembled FBI brass reaffirmed the unspoken rule that so long governed and sustained SOLO: Let the men who have run the case so brilliantly keep running it as they judge best.

REGARDING THE SOVIET MONEY, however, there was total openness and agreement among Washington, New York, and Chicago and all members of the SOLO team. Over the years, millions upon millions of dollars passed through the hands of Jack, Morris, Eva, Langtry, Boyle, and a few other agents who left their families on Saturday nights. Any one of them could have dipped into the cash with relative impunity but not one of them ever did, and all willingly abided by the most punctilious accounting procedures.

On Sundays, after a Saturday delivery, Langtry opened the packages of money in the presence of a supervisor and several other agents at the FBI office. Teams of two separately counted the bills, photocopied them, and logged the serial numbers of each. They then repackaged the cash according to denomination and locked it in safe deposit boxes at a branch of Hanover Trust Company. When Hall asked for money, agents removed the amount requested, counted it again, listed the amount withdrawn, wrapped it anew, and gave it to Jack or Morris for transfer to him. To accommodate Hall's demands on weekends or holidays, Jack kept up to $100,000 in a hole the FBI drilled into his basement wall. Later an FBI carpenter built a bookcase with a secret compartment, and Jack made sure Hall saw it in his study.

The New York office had to submit to headquarters by the fifth of each month an accounting of receipts, disbursements, and cash on hand. Accountants periodically came from headquarters for surprise audits and invariably found the New York records accurate to the penny.

Although Jack picked up the money from the KGB, Hall made Morris responsible for hiding and managing it. He didn't care where or how it was hidden so long as Jack and Morris produced cash on demand. Because both SOLO and Hall required Morris to be in New York so often, he and Eva rented an apartment there, and it became a kind of financial center. Hall would tell Morris that he wanted, say, $300,000. Morris would call Burlinson or Langtry, and at an appointed time agents would meet him and Eva on the West Side with cash in a shopping bag. Lagging a little behind, agents would follow the couple until they had safely entered their apartment building. Any mugger who accosted them would have been shot on the spot.

Eva usually carried the money because she thought it more appropriate for a woman rather than a man to be seen on the streets with a shopping bag. If Morris and Eva were not in New York, Roz occasionally carted it just as Eva did. Once Jack boasted to Hall that he had just received $500,000. "Give $250,000 to Elizabeth and $250,000 to Morris," Hall ordered. Trailed by agents, Roz marched into the offices of International Publishers, where Elizabeth worked, and handed over the quarter million. Later Hall flew to Chicago and with Morris drove to Minnesota to hide the other $250,000 at the home of Hall's brother.

Langtry more often than not had to work on weekends regardless of whether money was delivered. Unless Boyle was present, Morris and Eva were his responsibility when they were in New York, and he had to be available if they needed anything or had something urgent to report. Boyle came to New York often, usually on weekends, to consult and coordinate. Morris and Jack sometimes joined them for weekend conferences, which took place at the cover office on Battery Place, at Burlinson's home, or in hotel rooms.

As a consequence of these regular contacts and strategy sessions, the Chicago and New York offices at all times knew what the other was doing. Boyle kept Burlinson and Langtry fully apprised of Morris' travels and findings. They in turn informed him of all they learned about the KGB, its personnel, equipment, and methods. As Jack correctly pointed out, if the KGB does something that succeeds in one place it will repeat the action in many other places. So knowledge of the operational techniques observed in New York would be useful to counterintelligence sections in field offices all over the country.

THE PRESENCE OF HALL had precluded the International Department and Morris from conducting the annual budget review when he last was in Moscow, and Morris had to fly back in January 1967. "I want you to look at something," Ponomarev announced as he laid before him a batch of papers. Morris was appalled to see that they were American intelligence reports containing information he had supplied about activities of the American party. "This is serious," Ponomarev said. "How could it happen?"

"I don't know. Obviously, there's a leak somewhere and we have to plug it. Are you at liberty to say where you got them?"

"Someone threw them into the yard of our embassy in Washington."

"Then it could be a provocation."

"It could be. But the information is accurate, is it not?"

"In general, it seems to be."

Gradually, Morris sensed that he was not a suspect, that Ponomarev was alerting rather than accusing him. Nevertheless, he was furious and frightened.

The FBI ascertained the cause of the fiasco. It had enjoyed some success in mounting so-called dangle operations against the KGB and GRU; that is, dangling or parading one of its own before the Soviets and enticing them to recruit him. The Washington field office, which knew nothing about SOLO, was conducting such an operation, code named "TARPRO." After anonymously tossing documents onto Soviet embassy grounds several times, it planned to send a U.S. navy officer to the embassy and have him say to the Soviets: "Look, I'm the guy who's been giving you all those documents, and I can give you more if the money is right." The documents selected did not appear to those who picked them to be particularly sensitive, and there was no indication that they emanated from a sensitive source; they could have come from virtually any informant in the party. (Thereafter, all data produced by

SOLO was considered sensitive, and circulation was further restricted.)

During their last conversation before Morris left Moscow in January, Ponomarev candidly spoke of problems besetting the Soviet Union and the worldwide movement. He saw no hope of repairing relations with China; Castro was a real pain and his machinations in Latin America mainly were counterproductive; there was incipient trouble in Czechoslovakia. The Soviet economy constituted the biggest problem. Agricultural reforms promised by Brezhnev had yet to yield results, and the Soviets needed to buy grain, products, and technology from the West but they had little hard currency. Hall had requested from Brezhnev a subsidy of $1,740,000 for 1967; Ponomarev somewhat apologetically advised that the Soviets could afford only about $1 million. This time when he repeated his *bon mot*, "We can give you all the tanks and planes you want but we have no money," he did not smile.

THE KGB CALLED JACK to Moscow in April 1967 ostensibly for routine operational discussions. The KGB officer directing MORAT from Moscow at the time was Vladimir Kazakov, who had been stationed in the United States and spoke English superbly. In a tone connoting neither friendliness nor hostility, he announced that he wished to review details of the operation with Jack.

Burlinson and Langtry had anticipated that someday the KGB might ask Jack how he handled the Soviet money and suggested that they rehearse an answer. Jack dismissed the suggestion out of hand. "They're not interested in petty crap like that. We don't have to worry."

The first question Kazakov asked was, "After our comrade gives you the money, what do you do with it?"

Jack realized he was about to undergo an interrogation for which he brashly had left himself unprepared, and he strung out his answer, playing for time to conceive explanations for the inexplicable and to leave himself escape routes—or at least enough time to escape from the Soviet Union.

He did what his general secretary (Gus Hall) directed, and mostly that meant he gave the money to Morris. At the instructions of Gus, he kept some money hidden in the ceiling of his basement in case Gus or the party suddenly needed it on weekends.

Why did the general secretary want Morris to be custodian of the money? Jack attacked, "Why in the hell don't you ask him? If you think I'm a [obscenity] informant on my general secretary, you are full of [obscenity]. If you [multiple obscenities] can't do your homework, you are more stupid than I thought." Hall was, under American law, a convicted criminal and fugitive who had fled the law, been caught in Mexico and extradited, and locked in a U.S. prison as communist agent. What would happen to him if the FBI, the Internal Revenue Service, or the New York police found a few hundred thousand dollars in cash at his homes or in his safe deposit boxes? Gus relied on Morris to prepare the party budgets and sequester the party cash. The Feds thought Morris was a decrepit, useless old man and paid no attention to him. That was Jack's opinion; the (obscenity) comrades could decide for themselves.

Probably the interrogation was recorded, and Kazakov together with others that night analyzed Jack's answers and prepared new sallies. The second day Kazakov noted that Morris much of the time was out of the United States. What did Jack do with the money then?

Jack said that usually he hid it in the basement or attic until Morris returned. There were exceptions. Now and then the party needed money immediately. Once, upon orders from Gus, his wife Roz personally delivered $250,000 to Gus' wife Elizabeth. A few times Gus himself had driven to Jack's house on Sunday to get money. The leaders of the American party were not robots; they did what circumstances dictated. Generally, though, Jack turned over the money to Morris, who concealed and disbursed it as Gus ordered.

Later in the week-long interrogation Kazakov raised the broad question bright people on Pennsylvania Avenue had foreseen. Most "special comrades" in New York at one time or another were followed; most undertakings involving fallible humans now and then went awry. Did Jack have any opinion about why comrades participating in MORAT never seemed to be followed or why everything worked so perfectly?

How in the hell would Jack know? He and his brother always had done their jobs. He thought they ought to be thanked.

Like most professional inquisitors, Kazakov reserved the most potentially incriminating questions for the last. "When you give our comrade microfilm do you also give him an index of what it says?"

"I give him a brief list of the subjects."

"How do you make up this list?"

"I type it."

"But you didn't type this list, did you?" Thereupon, Kazakov produced a menacing piece of paper. The FBI put Jack's reports to the KGB on microfilm, and Langtry gave him a handwritten summary of the contents, which Jack was supposed to copy on the typewriter. Jack saw that instead of the typewritten version he had given the KGB Langtry's handwritten notes. With Kazakov staring at him, Jack feigned brazen indifference.

"Any idiot can see that it is not typed."

"Is this your handwriting?"

"No."

"Then who wrote it?"

"My wife."

"Why?"

"Goddammit, I sprained my wrist. It was in a cast. I couldn't type or write, so I dictated to her."

"You mean you have made her aware of our collaboration?"

"Look, Einstein, you guys made her aware. You had me bring her over here, and you talked to her. Remember? Don't you read your own [obscenity] files? She's been in the Party since she was a girl; she worked for the Comintern in Moscow; and there is no way I could do all I am doing without her knowing something about it. Besides, the list is meaningless to her."

On Jack's sixtieth birthday, April 15, 1967, the International Department gave a dinner party in his honor and at his request invited Kazakov. During the festivities, Jack went out of his way to introduce Kazakov to his friends Boris (Ponomarev), Mikhail (Suslov), and Nikolai (Mostovets). Kazakov watched as the most powerful men in the Soviet Union embraced Jack, and he listened as they drank effusive toasts to him.

With a single phone call, any one of these men could enhance his career and buy him a ticket back to the United States where he dearly wanted to take his wife and children, or they could destroy his career and impoverish his family. What was Kazakov to do? Risk antagonizing them by substituting his judgment for theirs, by confiding that, although he had no proof, he suspected that their dear American friend was an American spy who was making fools of them?

After Ponomarev spoke in tribute to Jack, Kazakov rose with the others to applaud. At the end of the evening, he wished Jack good luck and smiled. Jack thought the smile said, *For now you've won. But I know.*

Jack may have been completely wrong. No matter, he resolved, I'm never coming back.

ten

BIG BUSINESS RESUMES

THE INQUISITION OF JACK in Moscow simultaneously alarmed and mystified Burlinson, Langtry, Boyle, and Morris. Jack was the opposite of a coward, and they had never known him to lie to the FBI or his brother. He clearly believed the KGB suspected him, that only the patronage of the International Department saved him, and he was still uncharacteristically afraid.

The mistake Jack made in giving the KGB Langtry's handwritten note along with the microfilm instead of a typed index merited questions. But Jack so plausibly explained away the incident that he was questioned about it only once. What then prompted the unprecedented five-day interrogation? Review of radio messages and contacts with the KGB in New York during the past six months yielded not a hint of an answer.

Langtry submitted a hopeful theory, emphasizing it was only a theory. Kazakov appeared to be a rising star in the KGB, or else it would not have appointed him to supervise the servicing of MORAT in which Soviet leaders, from Brezhnev on down, personally were involved. Maybe he just wanted to familiarize himself with minute operational details so that he could do his job better and, if necessary, demonstrate to the Kremlin that he knew what he was doing. Jack was under extreme stress and maybe it, together with his guilt, caused him to misconstrue the purpose of the questions.

"I hope you're right and you may be," Morris said. "In any case, we must watch and listen to Gus very carefully in coming weeks."

The Soviets communicated with Hall almost exclusively through Jack and Morris because they did not want to associate with him in the United States and lend credence to charges by anti-communists that he was merely their puppet. But Morris believed that, if they ever concluded that he and Jack were actually U.S. agents, the Soviet ambassador at the United Nations or in Washington would warn Hall and, because he was not a subtle man, his behavior would change markedly. If he stopped using Jack as an errand boy or asking for money or calling Morris, if he went to the United Nations or Washington, if he convened unusual meetings at party headquarters, he would be signaling trouble.

Hall gave no such clues. Rather, he confided to Jack his conviction that the FBI had bugged party offices around the country and ordered Jack to hire a specialist to inspect them electronically. Jack duly engaged a private investigator and helpfully drew up an inspection schedule for him. Forewarned of when the investigator was coming to each office, the FBI removed the listening devices before he arrived and put them back after he left. Jack reported, "They're all clean, Gus."

Hall also asked Jack's advice about how to react to a cashiered FBI agent who, angered by his dismissal, approached the party with an offer to supply FBI secrets. Jack did not have to feign concern because he was very concerned. Again he thought quickly. He said that the approach was an obvious FBI provocation, an attempt to entrap Hall. If he accepted classified information, the FBI would arrest him for espionage. Hall told the former agent to stay the hell away from him.

Another good sign appeared in June 1967 after a chalk mark summoned Jack to an emergency meeting with his KGB handler that evening. The KGB officer handed him a copy of a speech Soviet Premier Kosygin planned to deliver to the United Nations about the Seven-Day Arab–Israeli War that had just ended. It was an apologia for Soviet actions and a denunciation of American actions in the Middle East. The Soviets wanted Hall to study the speech in advance so he would understand the positions the American party was to adopt regarding the war. Given the text, the State Department and U.S. Ambassador Arthur Goldberg prepared a devastating rebuttal before Kosygin spoke. Goldberg told the FBI that prior knowledge of just what Kosygin would say was enormously valuable: "I don't know where you got it, but if you get anything else like this, please let me have it."

Manifestly, the Kremlin still trusted MORAT. Whatever suspicions Kazakov may have harbored, the KGB had been unable or unwilling to pursue them, and its failure illustrated the Soviet vulnerability the FBI so long exploited. The KGB had responsibility for conducting the operation and determining operational procedures; it had no control over policy governing the operation. The Politburo, Central Committee, and International Department dictated overall policy, the content of messages, how much money the American party would receive, when Morris came to Moscow. And when he came he talked most of the time to members of the Politburo, Central Committee, and International Department— and to the KGB only at their behest and his convenience.

After a Saturday night exchange of money and microfilm in the New York countryside, the FBI, using a cipher and code the KGB issued to Jack, sent a message to Moscow in his name. Typically, a message said: "To Able-Kit. Received 300 pairs of shoes April 6. Spring." "Able-Kit" meant the Central Committee of the Communist Party of the Union of Soviet Socialist Republics; "300 pairs of shoes" meant $300,000; "April 6" meant April 3 (in messages, three days were added to the actual date of delivery); "Spring" meant Jack. The absence of other words meant the exchange occurred without incident and that Jack arrived home safely with the money.

The routine told the SOLO team much. Jack and Morris reported directly to the Central Committee rather than to the KGB.

The Central Committee asked them to verify for it that the KGB had followed its orders and had not purloined any of the cash. The Soviet leadership unwittingly had made Jack, Morris, and their FBI confederates superiors of the KGB by retaining all authority over the operation without accepting any responsibility.

Morris warned though that the breach could swiftly and fatally close at any time. Seeing Jack in the veritable embrace of his political bosses, Kazakov retreated. If he had suspicions, he had no proof and was afraid to proceed without it. But if, as a result of some leak in Washington or mischance with documents in Moscow, the KGB ever acquired hard evidence, the patronage of Soviet rulers could not save Morris and Jack. Indeed, the rulers would turn on both of them with a vengeance.

Between October 1967 and June 1968, Morris journeyed into the Soviet bloc four times and mingled with communist leaders from North Vietnam, Czechoslovakia, and Hungary as well as the Soviet Union. He reported that the Vietnamese were as determined as ever to wage war and that the Soviets were organizing all communist parties in the Western Hemisphere into a campaign to force the United States out of Vietnam. He also brought back seven thousand feet of film that showed imprisoned crewmen of the USS Pueblo, which had been seized off the high seas by the North Koreans.

In Moscow, Ponomarev expressed concern for the safety of Morris and Jack and the security of MORAT. He said that Morris should continue to deal personally with chiefs of foreign parties and attend international communist conclaves as a secret delegate. However, in the United States the Soviets intended to use MORAT "only for confidential, urgent, and illegal matters."

Shortly after Morris returned from Moscow on June 29, 1968, Jack's KGB handler, Vladimir Aleksandrovich Chuchukin, signaled Jack to come to an emergency meeting. The Soviets wanted Hall and Morris to know the political situation in Czechoslovakia was rapidly deteriorating and there might be trouble. Referring to the Czech leadership under Alexander Dubcek, Chuchukin angrily declared, "If those revisionists don't stop, something will have to be done." Chuchukin summoned Jack twice more in the next ten days to advise him that Soviet efforts to reason with the Czechs and persuade them to return to the party fold, as defined by Moscow, had failed. All Chuchukin said proclaimed to Jack and Morris that the Soviets were about to act against Czechoslovakia. Accordingly, Burlinson notified headquarters that "A Soviet invasion of Czechoslovakia appears imminent."

At the time, Assistant Director William Sullivan controlled dissemination of SOLO intelligence and he deemed the report too vague to be forwarded to the White House, State Department, CIA, or anyone else. After Soviet tanks rolled into Prague in August 1968, New York and Chicago vehemently protested the failure of headquarters to circulate vital intelligence that the United States might have used to deter the invasion. Headquarters lamely responded, "You didn't tell us how and when."

When the invasion began, the Central Committee flashed a message to Jack for Hall, exhorting him and the American party to support the Soviet military intervention. If the Soviets had outlawed the baking of bread or sexual relations between husband and wife, Hall would have supported them. But he needed to know what to say and how to defend what in the eyes of many in the West, including many Western communists, was indefensible. To find out, he dispatched Morris to Moscow on August 23, barely two days after the invasion.

When Morris arrived, Ponomarev was engaged in discussions with representatives of the Czech regime newly installed in Prague with the help of tanks and bayonets. While waiting for him, Morris conferred with Mikhail Polonik, who had succeeded Kazakov as the KGB's Moscow manager of MORAT. Polonik spoke to him courteously and respectfully in excellent English, and asked whether he could recommend any operational changes and if he had any complaints about the performance of the "New York [KGB] comrades." Morris saw an opportunity and gently picked it up.

He had no complaints; he had only admiration for men who left their wives and children at night and on weekends to do their duty at personal risk. He also admired the sacrifices of the communications and cryptographic personnel who had to work nights and weekends to service MORAT. Morris had to account for the money, so he was familiar with the deliveries and their dangers, and he could recall only one time, a time when ice and snow made countryside roads impassible, that the New York comrades failed to deliver as scheduled. The radio messages always had been transmitted as scheduled. As for operational techniques, he really was not as qualified as Polonik and his comrades to judge—they had worked impeccably thus far—but he would ask Jack. And speaking of Jack: Sometimes he could be rude, even insolent, to your comrades. He really does not mean to be. He is just letting out emotions he cannot let out anywhere else. Remember, he is constantly risking the ruination of his wife, children, and himself.

Polonik politely interjected that everyone understood the pressures under which Jack labored and that everyone regarded him as a very able and devoted comrade. He thanked Morris for his evaluation of the New York comrades and hinted all might profit if it were repeated to some of Morris' confidants, i.e., members of the Politburo.

The final draft of a communiqué pledging solidarity of purpose and action between the new Czechoslovakian regime and the Soviet Union was completed August 26. Just an hour afterward, Ponomarev received Morris. He looked gray, haggard, and in need of sleep yet seemed glad to see his old friend, someone he could really trust. And he spoke personally and frankly.

The Soviets regretted the necessity of interceding in Czechoslovakia but they had no choice. The "revisionist" policies of Dubcek, his "socialism with a human face," were like a cancer that, unless excised, would grow and spread into Eastern Europe and even the Soviet Union. Unchecked, they conceivably could have propelled Czechoslovakia out of the Warsaw Pact alliance and splintered the international communist movement. Ponomarev acknowledged that the invasion had "created tensions with some parties" in Western Europe and asked if the Soviets could count on the "solidarity" of the American party.

Morris assured him that they could; under the leadership of Hall, the party was disciplined and reliable. A few dilettantes and poseurs might defect, but they did not matter.

"What is the general reaction in the United States?" Ponomarev asked.

Morris could have said: You probably have ensured that Richard Nixon will be the next president; you certainly have secured many, many billions more for the Pentagon; you have validated in the minds of the extreme Left the Chinese charge that the Soviet Union is just another chauvinist, imperialist power. But Morris was not in the business of giving the Soviets intelligence or analyses unless by so doing he served a clearly defined American interest. So he simply replied, "It is not favorable."

They then came to Hall's question about what the party line regarding Czechoslovakia should be. It was an embarrassing question, and Ponomarev disposed of it quickly. It ran: German revisionists, in connivance with the North Atlantic Treaty Organization (NATO) and the CIA, with Dubcek acting, wittingly or unwittingly, as their front man, attempted to organize a counterrevolution. Fraternal neighbors of Czechoslovakia detected the plot and requested the Soviet Union to join them in rescuing the Czech people from imperialist aggression.

Morris knew that, to a majority of Americans who paid any attention to it, this explanation would convict the Soviets of being congenital liars as well as a menace. A month after talking to Ponomarev, he found that the Soviet justification of the invasion had been just as ill received by West European communists.

Morris landed in Budapest September 30 as a secret delegate to a conference of European party leaders to plan a more grandiose, worldwide conference. These smaller, preparatory meetings were important to the Soviets because they wanted to guarantee the outcome of the bigger assemblies. But among themselves the delegates talked mostly about Czechoslovakia, and for the first time in Morris' memory their mood was anti-Soviet—not anticommunist, but anti-Soviet. Over dinner, a Soviet delegate gravely told Morris, "Revisionism is a virus infecting all communist parties."

At Budapest, Ponomarev or another Soviet delegate admitted to Morris that the Soviets had failed fully to comprehend what was happening in Czechoslovakia until it was too late to do anything except use military force and that they had miscalculated the political and international consequences of the invasion. "Our military intelligence is perfect. Our political intelligence is just the reverse." Soon Morris saw and read ominous and, to him, appalling signs that this assessment was accurate insofar as it pertained to "political intelligence" and political understanding of the United States.

The long, black limousine that took him from the airport toward his Moscow apartment on November 17, 1968, had to stop, and Morris parted the curtains to look at the passing convoy of tanks, armored personnel carriers, trucks, and artillery. Jets whistled low overhead, and he thought he was in the midst of a military maneuver. In some of the sections of Moscow he traversed, there were more troops than civilians and armored vehicles were everywhere. It was as if the Soviets expected the city momentarily to be besieged.

After a few hours at the International Department, Morris began to understand. The election of Nixon as president of the United States had stunned and frightened the Soviets. They viewed him as a fanatic anticommunist who might attempt to annihilate or overwhelm the Soviet Union by a surprise nuclear attack. Because the Soviets tended to act upon what they believed, this crazy belief was dangerous to everybody. Morris wanted never to appear to be trying to influence the Soviets, and he offered his judgments or analyses only when they requested them. But to the extent their questions allowed, he tried subtly to nudge the new czars in Moscow back toward reality without saying, "You're crazy."

No, the outcome of the election did not astonish him. He recalled telling everyone at the International Department back in the summer that the presidential contest appeared to be close and that either Nixon or Hubert Humphrey could win. True, Nixon was an inveterate anticommunist and he probably would turn out to be a tough adversary. He also was an astute politician adept at divining the mood of the American public, and the public, already deeply divided by the war in Vietnam, hardly was in a mood to start World War III. In any case, there was no immediate danger (i.e., no need to keep tanks rumbling around Moscow) because before undertaking any fundamental changes in foreign policy, Nixon would need time to organize and consolidate his administration.

Boyle hoped to take a few days off during the Christmas season of 1968 to be with his children, and no one would have faulted him for doing so; for years he had been unable to use all the leave to which he was entitled. As it was, he and Morris worked until December 23, driven by the conviction that the incoming Nixon administration needed to be immediately informed of the misapprehensions the Kremlin had about it and their dangers. Much more was required than a simple, straightforward recitation of facts.

Headquarters had instructed the SOLO team to accompany reports with their own explanation of the significance of the contents; no one had empowered them to recommend, much less make political policy. Their interpretations thus had to show policymakers what ought to be done and the likely consequences of inaction without presuming to tell anyone what to do. At the same time, nothing in the analyses could hint that they were made by someone with rare understanding of Soviet mentality derived from lifelong immersion in communism and someone Soviet rulers trusted with their innermost thoughts.

In essence, the analysis Morris and Boyle submitted that December said: The Soviets are proceeding from the irrational premise that upon assuming office President Nixon may order a nuclear attack upon them. Unless they are disabused of this irrational assumption, they are likely to act irrationally.

Morris and Boyle hoped that the Nixon administration would conclude that, by all available diplomatic means, the Soviets must be reassured that the United States had no intention of attacking them.

Evidently it did, for by the time Morris returned to Moscow in March 1969 Soviet attitudes had undergone a striking change that could not have occurred without some American initiatives. All talk about impending war had ceased, and the tanks and troops so conspicuous the preceding November had disappeared. Suslov and Ponomarev said that achievements of understandings with the United States had become a primary objective of Soviet foreign policy. They hoped that Nixon would "see the light of reality" and agree to arms limitations, and they intended to be patient in negotiating with the Americans.

For the first time, however, they explicitly expressed fears that the United States and China would unite against the Soviet Union. Morris could not ascertain whether their concern arose from concrete intelligence collected either in Washington or Peking or whether it was based solely upon analysis of the drift of world events. Regardless, the political intelligence or analysis that the Soviets only a few months before had pronounced abysmal in this instance was excellent.

As for the Chinese, the Soviets seemed on the verge of losing all patience. Never before in all their many conversations with Morris about China, spanning nearly a decade, had the Soviets alluded to the possibility of war. Now they did, declaring they were prepared to employ military force against the Chinese if that proved to be the only way to deal with them. They did not want war and they planned one last appeal to the Chinese, but they were ready for war.[‡]

[‡] An incident that occurred in Washington in early August 1969 illustrates that the Soviets really meant what they said.

KGB officer Boris Davidov, second secretary at the Soviet embassy, invited an American specialist in Sino–Soviet affairs to lunch and put to him a chilling question the Soviets at the time could not ask officially.

Referring to armed clashes along the Soviet–Chinese border, Davidov said, "The situation is very serious. In fact, it is so serious that my government may be forced to take much stronger action."

"What kind of action do you envisage?" the American asked. "A preemptive strike?"

Davidov answered deliberately, "Yes. A preemptive strike is being contemplated, and the use of nuclear weapons is not excluded." Then he put to him the question the Politburo through the KGB had sent him to relay, "What would be the attitude of the United States government if we made such a strike?"

The Soviets knew that the American would report the conversation to the White House, and within hours he did. SOLO intelligence fully and continuously informed President Nixon of the status of Soviet–Chinese relations, and Nixon recognized that an answer of any kind could be construed by the Chinese as evidence that the United States was conspiring against them. Thus he ordered that no response whatsoever be made to Davidov's inquiry or any other like it.

The Soviets elaborated upon these positions while Morris attended an international conference of parties in Moscow during May and June. They were still afraid that Nixon might revert to policies of "Cold War and containment"; they worried increasingly about an accommodation between the Chinese and Americans, yet they remained committed to improving relations with the United States and reaching some arms agreements. Developments in China appalled them. Ponomarev told Morris that Maoists had murdered the former president of China, Liu Saho-Chi, and his wife, and thereby virtually destroyed the Communist Party.

Morris heard more from Brezhnev in September. He had to fly to Moscow to arrange for Hall to go to the funeral of Ho Chi Minh in Hanoi, and when Hall came back to Moscow, Brezhnev briefed him and Morris about secret discussions between Kosygin and Chou En Lai conducted just a few days before on September 13, 1969. The Soviets judged it futile for the time being to try further to settle their ideological differences with the Chinese. So Kosygin proposed some relatively small, practical actions to rebuild civil relations—increased trade, sharing information about world affairs, exchange of newspaper correspondents, mediation of border disputes, and resumption of contacts between friendship societies. Chou listened sullenly and agreed to nothing, and Brezhnev predicted the Chinese would continue to agree to nothing.

In December 1969, during the annual review of the next American party budget, Ponomarev confirmed that the negotiations in Peking had come to naught. The Chinese had resumed their nasty calumny and bellicose propaganda against the Soviets, and Ponomarev despaired, "China is our most important international problem."

He was more optimistic or at least hopeful about relations with the United States. Both Soviet and American negotiators engaged in the Strategic Arms Limitation Talks (SALT) were "playing their cards close to the chest," but the possibility of some agreements existed and the Soviets were willing to make concessions if the Americans reciprocated.

Enabled by SOLO to read the thoughts of Soviet rulers, Nixon, Henry Kissinger, and confidants within a year had transformed the attitudes of Soviet rulers. In November 1968, this little band of oligarchs viewed Nixon as the devil personified, threatening them with extinction. By November 1969, these same men sufficiently trusted Nixon to make dealing with him the foundation of their foreign policy. They did not like him—they still regarded him and the United States as enemies—but they respected him.

By nature and nurture, Kissinger was a scholar not prone to adulatory or extravagant statements. Years would pass before the FBI revealed to him (or to the president) who Agent 58 was and just why he could do what he did. Kissinger had no ties to the FBI, nothing to hide from the FBI, and nothing personally to gain from the FBI. But on his own he went to the FBI and said, "What you are doing is fabulous. You have opened a window not only into the Kremlin but into the minds of the men in the Kremlin. This is unprecedented in modern history."

Through Missions 35, 36, and 37 to Moscow, Morris kept the window open during 1970 and précis of reports by him and Boyle show how wide the view given the United States was:

❖ A vicious feud rends the Soviet leadership. An ultra-nationalist faction opposes Brezhnev, advocates rehabilitation of Stalin, and reinstitution of his repressive methods. However, Brezhnev will prevail and purge his opponents.

❖ The Soviet people are not "pro-Israeli" but they are not "enthusiastically pro-Arab." In fact, they don't give a damn about the Middle East and they increasingly resent Soviet aid to Arab countries, believing that the money should be spent at home. For the Soviets, foreign aid is becoming a domestic problem.

❖ The Soviets believe they are falling behind the United States in the "scientific and technological revolution" and that, unless they "catch up," their military power and political influence will decline. They intend to allocate more resources to science and technology.

❖ The East Germans vow that there never will be a reunited Germany or free access to Berlin.

❖ The Soviet Union has no intention of helping the United States leave Vietnam gracefully and will not cooperate with the United States in any manner regarding Vietnam. On the contrary, the Soviets plan to increase the quantity and quality of their military aid to the North Vietnamese and Viet Cong.

❖ The Soviets now are convinced that the Chinese want to become a silent partner of the Americans in world affairs.

While Morris was in Moscow, the FBI received a communication from the Royal Canadian Mounted Police (RCMP), a service it regarded and treated as a brother. A well-placed member of the Canadian Communist Party, revolted by the Soviet invasion of Czechoslovakia, brooded and concluded that he long had been on the wrong side. In the words of Milovan Djilas, the Yugoslav political philosopher who once ranked just below Marx, Lenin, Stalin, and Mao as a communist ideologue, he "thought his way out of communism," just as Morris had. Conscience impelled him to go to the RCMP and detail what he knew about communist subversion. The Canadians naturally were most interested in what the communists were doing in Canada, but toward the end of his confessional the convert told a story that caused his RCMP listener/interrogator to ask, "Are you willing to tell that face to face to the FBI?"

The Detroit field office, being nearest to Toronto, took the testimony and filed a report, which roughly said:

The CPUSA has an "elder statesman" who has ties with many Communist parties throughout the world, including the CPUSSR. He is Morris Childs, who years ago was district organizer in Chicago and later became secretly active in the leadership of the CPUSA. Childs travels extensively for the CPUSA, including trips behind the Iron Curtain. When he travels, he uses assumed names, and when introduced in foreign circles, he is introduced as Mr. So-and-So or as Mr. Smith. Source believes that through the many channels of Childs, the CPUSA is able to obtain funds from Moscow. Source does not know how the funds are passed or handled. Source believes the CPUSA could not sustain itself without outside support. Source said Childs has intimate contact with the leaders of the Canadian Communist Party. Source said he met Childs several times in Prague and considered him a conspiratorial figure. His name never appears among those listed as attending international party conferences, even though he speaks at them. Source said Childs undoubtedly has contact with "elderly statesmen" in Soviet bloc countries.

THERE IS A GREAT old hotel in Ottawa, the Chateau Laurier, some of whose rooms have turrets overlooking the Canadian Parliament. At the hotel, the U.S. legal attaché (the senior FBI agent assigned to effect liaison with Canadian authorities) over lunch thanked an RCMP inspector for the leads concerning the "elderly statesman" and suggested the FBI investigation would be facilitated if his name was not mentioned by anyone, especially the defector from the Canadian party. The inspector glanced at his FBI friend as if to say, "congratulations"; he actually said only, "done." If the Canadians surmised any part of the truth about Morris, they forever kept it to themselves.

MORRIS ALIGHTED AT KENNEDY Airport in New York December 13, 1970, pale and depleted, as he always was after long flights from Moscow through Europe. Boyle asked if he would like to rest before they talked. "No, let's just get to the motel. I have something you may want the right people to see before they begin the holidays." Without unpacking or showering in the motel suite, Morris proceeded to summarize the most important intelligence and his thoughts about it.

The Soviet attitude toward the United States suddenly had become "belligerent, even combative," and among themselves the

Soviets were throwing a tantrum out of exasperation at failure to swiftly euchre the United States into the kind of disarmament and other agreements upon which they banked so much. Through the agreements, they hoped to slow the strategic arms race in those spheres where they felt at a disadvantage and thereby gain time to improve their technology. At the same time, they hoped to use the agreements as a shield from behind which they could attempt to neutralize Western Europe, undermine NATO, and isolate the United States politically. But so far the United States had refused to buy.

Here Morris offered another prescient analysis. The Soviets in the coming months might wail and flail about, making all sorts of menacing noises about the perils (unspecified) to the United States of not promptly coming to terms with them. It would be a mistake to be intimidated by such theatrics because ultimately the Soviets, who could not go to Peking, could only turn to Washington if they wished to treat with a Great Power—and they did. So however loud their bombast, they eventually would quiet down and come around.

"Of course, this assumes they act rationally," Morris said. "We must watch carefully for any signs of irrationality. Walt Boyle, the next year will be interesting."

FBI Headquarters, Washington: February 29, 1988. Seated is Morris Childs, Agent 58, age 85, who has just become the fifth man in history to receive the National Security Medal, which he wears on his left lapel. To the right stands Carl Freyman, the senior surviving FBI member of the SOLO team. He holds the National Security Medal awarded posthumously to Jack Childs. Behind Morris stand Mr. and Mrs. Max Schlossberg.

(Left to right) Leonid I. Brezhnev, General Secretary of the Communist Party of the Soviet Union; Boris N. Ponomarev, head of the International Department of the Central Committee of the CPSU; Nikolai V. Mostovets, head of the North American Section of the International Department; Morris Childs; Gus Hall; and Igor Mikhailov, Deputy Chief of the North American Section of the International Department. This photograph was taken April 21, 1973, in the Kremlin.

(Left to right) Mikhail Suslov, Leonid Brezhnev; Boris Ponomarev, and Gus Hall. Note that the chair to the right of Hall is not visible. That is because Morris Childs was sitting in it and the Soviet technicians blacked out his image.

(Left to right) Morris Childs; Eva Childs; and FBI Director William Sessions. The photograph was taken at FBI headquarters on February 29, 1988, after Morris received the National Security Medal.

This is the torn half of a postcard replicating the painting, *Landscape with a Wagon,* by Peter Paul Rubens, on display at the Hermitage in Leningrad. The KGB gave it to Morris for his last mission. The Soviet officer who met him in Eastern Europe identified himself by presenting the other, matching half of the torn card.

This typifies the myriad clandestine messages the Russians left for Jack Childs in hiding places or "drops" around New York. Translated, it meant that Jack should affix a little strip of tape at the site pictured, then call a telephone booth to signal that he and "Hub" (Morris) were prepared to rendezvous with the Soviets at "Berkman," code name for a meeting place in Westchester or Nassau County. FBI Agent Langtry picked up most messages and afterward phoned the Soviets: All is well.

Morris Childs campaigning for a seat in the United States Senate in 1938 as the Communist Party candidate from Illinois.

Morris Childs when he was editor of the Communist Party newspaper, the *Daily Worker*, after World War II.

Morris Childs after he became Agent 58.

Eva as a young woman.

Agent 58 riding a camel while touring Mongolia.

Eva Lieb Childs as she appeared about the time Morris met her in 1961.

Morris and Eva Childs shortly after their marriage in 1962 and shortly before their first joint mission to Moscow.

(Left to right) FBI Agent Alexander Burlinson, FBI Agent John Langtry, and FBI Agent Steven Bradford.

FBI Agent Carl Freyman.

FBI Agents Alexander Burlinson (left) and John Langtry during an operational crisis in the early 1970s.

(Left to right) Senior Agent in Charge of the FBI Chicago office, Marlin Johnson; track star Jesse Owens, hero of the 1936 Olympics in Berlin; and FBI Agent Carl Freyman.

Walter Boyle when he was commissioned an FBI Agent in 1954 at the age of 25.

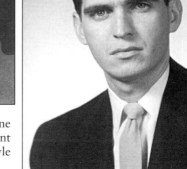

The commanding general of the First Marine Division, E.A. Pollack (left) awards Lieutenant Walter Boyle the first of seven decorations Boyle received for heroism during the Korean war.

(ABOVE) Special Agent in Charge of the Chicago FBI office, James Ingram (left), in November 1979 presents another of the many FBI commendations Walter Boyle earned.

(TOP RIGHT) Former Assistant Director of the FBI, James Fox.

(CENTER) During the two decades Walter Boyle devoted to Operation SOLO, through Catholic Charities he also adopted and nurtured these six children: (from left to right) Mark, Beth Ann, Matthew, Jeannie, John, and Christopher.

Oleg Gordievsky (right) is introduced to Ronald Reagan by David G. Major at the White House. After the "window" that Operation SOLO opened into the Kremlin closed, Gordievsky and the British brought to President Reagan horrifying information. Reagan acted immediately and decisively upon it to the benefit of all people. *Photo courtesy of David G. Major.*

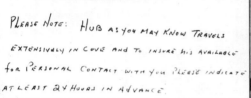

Below is a portrait of HUB for Identification. This is in the event of my absence at a time when a personal contact must be made. Should such a contact be made for the first time HUB will carry a copy of Life Magazine under his Left arm and have a Bandaid on his left index finger. The recognition code words will be, " Do you have the time" ----answer, "its 7:05" You will then show him our Business card.

PLEASE NOTE: HUB AS YOU MAY KNOW TRAVELS EXTENSIVELY IN COVE AND TO INSURE HIS AVAILABLE FOR PERSONAL CONTACT WITH YOU PLEASE INDICATE AT LEAST 24 HOURS IN ADVANCE.

The Russians gave Agent 58 this identification note for use in meeting a comrade he did not know. The coded message told anyone from the KGB or the International Department to afford Morris all assistance possible.

(RIGHT) Agent 58 (left) meets a KGB agent in New York after his brother, Jack Childs, died in 1980.

Pictured here are left to right: Nikolai Mostevets (Chief of the North American Division of the International Department a/k/a Comintern); Mikhail Suslov (Chief Soviet Idealogue); Gus Hall (Head of U.S. Communist Party); Leonid Brezhnev (Ruler of the Soviet Union); and Boris Ponomarev (Head of the International Department that controlled all foreign communist parties, except the Chinese, and was one of Agent 58's most intimate friends in Moscow).

eleven

A CROSSROAD IN HISTORY

WHEN RICHARD NIXON ASSUMED the presidency and selected Professor Henry Kissinger as his national security advisor, the SOLO file offered a clear road map to China. SOLO kept showing the way.

National leaders, particularly Americans, prefer to make great foreign policy decisions on the basis of scientific or objective, verifiable evidence rather than the word of fallible human spies. Stalin in 1941 dismissed warnings from his own and British spies that the Nazis were about to attack the Soviet Union. The Kennedy administration in the summer of 1962 ignored reports from CIA spies indicating that the Soviets intended to emplace nuclear missiles in Cuba. It did not accept the truth until months later when U-2 reconnaissance photographs showed the missile sites and bunkers for storage of nuclear warheads being constructed. Throughout the 1960s the United States emphasized intelligence gathering by technological means rather than through human agents.

But the camera that can photograph the thoughts and intentions of men has yet to be invented. For more than a decade

Operation SOLO had read very accurately the thoughts and intentions of communist leaders. All the readings were consistent with one another, and collectively they predicted that the United States had a historic opportunity to convert China from an enemy into an ally against the Soviet Union.

Just as the solution to a riddle or puzzle seems simple once the riddle is solved, the wisdom of exploiting that opportunity today may seem self-evident. At the time, though, Nixon risked alienating his core constituency, which was militantly anticommunist, and antagonizing liberals sensitive to China's human rights abuses. Additionally, the Chinese were aiding the Vietnamese fighting against the United States (although the aid was less extensive than most imagined). If overtures to China became known and failed, Nixon would expose himself to charges of political treachery and personal perfidy. But the SOLO files made clear that the Chinese were likely to welcome American overtures.

Because the United States and China did not maintain diplomatic relations, first there was the practical problem of how to open up a line of communication. It appears that an American emissary made the first contact through the Chinese embassy in Paris. Other contacts continued as the two nations searched for a mutually acceptable intermediary who could broker arrangements for direct, secret talks.

When Morris visited Moscow in 1971, he discovered that the Soviets had a source in Peking who kept them apprised of these exchanges. The Soviets expressed alarm and anger at what they termed the "growing improvement" in American–Chinese relations and declared that the new U.S. policy was a "slap" at them. They now distrusted the United States more than ever and doubted that it was sincere about disarmament. The Soviets planned to counterattack by organizing a worldwide anti-American propaganda campaign, by arranging a European Security Conference to isolate the United States, and by seeking better relations with Japan.

Pakistan, which had close ties to both the United States and China, ultimately acted as the intermediary in negotiations that culminated in Kissinger's secret trip to Peking in July 1971. The

Chinese in general, and Chou En Lai in particular, accorded him the most cordial and heartening of welcomes. Of all the communist figures Morris ever met, he considered Chou the most brilliant, profound, and engaging. Nixon ranked Chou as a statesman alongside Winston Churchill and Charles de Gaulle. Kissinger characterized him as "electric, quick, taut, deft, humorous," and from the start the two got on well.

Their initial discussions demonstrated the accuracy of all Morris had reported over the years about the irreconcilable enmity between China and the Soviet Union, and about Chinese willingness to ally itself with the United States. The Chinese were not only willing; they were eager. Kissinger later wrote: "China identified security with isolating the Soviet Union, and with adding the greatest possible weight to its side of the scale—which meant rapid rapprochement with the United States."

Chou and Kissinger agreed to communicate through the Chinese embassy in Paris and the Chinese Mission to the United Nations in New York. Chou proposed that they begin to consider establishing formal diplomatic relations and indicated that the problem posed by U.S. recognition of the government of Taiwan as the legitimate government of all China could be ignored for the foreseeable future. Finally, they agreed that Nixon should make a state visit to China, prior to which Kissinger should return in October 1971 for broader, private talks.

Shortly before Kissinger's second journey to Peking, Morris flew to Moscow on Mission 39, one of the most significant of all SOLO operations. Morris intended to prepare for a "state visit" by Gus Hall, during which Soviet rulers wanted to brief him personally. Just before his scheduled departure from New York, Hall suffered gall bladder problems and was hospitalized. Consequently, the Soviets told Morris what they meant to tell Hall and gave him documents to study for the benefit of Hall. Again, he dared to take copious notes, recording long passages of conversations verbatim.

Suslov began by saying, "First of all, just between you, me, and Gus—we don't intend to make this public but we may—Comrade Brezhnev received a letter from Nixon during the latter part of

August. He raised a number of questions but the idea was 'Why don't we get together?' We took our time, and Brezhnev did send a preliminary answer in which he indicated that just getting together could be pleasant but unless we are ready to discuss some concrete questions and solutions, we doubt the advisability of a meeting at this time. As time goes on, we will undoubtedly lay the basis for such a summit meeting in Moscow."

Suslov recounted a recent, unexpected visit by Senate Minority Leader Hugh Scott, a large, jocular man who evidently charmed the Soviets:

> I am glad to say that Senator Scott was not in a combative mood and was not fighting our arguments too much as we presented them to him and the [American] ambassador who was present. In fact, we might say he was passive when we became argumentative. We criticized U.S. aggression in Vietnam; we criticized U.S. policy in the Middle East. In fact, we couldn't get any arguments from either [Scott] or the ambassador. Whatever discussion they did participate in was more or less defensive. We talked in a very friendly manner.
>
> I told Scott that Nixon's visit to China will be a complicated thing. It is not as simple as a social call. There is the war in Indochina. It is difficult for the U.S. It is also difficult for the Chinese... We know that Scott was sent by Nixon to see if he can sense our mind. We explained to Scott our principles. We know that Scott did speak on the floor of the Senate in which he truthfully reflected some of these things.

Suslov then meandered away from the conversation with Scott and onto the subject about which Morris most wanted to hear: Soviet reaction to American–Chinese negotiations.

> For the Soviet Union, China is a big problem. But we are calm about the whole problem. As you might say, we are keeping our cool. However, we are not passive.

We do not know if Nixon and the Chinese will reach agreement or not. We really don't know. It is not a simple thing for the United States after all these years to reach agreement with China.

Then the next thing is, will it be an anti-Soviet agreement? If it is an anti-Soviet understanding, we will certainly oppose it and fight it. We hope that if there are agreements, they will not be harmful to socialist countries.

As you can see, our foreign policy nowadays is not a passive one. We are interested in all continents. We have people on all continents, working, keeping up ties, developing understandings and agreements with these nations on all these continents. In any case, we can assure you that whatever the agreement between the U.S. and China, we will not be taken by surprise. To put the thing in its political framework, I want to repeat again that we are going to pursue our policy and our principles of peaceful co-existence. We are going to negotiate with the United States constantly and we will continue to do so... Serious negotiations are possible and are continuing on the reduction of strategic arms. Now, these negotiations will take time, but I think we can reach agreement. We are also discussing reaching agreement on anti-ballistic missiles, but on this too long discussions are necessary.

Glancing at his notes, Suslov said, "You will be invited to the Convention of the Indian Communist Party which opens October 3. We hope you will go. You should know that Indira Ghandi asked us for an invitation to visit here. We told her that she can come if she wants.

"You know the Japanese are very much worried about the United States' role in Asia again. They are very worried about Nixon's visit to Peking. We can tell by their changed attitude toward us."

The official business of the day had ended, yet Suslov wanted to talk a little more to his friend of forty years. He proposed that the two of them stage an impromptu dinner party that evening at the "Captain's Cabin" and invite whomever Morris wished from the Politburo and Central Committee. If no one was free, then the two of them could dine and reminisce by themselves. The "Captain's Cabin" was an elegantly paneled and richly carpeted redoubt of the oligarchy, probably the most exclusive club in the Soviet Union, serving the best cuisine available in Moscow outside the Kremlin. Under regular circumstances, duty and personal inclination would have compelled Morris immediately to accept the spontaneous invitation. Some of the most meaningful intelligence or insights could be gained at these intimate, alcoholic séances with the rulers. But Suslov had overloaded Morris with intelligence that he wanted to put on paper before any detail faded, so he begged off, pleading fatigue and promising to join Suslov at a farewell luncheon in a couple of days.

Except that he could not sell or bequeath it, Morris by now in effect owned an excellent apartment in Moscow, just as he did in Chicago and New York. The party set it aside exclusively for him, and he kept there a full wardrobe, including a heavy coat and fur cap that made him look like a Muscovite, and expensively tailored suits that identified him to Soviet associates as what they thought he was, a devout communist clever enough to beat the capitalists at their own game of making money. In the armoire, he left a house robe and slippers that he liked to wear while writing because in the colder months the apartment was overheated and the windows sealed shut. In the bath, he left toiletries and a veritable pharmacy of Chicago drugstore nostrums that he passed out to guests.

The Moscow apartment was attended by a staff, but for this evening of work he wanted to get rid of his favorite staff member, Yekaterina, his cook/nursemaid, who would linger after supper to see that all was well—and to take home food after he retired.

This evening Morris told his driver to stop at the "speakeasy"—the Kremlin store where, with a special card, he could walk in and collect imported luxuries, which were promptly delivered, all for free. Morris never entered without feeling

hypocritical, and normally he went there only to replenish his supply of presents for his Soviet hosts and hostesses. But that afternoon, he acted just like any other greedy oligarch, ordering
piggish quantities of sausage, wurst, caviar, smoked fish, and
chocolates. At the apartment, he gave the package to Yekaterina
as a present from Eva and sent her home.

After writing down all Suslov said to him, Morris began the
analysis he would give to Boyle. In July, Kissinger and Chou En
Lai had concluded substantial agreements; yet in September, the
Soviets remained ignorant of them. Neither did they seem to know
that Kissinger was about to return to China. Morris concluded
they either had lost or been unable to communicate with the well-
placed source he believed they had in Peking.

Suslov said the Soviets were not sure whether Nixon and the
Chinese would "reach agreement" and, if they did, he wondered
whether it would be an "anti-Soviet agreement." Morris thought,
What other kind of agreement could it be? When Morris last spoke
with the Soviets in April, they were angry, bitter, and mistrustful of
the United States, and contemplating actions to undermine it. Now
they were confident that they could trust the United States to come
to acceptable terms with them. And Suslov vowed that no matter
what Nixon and China agreed to, "We are going to negotiate with
the U.S. constantly, and we will continue to do so."

Morris did not know what produced such a stark reversal in
attitude in such a short time. He did know that the White House
forthwith should be informed that in dealing with China it need
not be inhibited by apprehensions about Soviet reactions.

The next day, the Central Committee entrusted Morris with a
position paper regarding China, and he copied it almost verbatim.
The paper recited the history of failed Soviet efforts to negotiate
with the Chinese and dramatized once again the intractable
enmity between the two former allies:

> One cannot forget that Mao Tse Tung is trying to
> make a deal with Washington. Not once but on numer-
> ous occasions the Chinese have made it clear that they
> are going to support Vietnam up to a certain limit but

they are not prepared to enter a direct conflict with the U.S....

The Chinese in the recent period attempt to achieve their aims by slogans of struggle against the two "super-powers." They are trying to set up a bloc of smaller and middle states to struggle against the two super-states. But the desire for Chinese–U.S. relations testifies to their real intention: to conduct their struggle mainly against the Soviet Union; not against the two "super-powers."

In considering Soviet–Chinese relations, one must consider the fact that an atmosphere of China as a "besieged fortress" is being artificially developed in China, while the reality is that they are developing their militarism. For example, the Chinese army occupies almost every key position in their country. There are no democratic forums in China. There are no elections. A bureaucratic and military dictatorship has been set up in China. [Morris found the Soviet concern at the lack of democracy and elections in China touching.]

Do not exclude the possibility of an alliance between Peking and the U.S. on some questions, having in mind the Peking anti-Soviet policies. But one cannot ignore the deep-seated contradictions between China and the United States.

For Morris, the position paper affirmed conclusions drawn from Suslov's statements and stimulated a few more. The Soviets did not understand that China and the United States in principle already had made a profound deal and had only to elaborate and formalize it. By keeping the Soviets ignorant, the Chinese were exhibiting competence and good faith toward the United States. The Soviets were vulnerable to great self-delusion. For years, the specter of American technology, wealth, and "cowboy violence," as Mostovets once said, aligned with a billion Chinese enemies on their borders, had tormented them. In the past couple of years, they repeatedly had told Morris that this nightmare very well might become reality. Though they did not know what Kissinger and Chou En Lai said to each other, there were conspicuous signs that what they themselves predicted was coming true. Mao, Chou, Nixon, and Kissinger were not sitting down with each other just for herbal tea and roasted duck. But the Soviets could not accept the indications that their own calculations were correct. They preferred to comfort themselves with the hope that the Americans and Chinese might not be able to get together, after all, because of "deep-seated contradictions."

Morris realized that the FBI first would want any information that might benefit Kissinger and the United States in the next secret negotiations with the Chinese, and that he had no right or reason to dispute this priority. But he did scribble a reminder on the back of the envelope containing his plane tickets, "TWA-DD." To him, the notation meant after we've answered all the questions, after I'm finished with the technocrats, tell Walt about dangerous delusions.

MORRIS AND BOYLE WERE still filing reports and answering queries from Washington when Kissinger returned to Peking in October 1971, ostensibly to arrange for Nixon's forthcoming visit. Actually, he and Chou engaged in cordial, candid, and wide-ranging dialogue about major world issues. At the same time, they established an enduring and friendly personal relationship.

Back in Moscow in December for the regular year-end review, Morris found the Soviets again drifting away from reality. The impending accords between China and the United States in a few weeks would dramatically alter the balance of power against the Soviet Union. Yet the Soviets had convinced themselves that the "crisis of capitalism is deepening and that imperialism is in retreat." A relatively minor economic recession in the United States persuaded them that the West was verging on collapse.

What the Soviets long had feared and forecast came to pass in February 1972 when Nixon, Mao, Kissinger, and Chou achieved understandings that, from the perspective of the Soviets, were worse than their gloomiest predictions. In a joint declaration issued at the end of their talks—the so-called Shanghai Communiqué—China and the United States pledged jointly to oppose "the hegemonic aims of others [i.e., the Soviet Union] in Asia." As Kissinger wrote, "In plain language, the United States and China agreed on the need for parallel policies toward the world balance of power." In plainer language, the two nations publicly and formally entered into an anti-Soviet alliance.

That was bad enough, but much more went on in private. The Chinese made it clear that they did not want China and the United States just to be "former enemies," but real friends and partners. Domestically, each nation should abide by its own political, economic, and social principles. Internationally, they should act jointly despite their ideological differences. Kissinger wrote, "Mao took the proposition a somewhat cynical step further by indicating that we would strengthen domestic support for our cooperation if we took occasional potshots at each other—so long as we did not take our own pronouncements too seriously." The Chinese exhorted the Americans to maintain the strongest possible armed forces and weaponry, to stay close to Western Europe and NATO, to forge an anti-Soviet alliance stretching from Pakistan through Iran and Turkey into the Middle East, and, above all, despite domestic pressures steamed up by an unpopular war in Vietnam, to assume and maintain a preeminent role in world affairs. In sum, they did everything within their power to encourage the United States, short of singing "The Star Spangled Banner."

At the same time, the Chinese wished to be a worthy and constructive partner. Insofar as their resources permitted, they would covertly abet Sino–American policies around the globe. Delicately, they hinted they would assist in solving mutual problems in Vietnam, Cambodia, and Laos. And they noted that the United States and China were natural trading partners who had much to offer each other commercially.

Morris at the time knew nothing of these historic negotiations because in February 1972 he and Eva were in Poland and Moscow, dispatched there by Gus Hall on an important mission— laying the groundwork for acquisition of Arabian horses to be sold by the American Communist Party (or Hall himself). But in Moscow Morris gathered some truly important intelligence showing that the Soviets really had gone 'round the bend. Three disparate and relatively trivial events persuaded them that the United States had set out "to worsen relations" on the eve of disarmament negotiations: (1) A U.S. Coast Guard cutter had hauled in a Soviet fishing vessel flagrantly poaching in American territorial waters; (2) the FBI had caught and arrested KGB officer Valery Markelov as he tried to steal designs for the new Navy F-14 fighter plane; and (3) the State Department had denied visas to Soviets seeking to attend a convention of the American Communist Party.

Awareness of the Soviet delusions enabled the United States to dispel them by communicating with the Soviets through different channels. Privately and repeatedly, the United States had requested the Soviet Union to keep its trawlers and "factory ships" out of U.S. waters. A Coast Guard officer, acting on his own in compliance with standing orders, simply did his duty in corralling the intruding Soviet trawler. The FBI by law was charged with catching spies, and when it caught a spy, it arrested him without consulting anybody. Markelov was guilty as hell, and if the Soviets had any doubts they could consult the KGB. Nixon was being upbraided by many of his supporters for consorting with Chinese communists who were contributing to the deaths of American soldiers in Vietnam. Why should he invite more outcries by helping the Communist Party stage its convention?

The "TWA-DD," "tell Walt about dangerous delusions," again worked.

THOSE WHO KNEW MORRIS and what he really did knew him to be an extraordinarily brave man, all the more brave because he fully understood the risks he took and the consequences of being found out in the Soviet Union. At the Lenin School in 1930 when his teachers included bomb-throwing, bank-robbing, old-time Bolsheviks, he heard a lecture by a professional Cheka/OGPU torturer. He thought the torturer evil incarnate until he realized that the man, who spoke calmly and smiled frequently, was an insane pervert, a classic candidate for a mental institution. But the torturer obviously was good at his trade. He explained that the trick in torture is not to kill or render a victim senseless until you have extracted what you want. No one can resist skilled, prolonged torture, and you don't have to have sophisticated equipment—a set of chains, a pair of pliers, and a box of matches would do just fine. "Give me a night with a man and I don't care how brave or strong he is, by morning he won't have any teeth or fingernails and he'll wish he didn't have any scrotum, and I'll have him confessing he's the king of England."

Morris also knew that under his friend Yuri Andropov, the KGB had perfected techniques of destroying minds and wracking bodies with deranging drugs. The FBI promised that, were he arrested, it would try to ransom him by releasing jailed Soviet agents. But Morris believed that Soviet rulers would never agree to an exchange that would show how completely they had been duped. Rather, he was certain that should he be caught in the Soviet Union, his death was guaranteed—and it wouldn't be painless. Yet he kept going back.

For all his courage and audacity, he gave to those who did not know him well the impression of being a reticent, even shy man. It derived in part from his habit of listening to others rather than talking himself. When he did talk, he spoke sparsely and rarely delivered speeches, although he was an experienced and able public speaker.

Morris made an exception on an evening in early March 1972 while he, Eva, and other team members were guests of Al and Ann Burlinson at their lovely old house in Scarsdale, New York. Morris was among his best friends, his mood was expansive, and he spoke as a coach might in addressing a team that had just won the championship.

Everyone could be proud of what they together had accomplished over the years and especially proud of their accomplishments regarding China. He said anyone could speculate about "what might have been." He proposed to talk only about what he was sure "had been." Recounting his first visit to Peking in 1958, he reviewed the history of SOLO reports about China and Sino–Soviet relations. From 1958 to now, they gave the United States the benefit of the highest and best Soviet intelligence and estimates pertaining to China while revealing the thoughts and intentions of Soviet rulers toward China. The reporting accurately charted the degeneration of the Sino–Soviet partnership into implacable enmity while tracking the evolution of Chinese attitudes toward the United States. Ultimately and collectively, the SOLO reports showed that, if the United States wanted the Chinese as allies against the Soviet Union in international affairs, it need only ask. And it could be confident of China's answer.

Morris pointed out something else that few others were in a position to appreciate. In personal dealings, the Chinese had for years treated the Soviets rudely or scornfully. As Kosygin complained after another futile negotiating session in Peking, they displayed "none of the characteristic Oriental civility and politeness." Instead, they barely masked their raw contempt. Even the cultured Chou remained frostily aloof and refrained from any gesture suggesting the least goodwill. But from what Morris had been told, he concluded that the Chinese from Mao and Chou on down received Nixon and Kissinger warmly and graciously, speaking to them as if they were old colleagues. Chou and Nixon were well on their way to becoming personal friends. To Morris, that meant the Chinese were trying to tell the Americans, *We really mean it*.

"The new relationship between China and us is a crossroad in history," Morris declared. "We are looking at a historic change. I hope we can say we helped a little to bring it about. I think we can."

twelve

CRITICAL
INTRIGUES

THE INTERNATIONAL DEPARTMENT in March 1972 again summoned Morris to Moscow, supposedly to arrange for Gus Hall to travel to Hanoi and Havana via the Soviet Union. Actually, it wanted him available before, during, and after the secret talks between Kissinger and Brezhnev that were to take place in April.

After shepherding Hall around during his Moscow stopover, Morris received a briefing from Ponomarev about current Chinese machinations. The Chinese were just as virulently anti-Soviet as ever, but now they were scheming more cleverly. Instead of reviling the parties of both Eastern and Western Europe as Soviet stooges, they were courting them, enticing them to enter into an anti-Soviet alliance.

"They found a few Italians on *L'Unita* [the Italian party newspaper] whom they bought for five cents, as we would say. One of them spent a month in China and wrote ten pro-Chinese articles for *L'Unita*. They were very well done and very clever in justifying Maoism. The Chinese took the writer to a concentration camp where he saw a professor. This professor said that during the Cultural Revolution he was beaten, forced to clean toilets, etc. But now the professor agrees this was the correct thing to do." The Italian party had brushed off Soviet protests about the articles. The Chinese also were making inroads into the Spanish and Rumanian parties.

Ponomarev declared that Mao had converted China into an armed camp seething with anti-Soviet animosity and that he was murdering anyone who disagreed with him. "Lin Piao was Mao's designated heir but he spoke out against Mao's position. We do not know all the details but Lin Piao was against their anti-Soviet line. So Mao eliminated him like he did Liu Shao-Chi. Liu's flight didn't reach its destination; he was shot down by a Chinese fighter plane."

In passing, Ponomarev confided, "We have good relations with the Cambodian resistance movement" (the Khmer Rouge, who were about to annihilate between 1 million and 2 million men, women, and children, primarily by driving the entire urban population of Cambodia into the jungles).

Kissinger came in April to discuss disarmament agreements that the Soviets hoped Nixon would sign during a summit conference with Brezhnev in May. Brezhnev reviewed the discussions with Morris and asked for advice about how to deal with Nixon. He reported that, because of U.S. actions in Vietnam, parties around the world were screaming at the Soviet Union to cancel the summit conference, but the Soviets intended to proceed unless some cataclysmic event in the next couple of weeks made the conference politically impossible. Brezhnev also said that he had "great respect" for Kissinger, whom he characterized as a "vigorous and smart negotiator not to be underestimated."

From the conversations with Brezhnev and Ponomarev, Morris made three primary conclusions:

(1) The Chinese were keeping their part of the bargain with the United States by doing exactly what they said they would do and urged the United States to do.

(2) The Soviets craved agreements with the United States so much that they would proceed with the summit conference no matter what other communists said.

(3) Whatever Kissinger said to Brezhnev, he said the right things.

Morris arrived in New York on April 30, and the intelligence and analyses he brought were delivered by hand to the White House and put to good use forthwith.

Without consulting or informing the Soviets, the North Vietnamese initiated a massive offensive against South Vietnam. Nixon had to decide between the military necessity of countering the offensive and the perceived political desirability of the summit conference. SOLO told him the Soviets would meet, almost no matter what he did, and on the eve of the summit conference he ordered North Vietnamese harbors mined and blockaded and the aerial bombardment of North Vietnam intensified. Foreign communist parties, privately and publicly, shouted at the Soviets to cancel the summit conference. The Soviets, just as Morris predicted, sent word to Kissinger that the meeting still was on.

On May 26, 1972, in Moscow, Brezhnev and Nixon signed an agreement (SALT I) that restricted the number of strategic ballistic missiles the United States and Soviet Union could maintain during the next five years and an agreement that limited the development of antiballistic missile (ABM) defenses. These modest agreements, which did little to reduce existing arsenals, enraged Gus Hall, who wrote a vituperative letter accusing the Soviets of conniving with the imperialists and selling out North Vietnam, and he ordered Morris to hand the letter personally to Brezhnev.

When Morris read the letter, he realized it had to be rewritten. Only two months before, Ponomarev declared that the Soviets were fed up with "deviationism" in foreign parties, and Hall's angry words could only brand him as a "deviationist." In rewriting the draft, Morris transformed Hall into a loyal acolyte anxiously requesting guidance, yet the revision satisfied Hall because it still conveyed all of his original points. Now, though, Hall himself was not accusing the Soviets of making squalid deals with Nixon and betraying North Vietnam. Such charges were being spread as part of anti-Soviet propaganda, and they had begun to worry members of the American party.

As Morris prepared to leave for Moscow, a seemingly minor incident occurred at the Washington, D.C., Watergate apartment complex in Foggy Bottom between Georgetown and the State Department. A security guard apprehended men trying to break into the headquarters of the Democratic National Committee. At first, the attempted burglary generally was regarded more as a sophomoric stunt than as anything sinister. Republican Senator Robert Dole commented, "I don't know why anyone would want to break into the headquarters of the Democratic Party. All they would find is a bunch of unpaid bills."

The Soviets took Hall's letter seriously, and Brezhnev instructed Ponomarev to give Morris a verbal reply pending a formal response. He said that the Central Committee understood Hall's concerns and wished to explain some facts. The summit conference long had been scheduled, and the North Vietnamese did not forewarn the Soviets of their offensive that provoked the American mining and blockade of Vietnamese harbors. At the time, nine Soviet ships were in Haiphong Harbor, and they barely escaped before it was mined. "When the blockade started, many Soviet ships were on the way to Haiphong. We asked the Chinese to allow these ships to unload at Von Pong [a Chinese port]. The Chinese refused and said they should go to Haiphong. The Chinese wanted a Soviet–U.S. confrontation and wanted us to war with the United States."

Considering all factors, the Politburo decided it was in the interest of Vietnam and worldwide communism to proceed with the summit conference, and the Vietnamese did not object. Far from abandoning the North Vietnamese, the Soviets were increasing aid to them. "Night and day, trains are going to Vietnam... We exerted tremendous pressure on Nixon. Comrade Brezhnev told him it is a barbaric, horrible war in which innocent people are being murdered, and so on. We told him categorically that our people are indignant, that world opinion is opposed to the dirty war in Vietnam, that there is world indignation. We demanded an end to U.S. aggression. This discussion went on for three to four hours, and there was danger that Nixon would leave the room. But he stayed and listened. He tried to justify the U.S. actions but failed. After Nixon went home, we gave hell to U.S. imperialism on our radio and television."

Lies concocted by the "bourgeois press," Ponomarev continued, had grossly distorted the results of the summit conference, and the Soviets needed to give Comrade Hall "more facts and arguments to counter the enemy." But he need not worry. "We have no illusions about U.S. imperialism or about Nixon or about Kissinger or any others. There is no difference between a Nixon and a Johnson—which devil is better? But as Lenin taught us, we can see the difference between aggressive and reasonable people... The Nixon speeches are chiefly demagoguery. But some parts of his speeches can be used."

Ponomarev also had some words about the agreements: "Of course, there is a difference between a document and deeds. But peaceful co-existence means that some documents need to be signed and implemented. We are aware that agreement on partial reduction of armaments and ABMs does not mean disarmament. We know that the number can be reduced but the quality can be improved. This is only a step in the direction of disarmament."

That was the Soviet message to Hall. Over lunch, Ponomarev spoke informally to Morris "as friend to friend," that is, for Morris' ears only. Hall had to be humored, but frankly the Soviets respected and even grudgingly liked Nixon and Kissinger because they were intelligent, they stood up for their beliefs—however wrong those beliefs were—and they gave the appearance of being honest. Of course, there was no such thing as an honest American politician but, so far as the Soviets knew, Nixon and Kissinger had not lied to them.

The Soviets did regard the May 26 agreements as merely a "first step." What they really wanted was a treaty whereby the United States and the Soviet Union each pledged never to launch nuclear weapons against the territory of the other. Morris marveled at Soviet chutzpah. Such a treaty obviously was unenforceable. But it would proclaim to Western Europe, Japan, and China that the United States was unwilling to risk its cities to protect theirs and thereby expose all American allies to Soviet bullying.

Ponomarev remarked that the Americans seemed to be stalling

and asked if Morris thought they might come around. Modestly noting his lack of military expertise, Morris asked, "If you were in their position, would you agree to such a treaty?" Ponomarev laughed and shrugged, as if to say *No harm in trying*.

Despite Soviet explanations, Hall remained unplacated, and in October 1972 he dispatched Morris to tell the Soviets that they were making too many concessions to the United States and undermining socialism everywhere. Morris again tried to represent these judgments as Hall's observations rather than opinions, but they nonetheless exasperated and angered the Soviets. They did not understand Comrade Hall's attitude, and, to be blunt, he did not know what he was talking about. Although the Americans had rejected a treaty banning nuclear strikes by the United States and the Soviet Union against each other, the Soviets were convinced that to date Nixon had dealt "honestly and fairly" with them; that Nixon and Kissinger tried to understand their concerns and candidly stated those of the United States. Soviet military and technical experts advised that the American concerns, from the American perspective, were in the main comprehensible and reasonable. In sum, the United States appeared to be negotiating in good faith, and no major foreign communist party, except the American and Chinese, opposed the ongoing negotiations, and the Chinese were hopeless in all matters. So what was the matter with Comrade Hall? Morris, who was well-versed in Sovietese, understood: Comrade Hall damn well better get in line.

Suslov and Ponomarev in many other discussions with Morris talked a lot about Nixon. They very much wanted him to win the presidential election only two or three weeks away but the Soviets had to be discreet in their support of him because if Democratic candidate George McGovern found out, he might get angry. Although they preferred to deal with Nixon and Kissinger above all others, Nixon still confused them. His feats in simultaneously "hijacking China," improving American–Soviet relations, and escalating an unpopular war in Vietnam awed them. How did he do it? Morris thought, *Maybe one reason is that he always knows what you're thinking and what you plan to do, insofar as you know yourselves.*

The Soviets theorized that Nixon's legerdemain was possible because his reputation as an inveterate anticommunist immunized him to charges of selling out to them. But what political tricks or acrobatics would he try next? If Nixon was reelected, the Central Committee wanted the American party to submit a "full analysis and evaluation" of his administration and its likely policies.

Morris and Eva returned to Chicago in time to vote for Nixon, who won the 1972 election by the largest majority ever, winning all of the fifty states except Massachusetts.

After the election, Morris pointed out more examples of Soviet detachment from reality. By October 1972, almost all rational, informed people in the United States knew that McGovern had no chance whatsoever of winning, yet the Soviets still thought he might win. Nixon had escalated the war in Vietnam; McGovern favored ending it on virtually any terms the communists dictated. Yet the Soviets preferred to deal with Nixon, the hawk, instead of McGovern, the dove.

The Soviets wanted the American party to tell them what Nixon was going to do. How on earth would the ragtag party know? Did they think that the party was more astute and knowledgeable than their Ministry of Foreign Affairs and the KGB?

Morris was seventy, and in the past thirteen months he had traveled to the Soviet Union and Eastern Europe six times. He looked forward to a surcease from danger, to rest, and to enjoying the holidays with Eva. But Hall had to go to Moscow in December to attend ceremonies celebrating the fiftieth anniversary of the founding of the Soviet Union, and he demanded that Morris be there with him.

A few days before he left, Jim Fox and his wife invited Morris and Eva to dinner. Fox was proud of his family, his career, and home, and after Eva came to know him and his background she realized that he had cause to be proud. Fox's father drove a bus for the Chicago municipal transit system, and his mother worked at whatever jobs a woman without a college education could find in those days. The family on Sunday morning attended a Baptist church, no matter how inclement the weather or how late his father had driven the night before, and when he was thirteen Fox went to a summer camp sponsored by the church. One of the counselors was an FBI agent, and by the campfire he enthralled the boys with accounts of how the FBI chased gangsters, spies, and Ku Klux Klansmen. Fox came home from camp resolutely sure of what he wanted to do in life.

The counselor told him that the FBI accepted maybe one out of every one hundred applicants and that his chances would be better if he had a law degree. So after making good grades as an undergraduate at the University of Illinois, Fox entered law school. At the end of his first year he was admitted to the law school at Georgetown University in Washington, where he could work as an FBI clerk at nights and on weekends. An assistant dean, however, tried to dissuade him from "throwing your life away" in the FBI and, having failed, refused to transfer to Georgetown the Illinois credits. The university upheld his appeal. After his graduation from Georgetown the FBI accepted him; during training at Quantico, veteran instructors accurately put him down as a future star.

He became one of the youngest supervisors in the FBI (Boyle before his fall from favor had also been one of the youngest), and the Bureau in 1971 chose him to be Boyle's immediate supervisor and therefore a principal participant in its most important operation. By now, the White House, State and Defense Departments, and the CIA beseeched the FBI for SOLO data. Anyone intimately associated with SOLO could gild his or her career with gold. But Fox, in reports to the Chicago SAC and conversations at headquarters, made it a point of honor to stress that the accomplishments of SOLO were the accomplishments of Burlinson, Freyman, Jack, Morris, Eva, Boyle, and Langtry; he just happened along. Boyle says, "Jim always ran interference for us. If anything went wrong, he took the blame. When things went right, and they usually did, he gave the credit to others."

Fox and his family lived in a pleasant suburban house where Morris played with the children, his delight so evident and spontaneous that it was contagious. Eva said, "The family scenes there could have been painted by Norman Rockwell." She remembered the evening just before Morris' departure for Moscow on December 11, 1972.

Before dinner Fox usually said a simple, three-sentence prayer—Eva guessed he had learned it in Sunday School. That night he recited part of a hymn that began "Blest be the ties that bind our hearts in Christian love" and ended "When we are called to part, it gives us inward pain; but our hearts are joined in hope that we shall meet again." When Fox raised his head, Eva sensed he suddenly was embarrassed at having said "Christian love." Eva said, "Jim, that was a beautiful prayer. Amen." She noticed that Morris' head still was bowed.

EVA HAD BEEN IN Moscow, Prague, and Warsaw throughout October, and Morris had no intention of dragging her away from home and relatives in December. In an uncharacteristic lapse, he complained before Hall about having to leave her at Christmastide. Characteristically, Hall asked, "What the hell do you care about Christmas?"

Morris cared a lot. He did not observe Christmas in any religious sense, and as a supposedly devout communist and atheist, he couldn't afford to enter a synagogue or church, even if he wanted to. But he could enjoy the festivities of Christmas—the lights and decorations along Michigan Avenue and Fifth Avenue; shopping for Eva, her nieces and nephews, the children of Boyle and Fox; listening to the Salvation Army bands. In Chicago and New York, the Christmas season for Morris, culturally and spiritually, was a happy time. In Moscow, Christmas 1972 was for him a dreary time.

He had to sit through long, soporific speeches larded with communist clichés he had been hearing for fifty years and had to trail along with Hall to ritualistic and boring meetings. After Hall returned to New York, Morris did receive an enlightening briefing from Yevgeny Kuzkov, an assistant to Ponomarev.

Kuzkov began with a harangue about U.S. actions in Vietnam. "The same point is on our agenda all over the world: stop the bombing and end the war in Vietnam." Meanwhile, the Soviets intended to do all they could to strengthen the North Vietnamese with more weaponry and supplies.

The infernal Chinese still were at it, vilely defaming the Soviet

Union and conniving to splinter socialism. They had moved troops from coastal areas opposite Taiwan and from the Vietnamese border to the Soviet frontier and were trying to provoke new clashes. Maps being distributed in Chinese schools represented large swaths of the Soviet Union as Chinese territory, and the populace was being drilled and indoctrinated for war with the Soviet Union. Chou En Lai had rejected "friendship" overtures from Brezhnev and told the Japanese that the existing Sino–Soviet friendship treaty was a worthless "scrap of paper."

In the Middle East, the Egyptians had become both a joke and a pain for the Soviets. The Soviets had invested immense resources in Egypt, and what had they gotten in return? After Gamal Abdul Nasser died, his successor, Anwar Sadat, unceremoniously booted the Soviets out of the country "without prior consultations." Then, after unsuccessfully flirting with the West, they had the gall to ask the Soviets for "offensive" weapons. "We said to them: 'The same weapons you have work effectively in Vietnam. You even have some better weapons than the Vietnamese have. What you need as much as weapons, if not more, is morale and spirit. You cannot sit in coffee houses sipping cognac and expect the weapons to work by themselves.'" Kuzkov added that the Egyptians had proposed that Sadat and Brezhnev meet, and that the Soviets said no.

The Soviets were also wary or mistrustful of the North Koreans and the unpredictable dictator Kim Il Sung. The North Koreans' attitude toward the Soviet Union was "give, give, give," and they offered nothing in return. Kuzkov said, "For now, their line is for peaceful reunification of Korea. If they succeed, that is fine, but from what we can see up until now, only God can help. We support their line but from a practical standpoint, how can you unite bourgeois [South] Korea and socialist Korea? Maybe Kim has the answers; we don't."

From Kuzkov's statements, Morris made these deductions, which the FBI subsequently shared with the White House and State Department:

❖ The United States could expect no help from the Soviets in extracting itself from Vietnam. Despite all the

Soviets said about peaceful co-existence, improved relations, and reaching agreements, they were determined to inflict upon the United States the most humiliating geopolitical defeat they could.

❖ The actions of the Chinese toward the Soviet Union matched their venomous words. They were consistent with what the Chinese said to the United States and consistent with SOLO reports about Sino–Soviet relations. If anything, the Chinese were growing more belligerent and the Soviets more worried about the Chinese.

❖ The Soviets held the Egyptians in contempt and were unwilling to invest more in Egypt. The Egyptians might be willing to listen to the United States privately.

❖ The Soviets feared the unpredictable, and they considered North Korea unpredictable. Relations between the Soviets and North Koreans were not as close as they appeared; the Soviets would not support reunification of Korea by force; and they cared little about Korea except as a danger point.

Morris owed his one pleasant evening around Christmas to Nikolai, the KGB officer who came by for "general intelligence" and bourbon. Nikolai spoke English with an American accent, asked insightful questions about the United States, never talked party cant, affected to believe in nothing except his wife and children, and dared to ridicule the ridiculous: "They say we're about to catch up with America. If that's true, America must be running backward very fast."

However, Morris and Boyle figured Nikolai was important in the KGB; Morris was a very important man in Moscow and the KGB would not allow just anybody regularly to talk to him. So why not utilize him? SOLO constituted one grand deception;

Morris and Jack regularly told the Soviets tactical or operational lies. Morris never purveyed substantive disinformation to mislead Soviet rulers because his influence depended in part upon the accuracy of the information and the assessments he gave them. He might mislead them once but not repeatedly.

He did misrepresent to Nikolai the sources of much of the "general intelligence" he volunteered. Supposedly, it came from a corporate executive or scientist by whom he sat on an airplane, or from his stockbroker or a business associate, or from something Jack had picked up. Almost all facts he reported were gleaned from open sources such as *Aviation Week*, the *Congressional Record*, the *Wall Street Journal*, and the *Economist* of London. But they were interesting and made for commendable reports.

Morris also consulted Boyle about what he should say. Sometimes Boyle asked for advice from headquarters. But FBI agents were not about to saunter through the corridors of the White House, State Department, Pentagon, or CIA saying, "Hey, our man is talking to Brezhnev next week. Anything you guys want to tell him?" And the FBI was not formulating U.S. foreign policy. So whatever Morris said in Moscow, was, in the end, "58's call."

The relative success of the North Vietnamese in using Soviet weapons intoxicated the Soviets, and they boasted to Morris that their weapons were just as good or better than American weapons. Boyle explained to Morris—whose only military expertise came from the Lenin School, where he learned how to blow up trains and stick pins into police horses—that the American difficulties in Vietnam resulted from idiotic strategy and idiotic Pentagon procurement policies of the 1960s, not from technological inferiority, and he introduced him to *Aviation Week*. Morris thought it dangerous for the Soviets to exaggerate to themselves their military prowess. So Morris recounted to Nikolai a fictional conversation he had with a Grumman Corporation executive while flying first class from New York to Los Angeles and drinking a lot of champagne. According to the tipsy executive, whose name Morris unfortunately did not retain, the United States was developing a new generation of fighter aircraft that, the executive claimed, would "rule the skies for decades." But there was something more devilish about these new planes. They not only were fighters; they were bombers. Each could carry miniaturized nuclear weapons many times more powerful than those dropped on Hiroshima and Nagasaki. The Grumman man claimed that the coming planes had "special systems" (Morris here concealed his newfound knowledge of avionics, terrain-following radar, and electronic jamming) that would enable them to penetrate any air-defense system in the world. The executive bragged that one fleet of these planes flying from U.S. navy aircraft carriers alone could blow up every city in the Soviet Union. Unfortunately, Morris again could not remember everything; only that the planes were designated by an F followed by two numerals. (Morris well knew he was talking about the F-14, the F-15, and the F-16.) Of course, this was just gossip; the executive was tired and had too much champagne; and if he would give away such secrets to a stranger, how reliable a person was he? Still, to Morris all this seemed like something worth looking into.

Surely, the GRU or KGB knew about the diagrammed capabilities of the F-14, the F-15, and the F-16 (which in flight turned out to be equal to or better than the projections of the designers hovering over computers in New York, Texas, Missouri, and California). At the next Politburo meeting Andropov could announce important, verified intelligence gained from MORAT, which the Politburo itself had instigated and for which it deserved congratulations. Boyle says, "We [the FBI and Morris] played them like a harp."

After they finished the supper laid out by the housekeeper, they drank bourbon and Nikolai asked questions about America. "How much of a factor was religion in the United States?" Morris, a student of the Talmud, Bible, and Koran, lied and said he really didn't pay much attention to religion. But he had read surveys which showed that a large majority of Americans said they believed in God and that a majority said they went to church. Morris then asked how much of a factor was religion in the Soviet Union.

"It's like weeds in a garden," Nikolai said. "You can stomp them out in one place and they keep sprouting in some place else." The party controlled the hierarchy of what was left of the Russian Orthodox Church, but it could not control the feelings of the people. Even many party members wanted their daughters to be secretly married by a priest and themselves wanted to be buried by a priest. Then there were the "sects," the most pernicious being the Baptists because they practiced what they preached. They were sober, diligent workers who showed up on time, did their job honestly, and then went home to their religion. Consequently, managers coveted them as workers and tolerated, even tacitly encouraged, their proselytizing at work—the more good workers the better. "Maybe someday we'll be the Soviet Union of Baptist and Muslim Republics."

Morris thought, *I'll tell Jim that the Baptists are making as much of a nuisance of themselves in the Soviet Union as they are in America*. He also thought, *Blest be the ties that bind*.

One of the verbal agreements of the May 1972 conference between Nixon and Brezhnev stipulated that Brezhnev would visit the United States in June 1973. Brezhnev was both excited and apprehensive about the journey, and in April of 1973 the Soviets called Morris and Hall to Moscow to help him and them prepare for it. Hall in turn asked Morris to help prepare him for the talks at the Kremlin. Morris advised him to explain to Brezhnev that the growing Watergate scandal conceivably could result in the impeachment of Nixon or compel him to resign from office.

At the Kremlin, Hall did explain, but Brezhnev was mystified. He asked, "*Chto etot Vatergate?*"—"What is this Watergate?" Ponomarev replied that it was a petty matter Nixon's political opponents were trying to magnify out of all proportions; it amounted to nothing.

When Hall was present Morris usually deferred to him, saying nothing unless asked a direct question. Now he spoke up, "Boris, that is exactly what I thought until a few weeks ago. I believe Gus felt the same way. No one can be blamed for not understanding Watergate. Most Americans don't understand it or care about it. But things are changing rapidly, aren't they, Gus?"

Hall may have been thuggish, uncultured, avaricious; he was not stupid. He picked up the cue and proceeded with the recitation he and Morris had rehearsed. Nixon's political opponents were trying to exploit a trivial incident to reverse the results of the

1972 elections. He and Comrade Morris thought they might succeed. "There is a real chance that Nixon will be forced out of office and you can't be sure he will be around."

Brezhnev then asked of the assembled Politburo and Central Committee members, "Is this correct?"

Suslov answered, "If Morris [not Hall] says so, it probably is."

Brezhnev nodded at Morris but spoke to Hall. "This is an example of comradely cooperation between fraternal parties. It is an example of why we so esteem you, Comrade Morris, and your party. We will pay attention to this strange Watergate business."

They talked next about Brezhnev's trip to the United States, and, as Morris said to Boyle, Brezhnev "acted like a little kid going off to his first summer camp." He had confidence in Nixon and Kissinger; but what would happen to him in a land marauded by gangsters, drug addicts, and insane people who daily murdered people, even public officials? Hall, who had been briefed by Morris, who had been briefed by Boyle, assured Brezhnev that he would be accorded a respectful and secure welcome. The United States Secret Service would protect him just as securely as it did Nixon, and he could bring along his own KGB bodyguards with whom the Secret Service would collaborate. It would be good if a few of them went to Washington right away to talk to the FBI and Secret Service.

There were a lot of crackpots in America, and there might be some anti-Soviet demonstrations by a few lunatics walking around with stupid placards. But the U.S. military would keep them far away. "And our party has influence. We will persuade the press that these demonstrators are a lunatic fringe."

Morris thought, *Gus, you couldn't persuade a single American journalist to say that apple pie tastes good.*

Ponomarev invited or commanded Morris to lunch in his office suite, and there Morris discerned why Ponomarev, who only recently had emerged from the hospital, was so sprightly and happy. Morris always hid his knowledge of the Russian language from the Soviets and, except when talking to men of the International Department or KGB who spoke English, he conversed through an interpreter. The interpreters were invariably excellent and invariably male. Now Ponomarev had a new interpreter, Natalia, who was every boy's dream. She had golden hair and blue eyes, and her black dress, which could have come from Marshall Field's in Chicago, did nothing to conceal her lovely contours. She was twenty-five or so, she looked and talked like an American teenager, and Morris guessed she was the daughter of a Soviet diplomat or KGB officer and had gone to high school in the United States. He wondered just what sort of deal Ponomarev had made with her father. The male interpreters were efficient and emotionless; they tried to ease conversation and make it seem as though they didn't exist. Natalia had a sense of shame and humor, and she blushed or giggled when something embarrassed or amused her. Ponomarev indulged her, and you didn't have to be a genius to figure out why.

Natalia both blushed and giggled as she interpreted "delicate matters." Comrade Brezhnev had a pretty young niece of whom he was especially fond. She was an Aeroflot stewardess and a highly qualified nurse who examined Brezhnev at night. She longed to see America. Could Brezhnev bring her along, and could she examine him at night?

Morris replied that the U.S. Secret Service doubtless was not unfamiliar with such matters and that the KGB should talk frankly with the Secret Service. All could be arranged among gentlemen.

Morris, as would any male in the world, admired the physical beauty of Natalia. She won his heart by giggles that showed she recognized the underlying absurdity of the question she interpreted or translated. "What should Comrade Brezhnev wear in America?"

A man who held the power of life and death over the inhabitants of one-sixth of the world's land surface needed to be told by a little seventy-year-old Jew from Chicago what kind of clothes to put on!

Walt, you have to think like they do. Instead of giving the simple, commonsense answer any juvenile clerk at J.C. Penney's would have given, Morris poured out a polemic about clothes. The capitalists had duped American workers into thinking that any one of them could become a capitalist. Clothes in America were a symbol. Most Americans laughed at the goofy garb worn by Comrade Fidel; they wanted to wear clothes like those of a British prime minister or a fashion model. Soviet tailors should take Brezhnev's measurements exactly, then the "special comrades" should have dark suits tailored for him in London, Milan, or New York.

Ponomarev lost his temper and brought Natalia nearly to tears. "He says he is sick and tired, and he used a bad word, of hearing about how much better everything is in the West."

Morris, for the only time in Moscow, lost *his* temper. "Then you tell him to ask his own [obscenity] tailors what to put on Brezhnev's fat ass."

"Sir, I cannot use those words."

"Use any words you want."

Ponomarev rose, picked Morris up, and hugged him. The terrified and beautiful Natalia said, "He says, 'We both are old and tired and we have worked too long. Are we not still friends?'" Morris said that they were.

On the flight out of Moscow, Morris and Eva were the only passengers in the first-class cabin. They declined the champagne but accepted a copy of the *International Herald-Tribune*. As the plane ascended from the runway, people in the rear cabin began to clap, shout, and sing *La Marseillaise*. Morris asked a stewardess why the people were shouting and singing. "Because, monsieur, we are leaving the Soviet Union."

Morris said, "All right, bring us a bottle of champagne."

thirteen

THREATS FROM WITHIN

MORRIS THOUGHT HE UNDERSTOOD all the implications of Watergate, and that is why he had Hall warn the Soviets about its potential consequences. He never imagined that the scandal could affect him and SOLO. But as more and more government officials were hauled before congressional committees and grand juries, as more leaked secrets appeared in the press, Morris and Jack increasingly worried about the security of the operation and their own personal safety. In an effort to reassure them, the FBI convened an operational conference in New York on May 31, 1973, a few days before Brezhnev arrived in the United States. Present were Assistant Director Edward S. Miller, Section Chief William A. Brannigan, Burlinson, Langtry, Boyle, Morris, and Jack.

"We have tremendous concern about security," Miller began. "We have to provide extra special handling of this [SOLO] information because we are operating in special times. Many people are telling everything they know. Despite this horrible situation, we cannot let the whole organization go down the drain. The whole U.S. intelligence community is being tested. We cannot let these desperate people like [John] Dean and [H.R.] Halderman shape the destiny of our country. I assure you that security is absolutely the highest priority in the FBI."

Jack spoke next. "Over almost twenty-two years we have built an apparatus for our government and country and we built it to our specifications. We said we were going to the very top. This is exemplified by my brother's last trip. This is the apex. But the question is how can we save the apparatus in view of these 'desperate people.' We have had some great achievements and I am proud of them. But all the years of sacrifice could go out the window with a situation such as we have today."

Jack complained that since the death of J. Edgar Hoover in 1972, he and Morris felt they were functioning in a void and that they and their accomplishments were being ignored by the FBI leadership in Washington. "I remember a small thing. When my father died, Director Hoover sent a personal representative, an inspector, to express his sympathy. It was a small thing but to me, significant."

Acknowledging that the FBI had experienced turmoil, Miller declared, "When the history of the first one hundred years of the FBI is written, the highlight will be this operation, the people in this room. When the history is written, this operation will be unique, not only in the FBI, but in the world. Nothing could equal it."

Miller stressed how stringently the FBI guarded SOLO intelligence. "We are protecting this intelligence by hand-carrying it by armed messenger to the White House to the man who reads it. He reads it, and it is hand-carried right back to my office. This is how we are protecting the product. We know we have to do everything possible to preserve the security of the operation."

However, Jack for the time being refused to be propitiated, and he continued alternately to brag, then gripe. "We have built this apparatus, and we are very jealous of it. When I say 'we,' I mean all of us including people in the Bureau. It is an apparatus that runs smoothly. We practically think the way the Russians do. My wife is now more involved physically than I am and so is my brother's wife. My brother and I have come to the conclusion that we are prisoners, prisoners of the Communist Party, the Russians, prisoners of the apparatus. I cannot be more than two hours away from a radio message. The only real vacation I have ever had was when I had major surgery while Gus Hall and my brother were overseas. My brother has never had a vacation in twenty years.

"This thing so carefully built through so much dedication can be destroyed by lack of security. When I was overseas getting ready to go to Cuba, a column by Victor Riesel exposed the money operation. This article was shown to me in Moscow and they asked, 'How come?' When I came back from the mission, and it was a good mission, I was promised it would never happen again. But something happened again a few months later when my brother was on the other side."

Morris had additional complaints of his own. "The Russians used to call us in for training in special techniques, codes, radio, etc. When the Bureau would get wind of it, somebody would come running up from Washington and ask us about it. They paid ten times the attention to these little things as to important matters that could affect the fate of the nation. I don't know how much attention is paid to some of these documents my wife and I would spend hours copying." Next he decried security lapses. "So there I sit talking to Suslov, not below the number-three man in the Soviet Union, and he pulls out an excerpt from the *Congressional Record* with a report from the FBI director about the budget and asks about it. I passed it off and remarked that they have to say those things to get their money. But how often can we go through these things?" Finally, Morris said something that must have been hard for him to say. "Human beings, no matter how tough, have sensitivities. I think as you get older, you get more sensitive. We used to get letters from the director after these trips. In the last years, we have come back with all kinds of information. But we don't get these letters any more. This is not only a question of vanity, though we all have some vanity. I am talking beyond vanity—about friendship, loyalty, and esprit whereby you protect your own."

Miller seemed to meditate for half a minute or so before saying, "We could and should have done more. We will." And at once, he tried. Morris and Jack were just as much a part of the FBI family as he, Bill, Al, Walt, and John, and as family members they were entitled to be informed about family business, which of course was private. The death of Hoover naturally precipitated change and invited temporary organizational disarray. The new director, L. Patrick Gray, whose appointment had yet to be confirmed by a hostile Senate, was still adjusting to unfamiliar responsibilities. Gray, other FBI executives, and the FBI as an organization had fallen under severe political attack, which caused personal stress and diverted attention from normal duties.

Morris and Jack had emphasized the necessity of security; the FBI agreed and consequently enforced extraordinary security procedures to safeguard the operation. Because in the main they had succeeded, very few people either at headquarters or in the field, and nobody outside the FBI, had been fully informed of SOLO. Pending Senate confirmation of Mr. Gray and until "the clouds cleared," no one else would be admitted to the "inner circle."

The intelligence SOLO was producing—the verbal and documentary revelations of the thoughts and intentions of Soviet leaders and their reactions to the words and comportment of American leaders—was literally priceless. Miller said he seemed to recall reading in the top-secret files, now kept in special safes in his office, something to the effect that the CIA had offered to pay the FBI any amount of money to be a participant in the operation, even though it was ignorant of the nature of the operation and the identity of its principals. Morris himself that very morning eloquently had traced the effects of SOLO intelligence upon American–Chinese relations, and its contributions to a historic realignment in the balance of world power. Famous men, whose names were well known, hungered for their reports.

"I cannot mention their names," Miller went on. "I can remind you of what you said earlier. Whenever the Soviets talk to Nixon or Kissinger, they consult you before and after the talks. Do you think Nixon and Kissinger are disinterested in what they tell and ask you? Sometimes at the White House or State Department when people hand back reports to our messenger—he of course is more than a messenger—they send along handwritten notes of commendation or appreciation or congratulations. Sometimes we get letters or phone calls. But nobody can say anything about you because nobody knows anything about you; they only know what you produce. We can't tell anybody, not even colleagues I would trust with my life, what the president or secretary of state or director of Central Intelligence says to us in confidence. Maybe we have been remiss. Maybe we should have tried to find some way to circumvent this rule so we could let you know how much what you are doing is valued. But to do that, we would have to talk about you and SOLO. None of us can have it all ways at once."

On a scale of one to five, Boyle rated Miller's performance a six, and he sensed that it had placated Morris and revived his faith. Langtry, like Boyle, was a military man and, like Boyle, he had kept silent while superiors spoke. But he sensed it was time to speak up and rein Jack in.

Langtry really understood and liked Jack. Undoubtedly, Jack and Morris had conferred before the conference and agreed upon what each would say, so whatever concerns Jack expressed were also those of Morris. Jack worked best on a loose leash so he could exercise his native brashness, initiative, and ingenuity as a self-described con man; but he had to be kept on a leash.

In complaining earlier, Jack mentioned that he recently had been upbraided by his KGB case officer (Vladimir Aleksandrovich Chuchukin). Brezhnev had sent an urgent message for Jack to deliver at once to Gus Hall; the message arrived on a Saturday night, and the KGB had not been able to reach Jack until it signaled on Monday morning for an emergency meeting that afternoon. "We must be able to contact you seven days a week," Chuchukin had said.

Langtry said that the FBI could "guard" (monitor) any and all designated radio frequencies twenty-four hours a day, seven days a week if necessary. But he recalled that when Jack last underwent such intensive interrogation in Moscow, his KGB inquisitor had asked if Jack did not think it strange that everything about the operation always went off flawlessly. Jack should point out to Chuchukin that he precisely followed communication procedures dictated by the KGB and that the radio schedule issued by the KGB called for no transmission that Saturday night, so neither he nor his auxiliary radioman (NY-4309S*) had been by their receivers. Jack (actually Langtry) had checked the signal site on Saturday morning, and there was no call for a meeting. According to the KGB plan, if the right chalk mark did not appear, Jack was free for the weekend.

Jack had been willing to give up many a Saturday and Sunday to smuggle the money. But always he had advance notice; if the KGB wanted to revise the communications plan to provide for sudden, emergency contact on Saturday night or Sunday morning, swell, "peachy keen." In the meantime, *don't blame me for doing what you and your whole organization have told me to do.*

Jack should say something else that Chuchukin, an intelligent man, would have to report, both in the interests of the KGB and self-protection: By effectively demanding that Jack be on call around the clock throughout the week, the KGB was jeopardizing MORAT. While handling clandestine communications, accepting and hiding illegal cash coming in now at an increasing rate that exceeded a million dollars a year, being at the beck and call of Gus Hall, and while supporting Morris, Jack needed and wanted to take care of his own family and business. What would the neighbors think if he skulked around the house all day awaiting messages from Moscow, never going to work or the grocery store? He believed the FBI watched KGB officers whom it had identified and tried to listen to their telephone calls. For Chuchukin to call him at home on a Saturday night over an open line was, as they had taught him in Moscow, suicidal, amateurish, irresponsible, dangerous.

Langtry also played basketball, and with a glance he passed the intellectual ball to Boyle. As reflexively as when he captained championship teams, Boyle picked it up and shot, "Jack, after dumping on the KGB and going through your poor-me routine, why don't you apologize. Say you're sorry for being rude; say you are under a terrible strain; say that you know he, his family, and his organization are under great strain; say you know something about bureaucracy. Then say, 'If there are problems, do you want my brother to bring them up with Brezhnev, Suslov, Ponomarev, or Andropov?'"

Jack and Morris smiled, and Miller saw why headquarters had continued to let New York and Chicago run the case since its inception.

THE CONFIDENCE THAT ALL felt upon leaving the conference was shortlived. Through the summer and into the autumn of 1973, the ongoing Watergate circus, the disclosures of secret information, and the political attacks upon the CIA and FBI mortified Morris and Jack. A barrage of allegations, true or false, compelled Gray to resign as interim director of the FBI (he was accused, among other things, of removing documents from headquarters and throwing them into the Potomac River). At the behest of Boyle, Chicago SAC Richard Held warned headquarters that Morris and Jack again needed some high-level handholding. Morris was due to fly via Europe to Moscow on November 21, so the FBI arranged another operational conference in New York on November 20. Inspector Andrew Decker and Supervisor Brannigan came up from Washington to preside over it, and at first it was a repetition of the May conference.

Decker started by saying that SOLO intelligence was "invaluable and unavailable from any place else," that there were many means of tracking, numbering, and evaluating weapons and military forces, but that "insights into what people were thinking" were more important and rarely attainable.

Morris responded with a review of SOLO accomplishments in the 1970s: Every time there were negotiations about arms control or Vietnam or anything else, we knew in advance what they were thinking and afterward we knew what they thought. "We were always one step ahead."

Morris always had been scared; now Boyle more acutely than ever appreciated just how scared he was. Morris said he thought he understood the United States and the FBI; he understood political disagreements—after all, they were part of what America was about—but he could not understand politicians who struck at the institutions that existed to guarantee the right to disagree; and he frankly wondered whether the FBI still was functional. "This has

been a very bad year. How can a person feel secure in these circumstances? We have said if this thing blows, there isn't a place on
earth that could hide us. If they found out that for all these years
we have duped all of them—Mao, Chou, Khrushchev, Brezhnev,
Suslov, Ponomarev, the head of the KGB, and the whole KGB—if
it was the last thing they did, they would try to exterminate us.
Hundreds of men would vie for the honor of doing that. Tomorrow I leave for Moscow. It is not easy in Moscow. I am a member
of the club. I have my own apartment, servants, and driver, and a
card that gets me into the speakeasies and anything I want. I can
deal with *them*; I've done that most of my life."

The minutes of the meeting paraphrased Morris' next statements (and anyone is entitled to guess why). Despite these ameni-
ties, Morris and Eva, when she was along, lived in fear of making
the most minute mistake and the necessity of making every nuance
right. A little example of how careful they had to be: The Soviets
discerned that art galleries and exhibitions delighted Eva, and they
took her and Morris to an exhibition of paintings by a Jewish
artist who had been "rehabilitated." Several beguiled Eva, and she
asked Morris if he had enough rubles with him to buy one. Curtly,
Morris told her no; later he explained, "They know I am Jewish;
I don't want to remind them of it."

Still, they could manage in Moscow. But they could not manage in Washington; the greatest fear they had in Moscow was of
what might happen in Washington. They feared the politician,
the journalist, the climbing bureaucrat—the congressional or
White House aide—who, from ambition, ignorance, avarice, or
malice, might exploit any knowledge of SOLO and thereby
betray them.

Like Miller in May, Decker took his time and thought about
what to say, and like Miller, he was honest. "The FBI is back on
an even keel. Morale never was bad at the operating level. Pat
Gray used terrible judgment, abysmal; but we rode it out. If some
politicians knew about this operation they probably would exploit
it. But they never, ever will know... John Dean would have
betrayed his mother, if he had anything on her. There can be a traitor in any organization. Jesus had one. But so far as we know the

FBI has not had one. Doubtless someday we will. But he won't be part of SOLO."

Morris said that in Moscow he probably would be asked about a small story in one of the Chicago newspapers alleging that the Soviets were funding the American Communist Party. Decker replied, "The story was written by a notorious anticommunist, and their records will show that. The story offers no specifics or proof or indications of how the supposed funds are being delivered or what they amount to or what they are being used for. You can be sure that if the reporter had any specifics or evidence, he would have reported them. He did not and everyone ignored the story for just what it is: informed speculation by a young anticommunist. Anyone can ask, 'Who else would give money to the American Communist Party except the Soviet Union?' So it is nothing. You can say, 'The FBI would love to catch Jack or me with the money, and it would have all American television photographing us as they carted us off to jail and it would do that without asking anybody.'"

Decker asked if that would wash in Moscow. Morris answered in one word, "Brilliantly."

Burlinson, Langtry, and Boyle read Jack well; whereas in May he might have been theatrical, he now was earnest and seeking professional counsel. "The Russians have been keeping very quiet. The last time it took four days to meet my contact. When I did meet him, he kept questioning me about security. Then he talked about setting up contingency plans in the event contact is broken."

Jack paused, stared at Decker and Brannigan, and asked, "What did the Watergate committee see?"

Decker replied, "Absolutely nothing, zero."

"Well, the Russians' experience is that an apparatus lasts five years, no longer," Jack said. "But we are still going after five times five years. This gives them cause to reconsider this operation from every angle. My Russian contact worries all the time. He asks me how I am feeling. Then he begins to ask me about Morris. They are very vigilant. Gus is also very vigilant. Sometimes he lets out information to see what will happen. He is testing... The Russians have changed procedures. My Soviet contact will meet and ask if everything is O.K. Then he goes away and comes back in fifteen minutes or half an hour. Also there is a strict order: no messages or talking while handing over money."

Decker's response took Langtry back to the woodlands, rolling hills, and meadows of Virginia, to Quantico where Marines and future FBI agents trained, and he could hear his instructor: Someday you will have to be the director. There will be no supervisor or manual to consult; there will be no telephone. You alone will have to decide, then and there.

Within hours, Morris had to leave for Moscow. There was no time to assemble a committee or make a study; Morris and Jack would construe any ploy to lead Burlinson, Langtry, and Boyle out of the room for even a few minutes of consultation away from them as a sign of distrust; the FBI—the United States—very much needed the trust and services of these two men and their wives, all now in their seventies. So Decker on the spot decided and became for the moment the director. In essence, he proposed or ordered that the FBI and the SOLO team turn things upside down, that they turn quite rational Soviet concerns with security into American advantage.

"For a while, things should be quiet. Jack should miss a few meetings, ostensibly for security reasons. You must realize that their security on meetings is going to be tougher and tougher. They cannot afford to have this operation compromised. They must be scared to death that at any moment the FBI will jump on them."

After missing a meeting, Jack should signal through the "rubber duck" or micro transmitter that he was all right, that something made him think the rendezvous was unsafe, and that he would meet at the fallback date and place. When he met Chuchukin he should appear worried, but not paranoid. He should say that all of his concerns were perhaps irrational; nevertheless, he wanted to report them. Then he should recite a series of fictitious and unverifiable incidents: a van that did not belong to anybody in the neighborhood loitered around his house; a young man and woman parked near his house and kissed and caressed, but his street was not a lovers' lane; his telephone sometimes failed, and the telephone company said it was having problems with squirrels gnawing at its lines—all right, the squirrels were pests, but up until recently they hadn't cut his telephone service.

If the KGB interviewed Morris in Moscow, as it normally did during his year-end visits, he should express concern about security, ask if there had been any more defectors, and demand reassurance that knowledge of MORAT was being tightly held. However, a fine balance had to be struck between convincing the KGB that Morris and Jack were acutely concerned with security and frightening the KGB into believing that the operation had been compromised. Jack should make clear that he was willing to go on, but that everyone had to be very careful. Morris should not bring up security matters with his Politburo buddies; they didn't give a damn about such petty matters, but if they asked about them, he should defer to the KGB. In talking to the KGB, Morris should point out that he had not voiced his apprehensions to the Politburo; in operational matters, he put his trust in the KGB.

Moscow was as cold and laden with snow as when Morris first rode through its streets on a horse-drawn sleigh in 1929, and he and Eva welcomed the warmth and sanctuary of their apartment. By decorating the apartment with small Russian antiques and paintings, Eva had tried to make it into a second home, like the apartment in New York. They kept there extensive toiletries and clothing, including a plaid woolen robe, fleece-lined slippers, and flannel pajamas Eva had given Morris. Morris put them on while Eva gathered supper from the refrigerator, which as always was amply stocked with delicacies. Doctors told Morris that a couple of glasses of red wine a day would do him no harm, might do him some good, and were preferable to sleeping pills, so they uncorked a really fine bottle of Burgundy and before supper looked out on the falling snow that made the city appear pristine. Eva remembered because Morris, who would be seventy-two in May, suddenly and tenderly embraced her and said, "You are the greatest thing that ever happened to me. What a comrade you are." Hastily, Morris corrected himself. "I meant partner." They laughed and proceeded to enjoy the delicious borscht Yekaterina had prepared along with good, chewy Russian bread. Morris thought, *Bread is the one good thing communism has given the people. No, that's not right. In my childhood we had good bread, and we exported wheat instead of begging for it from the United States and Canada.* Before they fell asleep, Morris said, "Don't forget to make Irina [Eva's escort] get the postcards tomorrow."

Before an extended mission, Morris, with the help of Boyle, loaded big suitcases with all sorts of odds and ends as well as with the customary gifts. When Boyle asked why he was packing some peculiar items, Morris habitually replied, "Just in case." The FBI rented a post office box to which Morris would send cryptically worded picture postcards from Moscow addressed to Mr. Justin Case, as in "Just in case."

It took time for the cards to wend their way to Chicago, and Morris could write relatively few words on them. So the cards were not the ideal means of saying something to the FBI while in the Soviet Union; but they were the only means. By asking the escort to buy cards and the housekeeper to mail them, Morris could proclaim to the KGB his innocence.

Morris in the morning told Ponomarev that the American party needed $3.6 million for 1974; the Soviets, as Morris knew they would, agreed to $1.8 million. Ponomarev and Kazakov, not very delicately, instructed Morris to make Hall understand that "detente with the United States is now the cornerstone of Soviet foreign policy." They did not say it outright but they clearly conveyed a message for Hall: This is the party line and you had better follow it, whether or not you like it.

There was something else Hall must understand. The Soviets recognized that the United States, because of its relatively influential Jewish population, had a special interest in Israel and the Middle East. The Soviet Union also had strategic interests in the Middle East, which was "much closer to us than it is to them." Soviet and American interests in the Middle East conflicted and so the area was a "flash point," which Morris interpreted to mean an area where events could get out of hand and lead to war. The Soviets were prepared to accept American interests if the United States would accept theirs. In return for American concessions and acknowledgment of its right to have a say about what went on in the Middle East, the Soviet Union was ready to declare to the Arab world that Israel had a right to exist as a sovereign state and to establish formal diplomatic relations with it. Thus far, Nixon and Kissinger had been frank and honest in negotiations. True, they had not spoken about their "billing and cooing" with the Chinese ("billing and cooing" were the words used by an erudite and diplomatic Soviet interpreter; the Russian words were different and vulgar). But the (obscenity) Chinese had not been the subject of discussions; so they did not lie about that. Nixon and Kissinger also had honored their word about keeping negotiations and communications secret. But if the negotiations succeeded, everything, or most of it, would come out, and Hall should be ready for the results and ready to applaud them.

The Soviets, who liked Eva and Morris, exhausted them with hospitality. Almost every night there was a dinner with a member of the Politburo or Central Committee; at each Morris tried anew to explain Watergate. But to men who had colluded in the extermination of millions of their fellow citizens, including longtime comrades, Watergate still made little sense.

They landed in New York on December 12, 1973. The heartening sight of Boyle at the airport; the general gaiety of New York preparing for Christmas; the relief from fear that hourly they were being watched and listened to; the comfort of being in an apartment that really was their own, of being able to walk a block or two to markets, delicatessens, carryouts where at almost any hour you could satisfy any reasonable hunger; the family evenings with Jack, Roz, and Langtry at the storybook home of Al and Ann Burlinson; and, compared to Moscow, the overall merriment and jocularity of the people they saw on the streets—all combined to make the first days back home happy.

They stayed the first days in New York because the demands from headquarters were so voracious there was no time to go to Chicago. The first mission reports, once they were circulated, elicited a succession of questions; far from perturbing Morris, they gladdened him because they proved that the intelligence was being seriously analyzed by intelligent people. Like Boyle, he awakened early and was at work at least by 8 A.M.

But on December 17, without consulting anyone except Eva, Morris made a pronouncement to the FBI: Tomorrow he and his wife were setting off on a vacation that would last until January 3. During it, he did not want to be disturbed.

Morris lived to work, and the belief that his work was vital to the United States probably kept him alive, against heavy medical odds. As a child he worked after Jewish school, helping in the cobbler shop of his father; at party headquarters in Chicago, to help after making his rounds as the "Red Milkman," he got up at night to stuff stupid communist leaflets into the mailboxes of Americans who would have skinned him if they caught him. Carl Freyman started the custom by which the FBI weekly assembled a package of Soviet publications for Morris to analyze. Sometimes Morris called as early as 7 A.M. on Sunday to excitedly explain the significance of something he had culled from publications delivered on Saturday. Doubtless, he would enjoy a few free days to visit relatives during the holidays. But that was not the real reason he declared a vacation. He intended to go nowhere, only to hibernate at home. But by making himself officially unavailable, he liberated Boyle to be with his wife and six children before, during, and after Christmas.

After the tranquil holidays, on the night of January 18, 1974, Morris received a telephone call, and when he put the phone down his hand shook. The FBI had just deciphered a message from the KGB to Jack for MORAT: "Suspend all contact until further notice."

Headquarters demanded to know what had happened. In the first hours, Burlinson, Boyle, and Langtry had no answers. Then agents uninvolved in SOLO reported that, on the afternoon of the eighteenth, Chuchukin, Jack's KGB handler, without bothering to pack, bolted from New York for Montreal. The Royal Canadian Mounted Police advised that he flew from Montreal on a ticket that listed his final destination as Moscow. Why? The next day Burlinson or Langtry found the answer.

The morning of the eighteenth a large bookstore on Fifth Avenue displayed in its front window copies of a new book about the KGB.‡ The book contained a photograph of Chuchukin captioned, "Vladimir Aleksandrovich Chuchukin, a KGB officer assigned to work against Western journalists under the cover of a United Nations appointment." An art or photo editor had placed his picture on a page with photographs, surreptitiously snapped and therefore unflattering, of three other prominent KGB officers who looked like snarling thugs. On the adjoining page appeared photographs diagramming a sinister KGB espionage device. The net effect portrayed Chuchukin as a candidate for the FBI's "Ten Most Wanted" list.

It is hard to say who was more dismayed—people in the Politburo, Central Committee, and KGB headquarters in Moscow, or people at FBI headquarters and the Chicago and New York offices. Something they all prized, for different reasons, seemed imperiled.

During the crisis, communications from headquarters to New York and Chicago were calm, reasoned, and encouraging, in part because of the changes in Washington. Plagued by scandal, the Nixon administration undertook to select as a new director of the FBI a man of unimpeachable rectitude, and it chose the police chief of Kansas City, Clarence Kelley, a former FBI agent. Kelley set out to surround himself with the strongest men he could find, and he appointed Raymond Wannall to be assistant director in charge of intelligence.

---

‡ Author's Note: The book was *KGB: The Secret Works of Soviet Secret Agents*, written by me. A European intelligence service identified to me Chuchukin as a premier example of an excellent KGB officer plying his subversive trade out of the United Nations headquarters in New York, and another foreign security service confirmed that Chuchukin indeed was an excellent KGB officer. Neither of these services knew what Chuchukin was really doing in New York and, of course, neither did I. Professional researchers, tasked with documenting or verifying the manuscript, queried original sources. Because the FBI had supplied no information about Chuchukin, they did not ask the FBI for corroboration of the references to him. Thus, the FBI had no forewarning of the exposure of Chuchukin and no chance to ask that he not be exposed.

Wannall had worked in intelligence or counterintelligence for more than twenty years. In all those years, he never heard even an elliptical hint of the existence of SOLO. When he became assistant director, he was fully informed and he in turn briefed Kelley, who was amazed, and said, "Ray, you have the most interesting job in the FBI."

Kelley granted Wannall broad authority to make policy decisions governing SOLO and told him that the management and protection of the operation would be one of his principal duties during the remainder of his FBI career.

Wannall began by trying to pick up the pieces and put them back together again.

fourteen

THE TRIAL

GUS HALL CONSTRUED THE ABRUPT, unexplained suspension of MORAT (SOLO) as a personal affront and a threat. Morris and Jack provided his main communications link with the Kremlin; they formed the conduit through which the indispensable Soviet cash flowed; and Morris, because of his standing and influence with the Soviets, enhanced Hall's status in Moscow. As weeks passed without any word whatsoever from the Soviets, Hall's apprehensions multiplied and, despite the order to cease all contact, he demanded that Morris by whatever means contact the Soviets to find out what had happened and why.

Still having heard nothing from the Kremlin or KGB, Morris on February 18, 1974, departed New York for Prague. Upon landing he asked to see the chief security officer at the airport and handed him a typed statement previously provided by the Czech Party commanding anyone who read it to help the bearer in all matters. Morris then gave the security officer a telephone number, and rep resentatives of the Czech Party soon arrived and contacted the Soviets, who arranged for him to go on to Moscow.

When Morris entered Ponomarev's office, he was surprised to see Chuchukin grimly sitting there, like a prisoner in the dock, his eyes pleading for help. Defying protocol, Morris strode straight to Chuchukin and greeted him as if he had recovered a lost son. He was overjoyed to see Vladimir safe and well. "Jack has been worried sick about you. Why did you run away without even saying goodbye?"

Before Chuchukin could respond, Ponomarev curtly spoke in a tone communicating that the meeting had not been convened for purposes of good fellowship. "We have a grave and complicated situation."

There ensued what Morris likened to a kind of trial. He was the expert witness, Chuchukin the defendant, Ponomarev the prosecutor or interlocutor. Seated next to Ponomarev was a big man who welcomed Morris with formal politeness but did not identify himself; periodically, he whispered to Ponomarev, probably telling him what to ask next. Morris guessed he was a KGB general acting as judge, jury, and counsel to the prosecution.

Ponomarev, referring to the book *KGB*, began by saying, "We believe you and Jack are in great danger and could be arrested at any time. If you are arrested, the cause of détente will be set back, maybe for many years. We believe this book is part of a plot by reactionary U.S. circles to sabotage détente." He added that they were assessing its consequences and investigating to determine whether mistakes by the "special comrades" (his euphemism for the KGB) brought about this sorry state of affairs. Giving Chuchukin a hangman's stare, he asked whether Morris, Jack, or Comrade Hall found any fault in actions by the "special comrades."

Morris started at the back and worked toward the front. The book perplexed and concerned him too; he had studied it and reached some tentative conclusions, which he offered for whatever they were worth. In his efforts better to understand how the capitalists manipulated the masses, he had been reading the *Reader's Digest* for forty years; it was notoriously and irredeemably anticommunist and reactionary. Its sponsorship of a book slandering the Soviet Union and socialism, therefore, was not surprising. The magazine had been publishing condensations of the manuscript for some time; this publication of the book itself represented no change in U.S. policy. The author claimed to have gained assistance from the FBI, the CIA, "special organs" of other capitalist countries, and Soviet traitors (KGB defectors). Had the author known about the transfer of money, he certainly would have said something about it because that would have made the book more sensational. Morris therefore concluded that neither the author nor any of his sources knew anything about the money. He noted that the book contained a one-sentence reference to Vladimir alleging that he had engaged in "disinformation" operations abroad; if that were true, perhaps those activities brought him to the attention of the author. Since publication of the book, he and Jack had watched for any signs that they were under surveillance or suspicion; they detected none. As for the "special comrades," they had been supportive and efficient, and Jack especially liked and trusted Vladimir because he was so careful and punctual.

Chuchukin said nothing but his face expressed relief and gratitude. Ponomarev thanked Morris for his analysis and the comments about Chuchukin, and said that his judgments would be taken into account. The implications of the book and the question of whether contact could be resumed in New York nevertheless were still under evaluation, and he could not predict the outcome.

Here Morris issued a subtle threat, yet one to which nobody could take exception. He and Jack appreciated as well as anybody the necessity of security; after all, their "necks were in the noose." They understood that the "special comrades" would know best how to manage security, and they in good grace would accept whatever was decided. For fifty years, he and his brother had tried to serve the party; he hoped they had made some small contributions; and he was proud they had helped create a secret channel of communications that for more than fifteen years had proven impervious to the "imperialists" and the FBI. But he and Jack were now in their seventies; their work was dangerous; it was physically demanding; Jack and Vladimir before transferring money had to drive around the countryside for hours in rain, snow, and storms to make sure they were not being followed, and sometimes his brother did not get to bed until 3 A.M.; Morris now was making four or five trips a year to Moscow and Eastern Europe, and travel was arduous. If the "special comrades" judged that the existing channel of communications and money transfers could not be maintained, then an alternate one would have to be established from nothing. If so, then this might be an appropriate time for Morris and Jack "to retire from active service." For the rest of their lives they would of course do all they could to serve the party to which they had devoted most of their lives, but perhaps the time had come for younger, more vigorous men to take over their arduous and perilous duties.

Feigning slight embarrassment and indecision, Morris then took Ponomarev and the rest into his confidence and thereby made them co-conspirators. He was not authorized to speak for his general secretary, Comrade Hall, but in the strictest of confidence, he felt obligated to say that Hall was extremely upset by the severance of contact. Comrade Hall was a loyal and devoted man; he also was a man of principle, consistently reject-ing overtures from the Chinese, who wanted the American party in their hands, like the other parties they were courting around the world. So Morris thought that, if contact in New York was to be permanently ended, it would be prudent to have a long talk with Comrade Hall before the Chinese had a long talk with him.

Ponomarev, who rarely displayed emotion, except in voicing vitriol against the West, came from behind his desk, lifted Morris from a chair, hugged him in the Russian fashion, and said, "My dear comrade, my dear friend, you may never retire."

Walt, you must learn to think like they think. Doing just that, Morris in less than an hour had imparted to the International Department and the KGB a message that made all who heard and comprehend it need to run to the lavatory: If you cannot reopen the New York channel, then you lose MORAT, Jack, and me; you may lose Gus and control of the American party, possibly even lose control to the Chinese. You may explain that to the Politburo as you wish, or, if you prefer, Gus and I will explain when we see Brezhnev in May, as you know we will.

When Morris returned to Moscow in late April in advance of Hall, he was informed that things were not as bad as feared and contact would be renewed. A new and well-qualified "special comrade" (Yuri Zhuravlev) had been assigned to work with Jack, and before Comrade Hall spoke to Comrade Brezhnev he should be assured that $500,000 would be delivered to Jack shortly. Radio communications would resume and previous operational procedures remained in effect.

Brezhnev, along with Suslov, Ponomarev, Mostovets, and four Central Committee members, received Hall and Morris cordially on May 6 (Morris made detailed notes of the meeting). After pro forma greetings, Brezhnev remarked, "Life in your country is very interesting. Your press is interesting. I have been seeing all kinds of people, senators, etc., all good friends of your party."

"Many people are beating a path to Comrade Brezhnev's door," Hall responded. "You are seeing more senators than Nixon. This is good because it shows the world the role and power of the Soviet Union. Our relationship [with the Soviet Union] gives our party a much greater status and influence."

Having rehearsed with Morris, Hall briefed Brezhnev about economic and political conditions in the United States. "There is a great deal of political instability which comes from the Watergate affair. There are new revelations every day. This instability will continue this year and part of next year." Hall explained impeachment procedures and predicted political turmoil for another year.

"You are our dear friends and comrades," Brezhnev said. "We did not really appreciate Watergate until you explained it to us. John Reed wrote his book, *Ten Days That Shook the World*. Watergate is taking years shaking the United States and the world. You mentioned the book that has been published with transcripts of the Watergate tapes—we hear that people are lining up in the United States to buy these revelations. It is difficult to tell what will happen to Nixon. We ask all around about him but nobody knows. Even the editor of *Pravda* doesn't know."

"Even Nixon doesn't know," Hall interrupted.

Brezhnev said that no matter what happened to Nixon, the Soviet Union would continue to seek détente with the United States. "We cannot have one policy before lunch and another for after lunch." But there were problems. "During the last visit of Kissinger, we found many difficulties, especially on military matters, but also in trade and credits. We took these up in our Politburo. There were also problems in regard to the Middle East. I was very sharp in telling him that he cannot act alone—without partners—that the [UN] security resolution was a joint Soviet–U.S. resolution. Then Kissinger started his individual diplomacy, as if solving all world problems himself... Kissinger will be in Moscow again soon to finalize Nixon's [forthcoming] visit and to discuss limitations of armaments. The United States claims that there is superiority on the part of the Soviet Union. But he refuses to include U.S. strategic air power, and bases, etc. We do not have to make concessions to achieve balance; the United States needs to do that. I proposed withdrawal of nuclear forces from the Mediterranean Sea—to make it a 'Sea of Peace'—but Kissinger said no. We proposed that planes do not carry nuclear bombs or rockets—'No,' he said."

Kissinger obviously knew what Brezhnev had said to him. Nevertheless, the fact that Brezhnev repeated his proposals to Hall and Morris, as if he really believed in them, was significant, for it showed that he either was very naive or that by "disarmament" the Soviets meant disarmament of the United States. Soviet naval forces in the Mediterranean did not threaten the continental United States; American aircraft carriers and submarines very much threatened the Soviet land mass. Soviet ability to strike the United States with nuclear bombs delivered by aircraft was small compared to American capability to bombard the Soviet Union both from long-range bombers and tactical aircraft ringing its borders. Accepting Brezhnev's proposals would have meant giving up much for virtually nothing.

Seeming to enjoy exhibiting his mastery of foreign affairs, Brezhnev took Hall and Morris on a tour of the world, as seen through his eyes and those of the Politburo. He also recited stupefying statistics to demonstrate that the Soviet economy was sound and its prospects bright.

Upon alighting in New York May 23, Morris was able to tell the FBI what the Soviets oligarchs really thought—oligarchs who lived in total isolation from the people they ruled, who never set foot on a Moscow street except to get in and out of a limousine.

Brezhnev in his economic survey noted that the agricultural situation was still "complicated"—meaning in Sovietese "a real failure" or "an overwhelming mess." For fifty years, Morris had been hearing official excuses for the failure of the Soviet system of state and collective farms imposed upon once-productive farmers tilling and husbanding rich lands and orchards, and of new plans to correct the "complications," and always they were approximately the same. The oligarchs first tried to persuade the people that the agricultural problem was not as severe as the bare shops suggested, and to this end they broadcast statistics, just as Brezhnev had done (which inspired another Russian saying, "If you want milk, just take your pail to the radio"). Then there was the weather, almost always bad (communism apparently brought about an enduring change in the climate of Russia, Ukraine, and the sunny, southern Republics). Next there were boasts, quite justified, about the natural resources and fertile soil of the Soviet Union, whose territory, not including that of its foreign vassal states, occupied about one-sixth of the earth's land surface. Given this natural wealth, things were bound to get better—but they never did.

Always there were new plans to eliminate the "complications." Khrushchev, dazzled during his 1959 visit to the United States by the corn and wheat fields of Iowa, decreed that corn and wheat be planted in uncultivated areas of Siberia; uncultivated because centuries of farmers, tutored only by their fathers and mothers, understood that nothing could grow there. Huge investments in fertilizer and machinery here and there produced corn that grew about a foot high. Now in 1974, Brezhnev told Morris, "The policy in agriculture is very complicated. We are planning the use of areas not much used up to now, such as swamps and dry areas. Big sums of money are required for these projects; some on a broad scale, some on a smaller scale." In other words, we are going to solve our agricultural problems by cultivating swamps and deserts.

Morris did not mock or laugh at Brezhnev just as an oncologist does not laugh at a tumor. He says this is something to be examined and watched, and that basically is what Morris said to the FBI: This is another example of their propensity to dangerously delude themselves, and we had better watch that.

INITIALLY, PROSPECTS LOOKED good. While Morris was still in Moscow, the KGB, as Ponomarev promised, resumed radio transmissions three or four times a week, and on May 18 in dark woods outside Nassau City, New York, Jack's new handler, Zhuravlev, with a finger in front of his mouth— "don't speak"—handed him a package containing $500,000. The KGB again radioed on schedule the reassuring *SK* signals. (To recapitulate, *SK* meant: We have no message today; as far as we know, all is well.) But by June, the continuing fallout from the Watergate frenzy, the hemorrhage of secrets, congressional investigations, and interrogations of the intelligence community, coupled with the exposure of Chuchukin, so frightened Morris that Boyle warned headquarters he needed more reassurance.

Ray Wannall responded by assembling Section Chief William Brannigan, Assistant New York SAC James Ingram, Morris, Jack, Burlinson, Boyle, and Langtry for an operational conference in New York on July 11. Meeting Morris and Jack for the first time, Wannall declared that the value of SOLO, the existence of which he himself only recently had learned, was "tremendous, beyond measure." He had brought everybody together so Morris and Jack could voice any complaints they had and talk about anything they desired.

Morris first said that "the dramatic disclosures which appear from day to day in the press" made him and Jack fear for their lives. The book *KGB* severely harmed the operation and very nearly destroyed it. The book was discussed among Politburo members, and its effects were still being evaluated in the Soviet Union. He believed that mention of Chuchukin in it could only have resulted from a serious security breach.

Jack interjected, "If my contact [Chuchukin] is exposed, how am I not exposed?"

Again, Morris described the psychological pressures of dealing with Brezhnev, the heads of communist states in Eastern Europe, and the egotist Gus Hall; the pressures of having to produce reports virtually every day; his life with only one vacation in twenty years; his fears that the dearth of recognition or appreciation from Washington meant that his and his brother's efforts were not recognized or appreciated.

Morris also lodged a new complaint. Hall watched the money supplied by the Soviets like a miser and acted as if they were his personal funds. If he or Jack dipped into the money too often or too deeply for operational purposes, Hall might remove it from their custody and thereby reduce their power over him. Thus, he and Jack often had to defray operational expenses out of their own pockets. Neither was a pauper, but it did not seem quite right that they should have to subsidize the U.S. government as well as Hall.

The impromptu response by Wannall was worthy of Morris himself. Because of the trust the FBI reposed in Morris and Jack, he wanted to confide some in-house matters so they could understand the FBI rationale that now governed SOLO. Director Kelley had implemented a new concept of "participatory management." Henceforth, each assistant director would be directly responsible for operations and policies within his division. Although the director was to be informed of any major developments and consulted about any basic policy decisions, from now on Wannall was free to make most decisions regarding SOLO without approval from anyone.

The conspicuous rapport prevailing among Morris, Jack, Al, Walt, and John impressed Wannall. If in the future Morris or Jack had any complaints, problems or advice, they should tell Al, Walt, or John as if speaking directly to Wannall.

The security measures safeguarding SOLO were extraordinary, and with the exception of the Chuchukin matter there had been no leaks in a long time. The reference in the book to Chuchukin as a disinformation officer was "old information" that did not emanate from the FBI—it could have come from anywhere—and the FBI did not know it was going to be published (implicitly, this was a Soviet rather than an American security breach). Nevertheless, the Soviet reaction in jerking Chuchukin out of the operation was normal and understandable to everyone. The FBI was doing everything conceivable to protect them; still, the invaluable intelligence they gathered had to be disseminated to senior policymakers if it was to have value.

Brannigan spoke up. SOLO intelligence bore the highest U.S. security classification. Reports could not be copied or passed from one recipient to another. They could not be read outside the continental United States. The reports were hand-carried to the highest policymakers of the U.S. government, read, then returned to the FBI. Brannigan paused, then probably out of a lifetime of conditioning rather than any clever artifice, blurted out raw truth: "Despite all we are doing, despite unheard of safeguards, we cannot guarantee absolute security."

Morris and Jack nodded. They knew there could be no absolute guarantee, and that is why they were afraid. What they craved was the belief that their services were valued and headquarters was doing all it could to sustain them.

Concerning expenses, Wannall said that as a matter of principle he did not want either Jack or Morris to spend a cent of their own on SOLO. Here again he flattered them with honesty. There were bureaucratic procedures of accounting for peculiar expenditures, and sometimes they clashed with even more stringent rules enforced to keep virtually everyone ignorant of SOLO. Occasionally it might be difficult to reimburse a few expenses (how do you justify buying a $600 suit for the general secretary of the American Communist Party without telling accountants something about SOLO?). But if ever money was needed on the spot, Wannall would make sure it was forthcoming.

Morris and Jack should not misconstrue the many questions often asked for weeks after a mission as pressure to produce intelligence. Sometimes reports contained slivers of information which, when combined with many other slivers, yielded important intelligence. The questions, rather than manifesting any pressure, testified to the immense value of the reports.

Wannall's willingness to discuss in-house matters, his treatment of Morris and Jack as fellow agents, his candid and intelligent explanations, and his statement that they could speak to him at any time through Al, John, or Walt completely won over Morris and Jack. They left the meeting restored in spirit and ready to rejoin the battle.

Though he needed to get back to Washington quickly, Wannall asked the others to stay for a brief conference. It was not a conference at all; Wannall simply issued some policy directives. From now on, if Al, Walt, or John discerned in 58 or 69 any dissatisfaction or disillusionment, they were to alert him so the problem could be confronted before it worsened. Al, Walt, and John, in dealings with 58 and 69, were to emphasize that, as far as SOLO was concerned, Wannall was the "director"; when they heard from him, they were hearing from the director of the FBI. Finally, he ordered Boyle after each mission to draft for his signature congratulatory letters to be shown to 58 and 69.

In Kelley and Wannall, the SOLO team had two new champions at headquarters, the most powerful possible. Before long, the team very much would need them.

ON AUGUST 9, 1974, Richard Nixon resigned from office, the first American president ever to do so. In the aftermath of his resignation, Kelley and Wannall made a difficult decision— to violate a fundamental rule that had helped keep SOLO, Morris, Jack, Eva, and Roz alive for an improbably long time. The rule decreed that no one outside the FBI ever could know how SOLO worked or the identities of Morris, Jack, Eva, and Roz. The rule resulted not from distrust of anyone personally but from fear of an inadvertent leak and from awareness that someday the KGB might succeed in penetrating the staff of the White House, the State Department, or the CIA. In the prevailing circumstances, however, Kelley and Wannall concluded that overriding national interests compelled an exception to the rule.

As Brezhnev said to Hall and Morris, Watergate was shaking not only the United States but the world. The scandals and turmoil preceding his resignation had left Nixon virtually powerless in world affairs during his last months in office. Allies of the United States from Western Europe to China and Japan were confused and apprehensive about future American policy, as were Morris' friends in the Kremlin. In Southeast Asia, the North Vietnamese were exploiting internal American disarray by probing and testing to see just how brazenly they could flout the Paris Peace Accords without provoking U.S. retaliation.

Up until now, policymakers eagerly had accepted "Special Source" (SOLO) intelligence without demanding to know who the source was and how the information was procured, and they had submitted to the somewhat humiliating procedure of reading reports in the presence of an armed FBI agent, then handing them back. Now Kelley and Wannall reasoned that, given the international uncertainty and atmosphere of crisis, the new president, Gerald Ford, and Secretary of State Kissinger needed to know the origins of the "Special Source" intelligence so they could better judge whether to make major policy decisions on the basis of it. Accordingly, the FBI fully informed Ford and Kissinger of the nature and history of SOLO.

Wannall instructed Jim Fox and Boyle, without naming Kissinger, to tell Morris what Kissinger said: "This is a window not only into the Kremlin, but into the minds of the men in the Kremlin. This is fabulous."

HALL IN SEPTEMBER 1974 dispatched Morris to Moscow with a letter warning the Soviets that they were misinterpreting political events in the United States and that their misguided public statements were fueling an anti-Soviet campaign. Morris found Ponomarev in an ebullient mood; he believed the tide of communism was rising, even in America.

"You should know that we are getting volumes of communications from your new administration and we value these contacts. We intend to work constantly for the improvement of relations and détente," Ponomarev told him.

"We are well aware and apprised of the past thinking of Ford and Rockefeller. But they assure us that their thinking is quite different than in the past, that they think differently now."

Ponomarev solicited the advice and help of Morris in doing the impossible: persuading American Jews that the Soviet Union did not persecute or discriminate against Jews. "We are planning to send some Jewish persons to the United States. Please tell us what kind of people can we send to improve relations. We have some very famous ones you know about—artists, many writers, scientists. Please suggest to us who could invite them and help their trip. What should they do to overcome the bad anti-Soviet propaganda? We are really perturbed and sometimes surprised that even non-Zionist Jewish people don't understand us and are anti-Soviet. We have given the newspapers the facts. We want this material published. We really want to clarify the Jewish problem. We would like your help on this problem."

Ponomarev was also in high spirits because the Soviets and he personally had just achieved what they regarded, with some justification, as a coup in the United States. They had duped the U.S. Congress into receiving and meeting with a delegation of Soviet "parliamentarians," as if they were members of freely elected British, French, West German, Canadian, or other democratic parliamentary bodies. Heading the Soviet delegation was that great parliamentarian, Boris Ponomarev. As Ponomarev beamingly recounted, in Washington members of Congress fawned over their Soviet counterparts, their colleagues in democratic governance:

> You know that we really had a good trip, our parliamentary delegation to the United States. Our contacts with Congress were good and are continuing. After I came back, we sent letters to the Senate and the Congress. We told them of our hopes for continuing contacts. We invited them, Comrade Suslov and I, and said that it would be very useful to continue these. We also want to convince them that we deal not only with one Party or one administration or one individual. We were able to talk to some of their commissions [congressional committees] from our point of view. I took advantage of the opportunity to speak to them on economy, on cultural matters, figures on trade and industry, etc. We did not stick to just foreign policy questions.

I was very much impressed with the final reception at a meeting in Congress with a hundred congressmen. Senator Albert [Ponomarev probably referred to Representative Carl Albert] spoke up full of praise. I spoke before them for half an hour... When I finished, they gave me applause and they were not communists and I was somewhat surprised and even happy. So such contacts help to restrain the reactionaries and the anti-Soviet elements.

Ponomarev acknowledged that he did encounter some killjoys or spoilsports who complained about the recent swindle (accomplished in part with the aid of KGB eavesdropping on telephone conversations pertaining to the commodities market) by which the Soviets bought huge quantities of American grain at what critics of the deal called below-market or giveaway prices:

In San Francisco, there was a big reception given by the City Council and the Chamber of Commerce. There were all sorts of people there from government, industry and commerce. In the speeches, some of them were kind of hard on us on the sale of wheat by the United States to the Soviet Union, and that we were responsible for high food prices in the U.S., etc. But I was told in advance that some might raise that. We decided that we would not run away from discussing this. So we gave our views. We talked from a business point of view. We [I] said, you believe in free enterprise; doesn't a businessman like to get the best deal, the best price possible? Just because some Czarist idiot sold you Alaska for 3 million dollars [the United States bought Alaska for 7 million], should we criticize you for cheating us? Most of the businessmen agreed that when you are making deals, you make the best deal possible.

The chairman of the meeting... actually chastised those who had attacked us. Despite these things, altogether it was a very useful and pleasant gathering and

we believe more contacts should be made and would
help everybody. We, Comrade Suslov and I, got a letter
from the [Senate] Foreign Relations Committee signed
by [Senator William] Fulbright and he proposed to continue the contacts of the Foreign Relations Committee
of the Senate with the Foreign Relations Committee of
the USSR. Of course, there are no workers on the Foreign Relations Committee. Nevertheless, these contacts
are important.

Morris realized that they indeed were. Every member of the so-
called Soviet parliamentary delegation had to be a member of
either the International Department or the KGB or under their control. By establishing direct ties with Congress, these professional
Soviet sharks could turn Capitol Hill into a hunting ground and
possibly influence the actions of individual congressmen without
having to bother with the trained diplomats responsible for the
conduct of U.S. foreign policy. Of course, the very concept of a
Soviet parliament or Foreign Relations Committee was ludicrous.
Morris thought, *Is the U.S. Congress a nursery for children?*

On September 30, the day before Morris departed Moscow,
Ponomarev called him in, thanked him for Hall's letter and gave
him a formal reply: "On behalf of our leadership, we want to send
greetings to your leadership. We appreciate the work of your
Party. Although it is still a small Party, it is doing good work.
Most important, it is a principled Party. It stands fast, holds the
banner of Marxism–Leninism high, and in internationalism it is
second to none. We also want to tell you that we appreciate Comrade Gus Hall as an important figure in our international communist movement. We really want to tell him that we appreciate
your successes, especially that the CPUSA is breaking its isolation
from the masses and is on the road to increasing influence among
the people and to further growth. We believe that the situation is
more favorable for communists now than ten years ago. And,
therefore, we are convinced that you will succeed."

In Chicago, Morris asked Boyle if the FBI could warn members
of Congress that, in consorting with Soviet "parliamentarians"

and the Soviet "Foreign Relations Committee," they were dealing with skilled, hardened subversives bent on manipulating them. Boyle said he honestly did not know. The director of the FBI or his representatives could testify before congressional committees, and if an individual congressman requested assistance regarding a security matter, the FBI could provide it. But the FBI had to avoid the least appearance of trying to influence a member of Congress or of involving itself in politics. The most Boyle could do was ensure that Wannall read what Ponomarev said and hope that he could devise ways to alert the congressional targets.

Morris and Boyle scarcely had finished all their reports when Hall sent Morris back to Moscow in November with a letter begging for money; it said the party was almost broke and could not sustain itself much longer without an infusion of cash. The Soviets took the plea seriously and promised to deliver $500,000 in early February and $1.3 million more later in 1975.

Ford and Brezhnev had just concluded their first summit conference, and Ponomarev shared with Morris the Soviet assessment of the meeting and the new American president. They considered him a "nice" man with whom they could do business despite his record of anticommunism; in their judgment, he lacked Nixon's experience in foreign affairs and therefore it might be even easier to do business with him.

The Soviets feted Eva as a queen, and in early December her escort and interpreter, Irina, announced that wives of Politburo members had arranged a luncheon in her honor. That meant they wanted her out of the way for the day so the KGB could talk to Morris alone in the apartment. Vladimir Kazakov, the KGB officer who grilled Jack, greeted Morris with unusual warmth and, Morris thought, sincerity. He said the KGB had made an exhaustive analysis of the book *KGB* and determined that Morris was right— the references to Chuchukin doubtless sprang from his prior activities rather than from his work with Jack in New York, and those activities became known to the author not because of any fault of Chuchukin but from some traitor. The KGB was confident that MORAT had not been compromised and that no one involved in the operation had made a mistake. The crisis was over but everyone must redouble vigilance because what they were doing was both important and dangerous.

As he started to leave, Kazakov said, "By the way, Vladimir [Chuchukin] sends greetings and best wishes to you and Jack. And we all thank you." Both understood why he gave thanks: for absolving Chuchukin and the KGB of guilt during the witch-hunt caused by the book. More than ever, the KGB was Morris' ally.

After long dinners, Morris and Eva stayed up late copying documents revealing Soviet views of world affairs and the status of communist parties throughout the world. When they left the second week in December, they were tired and eager to go home to quiet and security.

But storms were about to burst upon them.

fifteen

UNDER SUSPICION

WANNALL FLEW TO CHICAGO on February 11, 1975, to personally congratulate Morris on the success of the last mission. In a meeting with Chicago SAC Richard Held and Boyle, he told Morris that the information gathered was immensely important and that it had been hand-carried to "the highest U.S. officials" (President Ford, Kissinger, and the director of the CIA, who then was William Colby).

The gesture heartened Morris, who understood that Wannall was sacrificing a whole day just to say kind words to him. In the security of the cover office and the camaraderie of men he trusted, he tried to tell them what a mission was like, how terrified he had been in Prague when ordered back to Moscow. "Over there, I am always worried. It is like being in a luxurious prison. I am a member of the club. I have my own apartment or, if I stay at the Central Committee hotel, I am given splendid accommodations next to the suite reserved for general secretaries of foreign parties. I am given a safe and a key. I am met at the airport by a special limousine. I don't have to handle my luggage or bother with arrival details. I am greeted by special contacts from the International Department. But when I go to bed at night, I never know what the next day will bring. I try to analyze just where I stand with the Soviets, whether certain people will agree to see me, why they would meet me, whether they would allow me to enter certain buildings if they didn't trust me."

Wannall replied that the few who were aware of what Morris was doing appreciated the enormous strains he had to endure, and again Wannall flattered Morris by sharing in-house matters. Director Kelley had appeared in closed session before the so-called Church Committee, the Senate committee investigating U.S. intelligence agencies. Kelley told them that there were certain subjects he did not want senators or staff members to ask about. If they asked, they would bear full responsibility for the consequences. Wannall emphasized, "SOLO will not be involved."

The conference lasted little more than an hour but in terms of its effects on Morris' spirits it bought more than money could have.

Afterward, over a pleasant lunch Wannall, Held, Boyle, and a supervisor privy to SOLO engaged in amiable banter, and the supervisor asked, "Walt, what would you do if you're on a plane and someone tries to hijack it to Cuba?" Because of hijackings, Boyle insisted on remaining armed while flying. Sometimes he had with him copies of documents Morris and Eva had copied in Moscow, and in any case the FBI did not want him subjected to the mercies of Cuban interrogators.

"The plane ain't going to Cuba," Boyle said.

"But what are you going to do?"

"I said, the plane ain't going to Cuba." They dropped the subject—some things are best left unsaid.

BOYLE KEPT READY A small bag packed with a fresh shirt, underwear, socks, and toiletries so that at any time he could leave immediately for O'Hare Airport, only some twenty minutes away from his home. Around 4 A.M. a call from the physician who relayed Morris' messages in code advised that Morris would arrive that afternoon in Los Angeles aboard a flight from

Oslo. The FBI issued agents a booklet of government vouchers that enabled them to write their own airline tickets to anywhere in the world, and by early afternoon Boyle was at the Los Angeles airport where Morris' flight was listed as "delayed." In the tower, air traffic controllers had no information about when it might arrive or the cause of the delay. Boyle stayed in the terminal through the night, calling the tower hourly until a controller told him the plane had been diverted and would land in Seattle.

In New York, Chicago, and Los Angeles, Boyle developed contacts among customs and immigration officials who gladly helped him and the FBI. In Seattle he didn't have any, but he persuaded authorities there to pass Morris and Eva without questions or inspection. Unbeknown to him at the time, one of the customs officials had second thoughts and panicked. Had he let in narcotics smugglers or Mafiosi or spies? To cover himself, he went to the FBI agent assigned to the airport, said that someone impersonating an FBI agent duped him into admitting two dubious characters and that the impersonator himself appeared to be "under the influence." This allegation was inherently implausible. Why would a trained customs inspector blindly obey the orders of some strange drunk? If he had doubts about the validity of FBI credentials shown him, he could have confirmed or dispelled them by a one-minute telephone call. Did Morris and Eva fit the profile of the types of people inspectors are taught to guard against? Without making any inquiries of his own, the Seattle agent relayed the allegation to headquarters as if it were credible and the FBI soon determined that the allegedly drunken impersonator was in fact Walter Boyle from Chicago.

Kelley was away, and his chief deputy directed Wannall, "Go out there and fire him."

Wannall protested, "But shouldn't we get the facts first?"

"All right, get the facts and then fire him."

Chicago SAC Held called just as Boyle was sitting down to breakfast after early Sunday Mass. "Ray Wannall is here and he wants to talk to you. Please come to the office, the sooner, the better."

It was to have been a family day—the park and zoo followed by hamburgers and sundaes for the six children—and Boyle was disappointed at having to disappoint them, but he was pleased that Wannall had flown out to discuss SOLO.

Wannall was interested in something else. After polite salutations, he said, "Walt, I'd like for you to go to your office now and sit down and write a detailed account of your trip to the West Coast. I want you to put down everything that happened, from beginning to end. You can't include too much detail. Take as much time as you need. Dick and I will be waiting."

Boyle started to exclaim Why! But a stare from Held said, *For your own sake, just do as he says.*

Dutifully, Boyle detailed the whole trip: Upon arriving in Los Angeles, he in accordance with rules notified the Los Angeles office that he was in the area and where he was staying. After learning that the flight from Norway had been diverted, he notified the Los Angeles office that he was leaving the area. When he alighted in Seattle he informed the local field office that he was there; he obtained assistance from customs and immigration officials; he told the Seattle office he was leaving.

Wannall read the narrative slowly and remarked, "It looks like you didn't get much sleep on that trip."

The anger welling within Boyle caused him to blurt out an impertinence that surely would have provoked a less gentlemanly and insightful superior than Wannall: "I didn't go out there to sleep."

"All right Walt," Wannall said. "I'll be here for a few days and I'm sure we'll talk again."

SAC Held was pure, old-time FBI, a Hooverite, relentlessly tough and courageously fair, and Boyle knew that if he could get to him he could get the truth. But every time Boyle peered into Held's office, there sat Wannall on the leather sofa. Finally Boyle persuaded a fellow agent to entice Wannall out of the office, and he was able to speak to Held alone. "What the hell is going on?"

"You're under massive investigation for being drunk on duty. Right now, Ray Wannall is the best friend you have. He and the Bureau are checking out every word you wrote and, thus far, everything checks."

To this day, Boyle refuses to disclose who called him at home late at night. Maybe the call came from Burlinson or Langtry or a secret SOLO ally at headquarters. A better bet would be that the caller's initials were R.H., as in Richard Held. Be that as it may, the caller was informed and spoke authoritatively. Everything Boyle wrote about the trip to Los Angeles and Seattle had been confirmed. Nevertheless, the FBI intended to remove him from SOLO on the pretext that his expertise was needed at headquarters. The caller offered some advice, "You didn't hear this from me, but it wouldn't hurt if you told 58 about the situation. In fact, if I were you that is exactly what I would do and I would do it right away."

IN SELECTING A PLACE to live, Morris had to satisfy the divergent demands of his multiple lives. He needed a home that was in keeping with his ostensible status as a wealthy businessman, which is what Hall and the Kremlin thought he was. But as a devoted proletarian he did not want to live ostentatiously on the North Shore like a greedy capitalist. The necessity of traveling so often and his inability, because of security reasons, to employ servants made maintenance of a house impractical.

Morris solved the problem by buying a penthouse in a handsome building occupied primarily by wealthy and friendly black families. In Moscow Morris was regarded as a comrade so principled that he was even willing to live among the "black asses," as the Russians called them.

Wannall visited the penthouse which Eva, with art, antiques, Oriental carpets, and fine crystal, had transformed into an inviting home. During dinner she flirted with him while Morris entertained with tales of adventures in the Soviet Union, including the story of how he and the director of the Leningrad Shipyard became so drunk that they got into a fistfight with each other. He recalled that, when he first saw Moscow in 1929, trees lined many boulevards and the beautiful architecture reflected the verve and imagination of Russians. But Stalin soon ordered the trees cut down and scarred the face of the city with huge, box-like buildings that glowered menacingly down at the people. Friends in 1947 told him that Stalin later persuaded himself that the felling of the trees, that he had ordered, was part of a plot to enable German aircraft to land on the streets and that he executed many of the "plotters." Eva piped up, "That Stalin, he was such a barbarian."

Over the years, some things had changed for the better; some had not. Ponomarev still expected Morris to bring aspirin, Alka-Seltzer, and Contac; everybody still wanted Camel and Chesterfield cigarettes, and cosmetics. "They want anything American," Eva interjected. "Secretly, they like us, really."

SOLO was not discussed until after dinner. While Morris excused himself supposedly to call Jack in New York, Eva remarked they had heard Walt might be leaving. Well, she understood, nothing is forever; Walt needed to get on with his career, and certainly if anyone ever deserved a promotion, Walt did. Doubtless the Bureau had more important things for him to do, doubtless it had operations more important than SOLO. And Walt had been stuck in Chicago a long time; let's see, how long had he been fiddling around with their little operation—about thirteen years? That was a long time. Of course, nobody understood Morris as well as Walt did, and Morris trusted him, and nobody understood the operation as well as Walt did, except maybe Al (Burlinson) and John (Langtry), but they also heard that Al was retiring.

Wannall, being a young man, might find it hard to understand, but old people tend to get into a rut, to expect, perhaps unreasonably, that things will continue the way they were. Sometimes old people start thinking of a young man as a son, especially when after many years they know they always can count on him. Still, Eva understood, but she wanted Wannall also to understand. Maybe the time had come for her to stop. She had traveled to Moscow at least twenty times; each time she was afraid, and when she wrapped documents around her body she was terrified. She was most terrified when Morris was over there without her. Outside of him, Walt was the person she relied upon most. If he were to go, she did not want to go on. If she did not go on, she was not sure Morris would; Wannall would have to take that up with Morris. Of course, if Morris quit, so would Jack.

To Wannall, it was clear Eva spoke for Morris. She starred in a cabaret written, directed, and staged by him, essentially a reprise of the blackmail he had perpetrated on the Soviets in Moscow. But Wannall was a forthright man, and so he spoke to Morris frankly: yes, the Bureau was considering transferring Boyle to headquarters—what did Morris think? Morris said Boyle was his best friend, and he could not imagine SOLO continuing without him.

Having listened to Wannall's report of his findings and his conversations with Morris and Eva, Kelley asked him if he thought Boyle was innocent. Wannall recited available facts: To the extent investigators could check Boyle's written account, they had corroborated all he said. They had not located any witnesses to the encounter between him and the complaining customs official in Seattle, but no one else interviewed there thought he had been "under the influence"; none of his present or past associates interviewed had ever seen him drink to excess, much less on duty. Boyle had received a disciplinary transfer to Chicago in 1962, evidently for threatening an inspector with physical violence, and not long afterward headquarters had reprimanded him—the reason was unclear. Ever since, his record had been exemplary, as outstanding as it could be. Boyle had for years maintained an intimate professional and personal relationship with the most important asset the FBI had, and the results spoke for themselves.

Do you personally think Boyle can and should remain a linchpin of SOLO?

Unequivocally and emphatically, Wannall said yes. Thereupon, Kelley ordered the allegation against Boyle dismissed and effaced, and decreed that he would remain in Chicago; Wannall was to inform everybody; and if there were any residual problems at headquarters, Kelley himself was to take care of them.

CONGRESS ENACTED LEGISLATION, effective in 1975, mandating that FBI agents retire by age fifty-five, and as Burlinson was nearing seventy, he had to leave after thirty-five years of service. He and Freyman were the fathers of SOLO, and for other team members his departure was akin to the death of a family patriarch. Headquarters continued to make the policy decisions and support the field offices. But in terms of daily operational decisions and the nurturing of Morris, Jack, Eva, and Roz, Langtry and Boyle were now the fathers.

In one of the most odious duties of their careers, the "fathers" soon had to put Morris and Jack under surveillance, placing wiretaps on their home telephones and otherwise looking for indicators that they might be double agents actually working for the Soviet Union. Neither had done anything whatsoever to warrant such suspicion. On the contrary, both had for more than two decades loyally, bravely, and brilliantly served the United States. Again and again, the intelligence they produced had proven to be accurate, and numerous evaluators likened it to intellectual gold.

The FBI decision to investigate its two most important assets and reassess its greatest operation resulted primarily from pressures exerted by CIA counterintelligence chief James Jesus Angleton. A man of formidable intellect, Angleton wielded considerable influence in the American intelligence community and had a personal following in other government agencies, including the FBI. Perhaps as a counterintelligence chief should, he looked skeptically upon defectors and Soviet nationals recruited by the CIA, viewing them as possible double agents sent or made available by the Soviets to purvey deceptive information or infiltrate U.S. operations.

There was a notable exception. Angleton reposed inordinate confidence in KGB Major Anatoly Golitsyn who in 1961 fled from the Soviet embassy in Helsinki where he processed intelligence reports. From these reports, Golitsyn supplied clues that eventually led to the arrest of dangerous Soviet spies in Western Europe, and as long as he presented factual data, he was a very valuable defector.

But there came a time when Golitsyn had no more new facts to give. He replaced them with imaginative theory and conjecture. According to one of his theories, the conflicts between the Soviet Union and China were not real; they were a hoax, a grand disinformation scheme. The trusting Angleton embraced this view until the end of his career. Golitsyn also asserted that the next Soviet defector to arrive in the United States would be a controlled KGB agent dispatched to worm his way into the CIA and to assist other spies on the outside.

The next significant defector to arrive was Yuri Nosenko, who came in 1964. After Angleton and his lieutenants thought they detected serious discrepancies and falsifications in Nosenko's account of himself, the CIA incarcerated and psychologically tortured him in an effort to extract a confession, but he never confessed. The FBI, which possessed information unavailable to the CIA, always considered Nosenko a bona fide defector and ultimately the CIA agreed, as did all other Western security services that interrogated him. Angleton, however, remained unconvinced.

The FBI had recruited a KGB officer, code named "Fedora," who posed as a Soviet diplomat at the United Nations. Queried by the FBI, Fedora confirmed some of what Nosenko had told the CIA and said he was a genuine defector. In Angleton's eyes, he thereby convicted himself of being a double agent participating in a plot to foist off another double agent on the CIA. Angleton thereupon commenced an unremitting campaign to convince the FBI that Fedora was a Soviet plant.

Fedora informed the FBI that the KGB had a contact in the American Communist Party and that it gave money to the party. A few times he notified the FBI that a colleague was preparing to meet the contact and urged the FBI to follow him and identify the contact. Some of those in the FBI swayed to Angleton's view of Fedora later argued that the fact that he provided information pertaining to SOLO indicated that the operation was "contaminated."

On the basis of a statement Ponomarev made to Morris, the FBI, without revealing its source, in September 1973 advised the CIA that the Soviet Union appeared prepared to grant diplomatic recognition to Israel. A short time later, on October 6, Egypt attacked Israel. Angleton then accused the FBI of disseminating disinformation spread to cause the Israelis to relax their vigil when war was imminent.

Finally even those in the FBI who rejected all of Angleton's theses as spurious, and they were a majority, acknowledged that SOLO had gone on for an extraordinarily long time and that a reappraisal might be appropriate.

While also trained to be skeptical, Boyle and Langtry leavened their professional skepticism with common sense, logic, and a regard for demonstrable facts, and both would have bet their lives on the honesty and fidelity of Morris and Jack. Boyle observed to Langtry that, even if Morris were conspiring with the Soviets rather than against them, this veteran conspirator would say or do nothing in the United States to implicate himself because he could talk to the Soviets securely in Moscow almost any time he wished. Hence, telephone taps would be futile. Langtry in turn pointed out that, if Jack were colluding with the Soviets, he gladly would accept their invitations to come to Moscow instead of dodging them, as he had done since 1967. Nevertheless, Boyle and Langtry could not argue professionally against an investigation of Morris and Jack. Espionage can be ugly, and they now embarked upon the new and ugly duty of helping to spy on their friends.

They could, however, argue for adoption of special procedures. Neither Boyle nor Langtry had any income outside their FBI salaries, and Boyle was raising six children. Over the years, both spent their own money on SOLO, in some months quite a bit relative to their incomes. Boyle was authorized to go anywhere at any time at government expense without having to explain why he went; and every conversation with Langtry in a way constituted "official business." Yet when he flew to New York to talk privately with Langtry about "what to do right" within the FBI, he paid for his ticket out of his own pocket.

After talking privately in New York on a Sunday, the two began making some demands of headquarters. The transcripts of conversations recorded by taps on the telephones of Morris and Jack should be read and evaluated by experienced field agents who had nothing to do with SOLO. Such evaluators could not be accused of bias. More important, those involved in SOLO should not see the transcripts because in talking to Morris and Jack they might inadvertently reveal knowledge that could only have come from private telephone conversations. The tapes and transcripts should be destroyed immediately after analysis, and no records of them should be kept anywhere. *Do you have legal authorization for these wiretaps? Would you like someday to discuss them with a congressional committee?*

Headquarters agreed, and the investigation began. Boyle and

Langtry dutifully watched for the least duplicity by Morris and Jack, as they always had—that was their job. Selected analysts in Washington reviewed SOLO files for reports that might have been inaccurate or misleading. The files dated back to 1951. Except for the first weeks when Jack was parrying with the FBI, they found no inaccurate reports. The analysts dismissed as absurd the CIA complaint that the FBI purveyed disinformation by reporting that the Soviets appeared ready to recognize Israel. The fact that war broke out in the Middle East shortly after Soviet Foreign Minister Andrei Gromyko, among others, told Morris this did not prove that what the Soviets said and Morris reported was untrue. It was preposterous to dream that Israel, then surrounded by fiercely hostile neighbors, would drop its vigil on the basis of a single report from an unknown, third-hand source about what the Soviets might do.

The transcripts of the telephone conversations of Morris, Jack, Eva, and Roz revealed not one incriminating word, not one incongruity or contradiction, not one suspicious item. The only thing the FBI learned was that Morris and Eva played a game with each other, much like children played the game "Monopoly." They took equal amounts of money and through separate brokers vied to see who could do better on the stock market. Eva played the game with girlish enthusiasm: "Now, don't you tell Morris I bought this."

In sum, all the taped conversations, surveillance, investigations, and analyses showed that 58 and 69 were just what Boyle and Langtry knew them to be. After about six months, someone at headquarters, probably Ray Wannall, in effect said: Enough. Stop it. Let's get back to fighting our enemies instead of our friends.

No one now challenged the loyalty of Morris and Jack, but doubters advanced a new thesis: SOLO had lasted so long that the Soviets must be aware of it. They were using the operation as a convenient means of smuggling money and using Morris and Jack as unwitting conveyers of disinformation.

Boyle and Langtry asked some questions. Did the Soviets want the FBI to know how much money they gave the American party, down to the penny? Did they want to empower the FBI at any time to create an anti-Soviet scandal and furor by proving that the American party was bought and paid for by them, and thereby effectively destroying the party? Would Brezhnev, Suslov, Ponomarev, Mostovets, and the Soviet leadership take time personally and repeatedly to consort with an American spy? Had they made the communist rulers of Eastern Europe collaborators in their scheme, or did they let them talk freely to Morris without revealing that he was a spy? What about Gus Hall? Had they informed him that his chief lieutenant worked for the FBI? And what about the KGB? Would it share with the FBI through Jack its most sophisticated equipment and communication procedures? And where is all this disinformation—just one example?

Well, the skeptics replied, if the Soviets had not yet realized that the FBI controlled the operation, they were bound to find out soon because the longevity and success of SOLO defied all odds.

When the FBI advised Kissinger of these fears—that SOLO might be or become a vehicle of Soviet disinformation—and that it was thinking of discontinuing the operation, he said nonsense (lore has it that he used another word). As Jim Fox said in his eulogy of Morris, Kissinger declared that no one was better positioned than he to evaluate SOLO intelligence and he would decide whether it was true or false. But he had to have the information SOLO produced. While he respected the judgment of the FBI, SOLO must go on and it would go on. Though Kissinger made no threats, the FBI comprehended that if it did not comply with his dictate, it doubtless would receive a comparable, and possibly less genial, one from the president.

THE THREATS TO SOLO from within the FBI abated, but the threats from without escalated as congressional committees expanded their investigations. Each morning Morris opened the newspaper, fearful of what he might read, and Boyle again warned Washington that he needed reassurance.

Accordingly, the FBI scheduled another conference in New York on October 10, 1975, four days before Morris was to depart for Moscow. Present were Deputy Assistant Director Thomas W.

Leavitt, Section Chief Brannigan, the new New York SAC James O. Ingram, Supervisors Raymond Ruckel and David E. Houser, and Special Agents Thomas J. Devine, Boyle, and Langtry.

Referring to the congressional investigations, Leavitt said, "The times in Washington are not the happiest at the moment but things aren't dull."

Morris, who never learned that he and Jack had been investigated by the FBI, jumped to defend the FBI. "Regarding these illegalities they charge the Bureau with, I would say most things were done by the book. That was a sustaining factor for me. I started a fight against communism because of their extralegal methods, the unbelievable terrors. Maybe there were some capers like COINTELPRO [a counterintelligence program aimed at what the FBI considered to be subversive or terrorist groups; the Bureau has been accused of acting unlawfully in some of its investigations of these groups]. But I am talking about the organization as a whole retaining a legal outlook."

Reiterating his daily fear of being exposed by some leak, Morris said, "It takes a pretty tough heart to work nowadays, especially inside the enemy camp, wondering whether you can go on when you see some of these stupidities. You ask, what are you working for?...

"If I am physically able, and unless Gus Hall has something different in mind, I should take off on a trip in a few days. The Bureau people in charge have to be on the lookout to prevent any bombshell while I'm on the road. With intelligence agencies on the griddle, you never know when someone will pull a boner or go crazy or give something out."

Leavitt emphasized that measures to safeguard SOLO were more stringent than ever and that the intelligence it yielded was distributed only "at the highest levels, to the White House, the State Department, and sometimes the military" (it is unclear whether Leavitt's failure to mention any distribution to the CIA was inadvertent or whether the Bureau had stopped sharing SOLO data with the Agency).

Ingram added, "You have men here in this room—your life is their life. Their entire life is devoted to you."

His words evidently moved Jack and Morris. Speaking of the SOLO team and the FBI, Jack said, "Regardless of the present turbulence, we have reached *a* peak but not *the* peak. I never thought we would reach this level of perfection. I think that means they still trust us, though they are being careful."

Morris said, "I have never run across anybody except dedicated men in the Bureau. The Bureau as a whole is the most dedicated organization I've ever known, maybe with the exception of the early Bolsheviks."

HAVING FLOWN VIA LONDON and Prague, Morris arrived in Moscow on October 17, 1975, and tried more than ever to read obscure signs: Who greeted him at the airport? Familiar friends from the International Department, or new faces that might be those of KGB officers? How was he greeted—with hearty embraces or polite handshakes? Did the reception party have personal messages for him from Ponomarev, Suslov, or Brezhnev? Where would he be lodged, in his apartment or a suite at the party hotel off Arbat street or some place lesser and new? Would his escorts, after taking him to his residence, stay for a drink? How soon would he see Ponomarev, who, barring illness, always was the first Soviet leader he saw? Who else appeared on his schedule? How soon did the "special comrades" (the KGB) want to see him, and just how was their request to see him phrased? Was there any hint that he might have to stay much longer than planned? Would the Soviets maintain or raise the level of payments to the American party?

Most of the first signs were good. Friends awaited him at the airport and were delighted to join him for supper at the apartment. Ponomarev expected him at lunch the next day, Mostovets was counting upon him for dinner the day after, and the schedule outlined was crowded. Ponomarev received him as cordially as ever and, so far as Morris could discern, was genuinely glad to see him. He did say that, because of an unexpectedly poor grain harvest (more bad weather), the Soviets next year might have to lower the subsidy to the American party (in 1975 it totaled $1,792,676).

Then at the end of lunch, Ponomarev mentioned that the "special comrades" had been making a nuisance of themselves and wanted to speak with Morris at his earliest convenience. Could he get them out of the way by letting them drop by the apartment that afternoon? Morris could only say, "Of course."

Kazakov, the KGB officer who supervised MORAT (SOLO) from Moscow, and another officer whom Morris had not met accepted his invitation to pour themselves brandies, thereby signaling that they had not come to interrogate him. They did want his opinions. How much did he think the FBI knew about him?

Morris said that because the party had no sources in the FBI he could not be sure. Doubtless the FBI recognized that he was a communist; after all, he had run for public office as a communist and edited the party newspaper. He assumed that the FBI had some low-level informants in the party; probably it tried to keep an eye on Gus and thus might know that he and Hall saw each other. However, he had not been active in overt party affairs since 1947; he was old and, as any investigator easily could ascertain, his health was not the best, and he owned a legitimate business. Therefore, in his judgment, the FBI did not have much interest in him. About one central fact he was sure: The FBI knew absolutely nothing about MORAT or the money.

Kazakov courteously said it would be helpful if he could explain why he was so certain.

Morris then confidently assumed the role of a professor lecturing the KGB. First, if you excluded Kazakov's comrades, the only people in the United States who knew about the money deliveries were Gus Hall, Jack, Morris, and their wives; and that "radio fellow" the KGB assigned to help Jack (the old Comintern radioman, NY-4309S*). The Central Committee of our party, Morris went on, knows we receive support, but outside the six or seven of us, no one knows how we receive it, and everyone who touches the money has to be extremely cautious. In America, you could commit almost any crime and, even if you were caught, chances were a clever lawyer or a stupid jury or a daft judge would spare you from jail. But the government and courts sternly enforced the income tax law. If you were caught with large sums of cash, whose origins you could not explain and on which you had failed to pay taxes, you went to jail. Thus, handling the money was so dangerous that nobody involved ever talked about it outside the tight little circle.

But there was a more basic reason why Morris was sure the FBI did not know about the money—the same reasoning Boyle and Langtry had used in speaking to headquarters. The FBI was a virulently anticommunist, semimilitary organization; in fact, most of its young agents were former military officers. If the FBI knew about the money deliveries, it could arrest everybody, including "special comrades," and stage a prolonged circus that would sabotage détente, ruin the party, and land everyone in prison. The FBI would love to do just that.

In Russian, Kazakov said to his colleague, "You see, I told you."

The other KGB officer replied in Russian, "Yes, he is remarkable."

Turning to Morris, Kazakov said that his explanation made eminent sense and was very reassuring. Kazakov asked if they could meet again to discuss technical operational details and apologized for burdening him with such matters. It would be better to discuss them directly with Jack, and he wondered if Jack could resume his visits to Moscow.

Morris feared he could not. Because of a combination of emphysema, heart trouble, and other ailments, doctors had warned Jack against attempting long flights. That reminded Morris of something: He hoped that in the future, money deliveries could occur in the spring, summer, and autumn so Jack would not have to expose himself to winter weather.

The preceding June, Morris had made a quick trip to Moscow to obtain Soviet approval of a report drafted by Hall for presentation to the national convention of the American party. While there he learned that Aleksandr Shelepin had been purged from the Politburo after instigating or participating in a coup aimed at dethroning Brezhnev. Morris gathered that the infighting in the Kremlin had not entirely subsided. Now in October Ponomarev told him Brezhnev had secured his position and unquestionably would be reelected general secretary of the party (something Kissinger very much wanted to know).

Ponomarev also told him that upon further assessing the summit meeting between Brezhnev and President Ford, the Soviets were gloomy about the results and additionally were pessimistic about the outcome of the arms limitations negotiations being conducted in Geneva.

As Morris prepared to leave in November, Ponomarev announced that the Soviets would not have to reduce the 1976 subsidy as he earlier indicated. In fact, they could increase it to $2 million and very shortly they would give Jack the last 1975 payment of $350,000.

Flying homeward, Morris mentally composed reports and looked forward to telling Boyle the good news—that the KGB had completely accepted his explanation of why the operation was secure.

But in the United States, very bad news about SOLO again awaited him.

sixteen

UNDER SIEGE

MORRIS ALWAYS FEARED MOST that which he could not control. During decades of dueling with the Soviets, he made not one operational mistake; Jack made just one when he gave his Soviet handler Langtry's notes instead of his own. Together, Morris and Jack long had outwitted the KGB and cynical tyrants who had helped raise the science of mass terror to a new apex. In difficult circumstances, they proved that if the outcome depended upon what they did, they could effectively control the outcome. They could not control the actions of the United States Congress or its ambitious young staff members. And there was nothing they could have done to prevent a Senate committee from demanding FBI files that would expose them and grievously damage the cause for which they continued to risk their lives.

The crisis that developed while Morris was in Moscow during October and November 1975 arose in part from events that occurred many years earlier and only tangentially related to SOLO. It had to do with civil rights leader and Nobel Laureate Martin Luther King. SOLO was never directed at King; neither

Morris nor Jack ever met King or even indirectly dealt with King; neither personally knew anything about him. A few SOLO reports did, however, mention King, and other reports concerned people who became close to him.

To see what happened, we must look back into history and into the communist underground of North America.

During the late 1950s, the FBI retargeted SOLO, aiming it at the Soviet Union rather than at the American Communist Party. Morris and Jack continued, passively and incidentally, to gather information about party activities, especially those that might illuminate secret Soviet actions and intentions. But they and the FBI were vastly more concerned with maintaining the flow of secrets and money from the Kremlin than with anything happening inside the American party; to all involved in SOLO, the party mattered most because through it Morris and Jack could tunnel into the Kremlin.

In the early years of SASH/SOLO, when the objective was to infiltrate the American party leadership, Morris and Jack did provide detailed data about party activities and personalities. One personality they identified was Stanley David Levison, a New York lawyer and business entrepreneur.

By 1946 Levison, then thirty-four, had gained admission into the inner circle of the communist underground. One of his sponsors and mentors was William Weiner, who administered party finances and the reserve fund, the cash hidden for emergencies. Weiner was a friend of Jack and of Sam Carr, the Canadian communist and Soviet espionage agent who attended the Lenin School with Morris and whom Morris and Jack later befriended.

Jack in early debriefings told the FBI that beginning in 1946 Weiner and Levison conferred frequently, and that Levison helped establish party business fronts and collected money from party "angels" in Hollywood and on Wall Street. (Morris confirmed that Levison consulted him while setting up party businesses in Chicago and Michigan.) Jack also advised that, in 1946, Levison gave Weiner $10,000 for the party and Weiner asked Jack to hide the money in a safe deposit box.

Weiner in 1952 instructed Jack to go to Levison's office and meet another underground member with whom he was to cooperate. In

1953, Levison warned Jack that an FBI agent had visited the party business front in Chicago and he offered Jack $200 to help him found another front. In 1954, during a meeting with Jack at the Statler Hotel, Levison said that, as a result of the death of Weiner, he had assumed responsibility for party finances. In 1955 Phillip Bart, the underground secretary who brought Morris back into the party, said that Levison was active in party work. And in 1956, Bart told Jack that Stanley Levison and his twin brother, Roy, who had changed his name to Roy Bennett, were now in charge of party business.

Jack in 1958 reported a conversation with James Jackson, the party secretary in charge of "Negro and Southern Affairs." Jackson claimed that he and Eugene Dennis had conferred with the "most secret and guarded people who are in touch with, consulting with, and guiding [Martin] Luther King." Though he pretended not to know their identities, Jackson characterized them as "party guys far removed from the top level but [who were] playing an important role in guiding these fellows [King and associates]." Jackson thought that "this group may be important in Negro work."

Unbeknown to Jack or Morris, Levison in the 1950s met King and subsequently attached himself to the young civil rights leader as a personal confidant and advisor. At the behest of Levison, King later employed Jack O'Dell in the Southern Christian Leadership Council. Morris identified Jack O'Dell as Hunter Pitts O'Dell, a secret member of the party's governing body, the National Committee. In November 1959 Jackson revealed to Jack that O'Dell was working full time for King and that Levison worked closely with O'Dell.

On May 6, 1960, Jack reported: "Hunter Pitts [Jack] O'Dell is working full time in connection with the King mass meeting to be held in Harlem on May 17, 1960. Working closely with O'Dell are Stanley and Roy Levison [Bennett]. The CP considers [the] King meeting of the most importance and feels that it is definitely to the Party's advantage to assign outstanding Party members to work with the [Martin] Luther King group. CP policy at the moment is to concentrate upon Martin Luther King."

At the time, King was not the object of FBI investigation but his intimate association with Levison and O'Dell sounded alarms, and in 1961 the Bureau decided it should alert the newly elected president, John F. Kennedy, and his brother, Attorney General Robert Kennedy. No one could have been more sympathetic to King than the Kennedy brothers. During the 1960 presidential campaign they publicly defended him and demanded his release from an Alabama jail, fearing he might be killed in his cell. The Kennedy administration had no higher legislative priority than enactment of a federal civil rights law forbidding discrimination against (or preferential treatment of) any citizen on the basis of race, creed, or ethnic origin and guaranteeing every citizen equal access to public accommodations. Thus, hoping to save King and the civil rights movement from embarrassment, President Kennedy and Attorney General Kennedy cautioned King that, by personally associating with and relying upon Levison and O'Dell, he was putting himself and the civil rights movement in jeopardy. King equivocated, then continued to associate with O'Dell and Levison, both openly and secretly.

Some have argued that there is no evidence that, after meeting King, Levison maintained his ties to the party or that in counseling King he acted in behalf of the party. Maybe so. Maybe the scales suddenly and miraculously lifted from his eyes. Maybe, *mirabile dictu*, he suddenly repudiated the ideology that for at least a decade had motivated him energetically to serve the party. Maybe he suddenly decided to devote himself to bringing about full freedom to a minority of Americans instead of trying to impose communist tyranny upon all Americans. Levison, after all, would not have been the first communist to abandon communism.

However, the president, the attorney general, and the FBI had to confront and evaluate some verifiable realities, in addition to maybes, illuminated by SOLO and New York surveillance teams.

And these showed that the party had such confidence in Levison's devotion and loyalty to communism that in the 1950s it still entrusted him with the sensitive duty of managing party finances and keeping all the secrets attendant thereto. What evidence was there that Levison had experienced a dramatic change of heart and outlook?

Usually, people who underwent an ideological metamorphosis and renounced communism did not care thereafter to hobnob with communist believers whose faith they no longer shared. The believers (and the KGB) in turn looked upon defectors from the party as moral lepers to be shunned or traitors to be punished. Yet Levison for years after 1956 enjoyed the comradeship and collaboration of at least two important party officials, Lem Harris, a friend of Jack, and O'Dell, a hidden member of the ruling council of the American party. Manifestly, he had done nothing to erode their trust of him. And Levison of course continued to see his brother, Roy Bennett, who remained active in party finances and donated substantial sums to the party well after 1956.

Then an FBI surveillance team discovered that Levison was seeing someone else—KGB officer Victor Lessiovsky, a sophisticated and engaging operative well known to Western security services. Lessiovsky specialized in influence operations, that is, in inducing influential foreigners to do, wittingly or unwittingly, what the Soviet Union wanted them to do. In Rangoon, he had cultivated U Thant, a talented Burmese who, as the KGB presciently divined, had a future on the world stage. After being elected, with Soviet support, the secretary general of the United Nations, U Thant, brought Lessiovsky to New York in 1961 as one of his three official personal assistants.‡ Regardless, the FBI well understood that the KGB did not succeed in ensconcing one of its best officers atop the United Nations with the expectation that he simply would serve as an altruistic advocate of amity among nations or as a cultural attaché eager to introduce the American masses to the undoubted wonders of Russian literature, music, art, and science.

---

‡ Switching his persona from that of a man worldly and wise enough to run the United Nations to that of an utter innocent from a small Asian country, U Thant later averred that no one ever told him that Lessiovsky was a senior, veteran KGB officer and that of course it never occurred to him to inquire about the background of a Soviet he was employing as one of his three personal assistants.

Immune from American law, at liberty to roam the corridors and chambers of the United Nations and speak with the imprimatur of the secretary general, Lessiovsky could freely stalk big game from all over the world. Would a skilled intelligence officer so emplaced fritter away his time and risk his career (the United States could not arrest him; it could only expel him), by repeatedly indulging himself in idle lunches or amusing cocktail conversation with an undistinguished lawyer (at least, publicly undistinguished) who had nothing to offer the KGB, or with someone who had deserted the party and its discipline, or with someone about whom the KGB knew nothing, someone who could be an FBI provocateur, someone Lessiovsky just bumped into on the street and thought was good for laughs? And why would an ordinary American lawyer and car dealer meet, again and again, with a Soviet assistant to the boss of the United Nations? And why would Roy Bennett consort with KGB officer Lessiovsky?

Despite friendly, personal explanations, pleas, and exhortations from the president and attorney general of the United States, King disingenuously persisted in relying upon a key member of the Communist Party and upon someone regularly dealing with the KGB. King announced that O'Dell was leaving the Southern Christian Leadership Conference, but stayed in contact with him. And he ostensibly severed relations with Levison, but then carefully arranged to maintain both of them surreptitiously through an intermediary and eventually renewed them openly. Why?

Judging that these questions must be answered, Attorney General Kennedy authorized an FBI investigation and electronic surveillance of King and Levison. Morris and Jack were uninvolved in the investigation and wholly ignorant of it. Voluminous SOLO data available to the author show that Jack and Morris made just one brief reference to King in their reports after 1960. On June 25, 1964, the KGB radioed Jack a message for relay to Gus Hall: "We were informed that Robert Kennedy demanded of Martin Luther King that he get rid of Jack O'Dell, who allegedly has close connections with the CPUSA or is a CP member. This is for your information." How did the KGB learn what Robert Kennedy said in a private conversation with King?

FBI listening devices planted in hotel rooms occupied by King and visited by others reportedly recorded words and acts inconsistent with those of a Christian minister and moral exemplar, and salacious rumors about goings-on in saintly hotel rooms spread. According to other rumors, the FBI in a calculated campaign of defamation offered selected journalists the opportunity to hear tape recordings featuring the Reverend Dr. King in action. Supposedly, all these journalists, being prim, proper, and uncompetitive professionals disinterested in scoops and scandal, refused the chance to listen with their own ears.

No matter how accurate or inaccurate these rumors, in 1975 they affected SOLO, as did other FBI actions of which Morris and Jack were ignorant. J. Edgar Hoover abruptly and furiously fired a close deputy, William Sullivan, who as chief of domestic intelligence operations knew all about Levison, O'Dell, King, and whatever the bugs told about activities in hotel rooms. On orders from Hoover, agents changed the lock on Sullivan's office so suddenly that he had no time to clear out his desk. Subsequently, Wannall told Morris this story: "I want you to know that Bill Sullivan has been less than truthful on certain things. When Sullivan left the Bureau, he left so fast that he left a drawer full of supposedly personal stuff behind. We inventoried the contents of that drawer. Among the stuff we found was a letter addressed to King." Wannall generally related to Morris what the letter said. Here are some verbatim quotations:

> KING: In view of your low grade... I will not dignify your name with either a Mr. or a Reverend or a Dr. And, your last name calls to mind only the type of King such as King Henry the VIII...
>
> King, look into your heart. You know you are a complete fraud and a great liability to all of us Negroes. White people in this country have enough frauds of their own but I am sure they don't have one at this time that is anywhere near your equal. You are no clergyman and you know it. I repeat you are a colossal fraud and an evil, vicious one at that. You could not believe

in God... Clearly you don't believe in any personal moral principles.

King, like all frauds your end is approaching. You could have been one of our greatest leaders. You, even at an early age have turned out to be not a leader but a dissolute, abnormal moral imbecile... But you are done. Your "honorary" degrees, your Nobel Prize (what a grim farce) and other awards will not save you. King, I repeat you are done.

No person can overcome facts, not even a fraud like yourself... You are finished... Satan could not do more. What incredible evilness... King you are done.

The American public, the church organizations that have been helping—Protestant, Catholic and Jews will know you for what you are—an evil, abnormal beast. So will others who have backed you. You are done.

King, there is only one thing left for you to do. You know what it is. You have just 34 days in which to do (this exact number has been selected for a specific reason). You are done. There is but one way out for you. You better take it before your filthy, abnormal fraudulent self is bared to the nation.

Wannall continued, "Well, we searched through the vouchers on the travel of agents and we found that an agent made a trip to Miami on November 21, a Saturday. We talked to that agent. He said he got a call from Bill Sullivan who told him to go to Washington National Airport where a package would be delivered to him. Sullivan told the agent to take the package and go to Miami and then call Sullivan. The agent called Sullivan and Sullivan told him to address the package to Martin Luther King at the address of the Southern Christian Leadership Conference and mail it. On that same day, there was another agent—I have the man still working in our division—and he was in the office on a Saturday and Sullivan came out and asked him for a sheet of unwatermarked paper. As you know, Bill did a lot of his own typing, and he typed something on the unwatermarked paper and put it in an envelope and told this agent to take it over to an office. That was the agent who took a package to Miami. Now, if you count thirty-four days from November 21, that Saturday, you come to Christmas... what he was saying was, 'Here is a man of the cloth in the pulpit talking about the birth of Christ,' when he really was an immoral man."

In other words, Sullivan composed and caused to be mailed a letter that sounded like a warning to King that he better confess his sins or commit suicide before Christmas.

At a different time, another package was addressed to King's wife, Coretta, who was never suspected of anything other than being a good wife and was never investigated by the FBI. The package reportedly contained materials a husband would not want his wife to see, materials doubtless compiled and sent by someone in the FBI.

Years later, in 1975, as congressional investigators set out to prove the FBI guilty of violating the civil rights of citizens, they focused upon its alleged treatment of King. While they might question or disagree with many acts of the FBI, relatively few ever were found to have been unauthorized or unlawful; many of the complex, legalistic issues raised were difficult for the public to understand and failed to excite popular wrath. But the degradation of a crusading clergyman who had become a folk hero to many people was something laymen could understand and condemn.

THE SELECT SENATE COMMITTEE on Intelligence Activities under the chairmanship of Frank Church on February 14, 1975, demanded the complete FBI files on fifty different subjects, including King. The demand was so sweeping and so affronted the concept of separation of powers between the executive and legislative branches of government that the FBI, upon the advice of Justice Department attorneys, did not reply. In the spring, Wannall began to receive reports from retired FBI agents that congressional staff members asked them about matters pertaining to King. Some of these agents knew Morris or Jack, or had been peripherally involved in SOLO. And they were aware that the complete King file would reveal to an informed analyst, American or Soviet, that the FBI had penetrated the innermost sanctum of the American Communist Party, and that it was monitoring secret messages transmitted by the KGB to the party. And although the names of Jack and Morris appeared nowhere in the King file, it would not take the KGB long to deduce that they were the penetrations. To a man, the retired agents refused to tell the committee staff anything. Frustrated, the committee issued a new, specific, and formal demand for the King file.

Meanwhile, in an understanding with the FBI, the committee agreed that the Bureau could withhold data that might identify sources or disclose sensitive investigative techniques, provided that two designated Justice Department attorneys concurred that their suppression was justified. Accordingly, the FBI deleted all references that might point to SOLO and so much other material that only about a dozen pages remained. Even though the Justice Department approved the deletions, the sparsity of the few innocuous pages infuriated the committee. It accused the FBI of gamesmanship and duplicity and threatened to subpoena the entire file and to interrogate FBI agents under oath in public session.

Accompanied by Deputy Director James Adams, Wannall briefed Director Kelley about the crisis.

"Do you feel they are going to get the papers?" Kelley asked.

Wannall replied, "Yes. If they are going to subpoena Kissinger then it looks as if they can subpoena and get this material."

As Wannall saw it, the Bureau had two choices. It could abandon SOLO before the committee exposed it and immediately hide Morris, Eva, Jack, and Roz. Or it could gamble by telling Senator Church about SOLO in hopes of persuading the committee to drop its demands for the King file.

Kelley chose to gamble and authorized Wannall to tell Church as much as he judged necessary.

Given the prevailing political climate, the decision to trust an unfriendly senator with information that until recently had been withheld even from the president was not easy. From Capitol Hill a stream of venom poured down on the FBI and the intelligence community in general. Senator Robert Morgan called the FBI "the greatest threat to the United States" and "rotten to the core." Kelley sent him a polite letter suggesting that he had been misquoted. Morgan curtly replied, "I was quoted correctly." Young people who not long ago had joined throngs in the streets to chant "Ho! Ho! Ho! Ho Chi Minh is going to win," now held positions on congressional committees, and defamation of the United States had become a popular Washington sport.

Although Church had treated Wannall courteously, he and his committee appeared aligned with congressional elements hostile to the FBI. He had allowed staff members to violate agreements with the Bureau by attempting to interrogate former agents around the country and by reneging on the pledge to abide by the judgment of Justice Department lawyers about which data could be released. And any politicians, by selectively extracting from SOLO files, could grab headlines such as "FBI Funds U.S. Commies." Yet, to do nothing was disaster.

Wannall waited until Boyle signaled that Morris and Eva were safely out of Moscow and on their way home. Then he called Church and said he urgently needed to discuss a sensitive matter. Before leaving headquarters, he removed from a SOLO safe something fewer than ten Americans ever had seen.

In an ornate and secure chamber of the Senate Office Building, Wannall announced to Church that his committee unwittingly was about to destroy the most important of all American espionage agents and the most vital intelligence operation the FBI ever had sustained against the Soviet Union. Astonished, Church asked, "Can you explain?"

"I can show you." Thereupon, Wannall displayed a photograph of Morris seated with Brezhnev in the Kremlin. Normally, Soviet technicians blanked out or erased the face of Morris from official photographs. But once, in a comradely mood, Brezhnev insisted that a picture of him together with Morris be taken and that Morris be given a copy as a keepsake. As Wannall stressed, the photograph illustrated the kind of access "our man" regularly enjoyed. He proceeded to outline the history of SOLO, its enormous success, its continuing value to policymakers, and the reasons why opening up the King file would collapse the operation and endanger lives.

Having grasped the importance of all he had heard, Church finally said, "I only wish the American people could know. This certainly would open their eyes. It has opened mine."

They agreed that Wannall should also talk to a few selected staff members without disclosing any details he felt should be suppressed. Church picked three aides, and the ranking Republican on the committee, Senator John Tower, sent a fourth. At the outset of the secret meeting, Church gravely admonished all four: What they were about to hear was extraordinarily sensitive, and not one word of it ever was to be repeated.

While omitting many details, Wannall for nearly two hours entranced Church and the staff with the story of SOLO. He explained why FBI assets (he never named Morris or Jack) had to participate in the deliveries of Soviet money in order to continue the operation. Finally, he again laid out the reasons that caused Robert Kennedy, with the concurrence of his brother, the president, to order the investigation of King and why the file would expose SOLO. The FBI remained ready to cooperate with the committee by all means consistent with national security, but it respectfully requested that the committee steer clear of the issue of Martin Luther King and do nothing that might compromise SOLO.

Church pronounced the official verdict in two words: "I approve." He added, "I am satisfied that there was every reason in the world for the FBI to be investigating King [he later made the same statement to the entire committee]. Of course, I want none of this talked about. None of this is to leave this room."

Church categorically assured Wannall that neither he nor any staff member would ever ask any question, publicly or privately, that might imperil SOLO.

A test occurred on November 19, 1975, when Adams and Wannall testified before the committee in open session. A senator raised the issue of FBI actions pertaining to Martin Luther King.

Adams spoke up, "You're getting into a sensitive area."

"That's right," Church declared. "We will move to another subject."

It appeared that the FBI had won the gamble. But to win it, the FBI had to betray its solemn word so often given to Morris and

Jack over the years: *Outside a few of the highest people in government, we never will tell anybody about SOLO.* Now somebody had to tell Morris and Jack, an unwelcome task.

Leavitt, Brannigan, Boyle, and Langtry undertook it at a conference with Morris and Jack on December 12, 1975. Leavitt told them just what happened, explaining that the FBI had no choice if it were to prevent them and SOLO from being exposed. No identifying data about Morris and Jack were provided. Wannall had quoted State Department and CIA evaluations and numerous letters from Kissinger attesting to the great importance of the operation. Ultimately, the committee agreed with the investigation of King, dropped its demands for files showing why it began, and pledged to keep the secret.

Then Leavitt acknowledged, "But there are five people in the Senate and two Justice Department attorneys who now know about the operation."

As Jack's face reddened with anger and Morris stared incredulously, Langtry tried to mollify. The committee could subpoena the agents who wrote the reports about Levison and his management of the reserve fund, his continuing ties with Lem Harris and reports by Harris to the party about him, and his relationships with King and the KGB, and could compel them to tell all under oath and in public.

Brannigan also tried. "We told them this was a sensitive operation and that if they exposed it, the country would be the loser."

Unmollified, Jack shouted, "This is serious and shocking."

"I also am surprised and shocked," Morris said. "Once something goes beyond a tiny group of people we no longer have a secret. The danger is that politicians or staff members will betray information for their own self-aggrandizement. We know little about these staff members or their relatives. We must admit to ourselves that we no longer have a secret."

"I would be a fool to disagree," Leavitt said.

"It could reach other senators and congressmen with bigger ambitions. One of them could leak it to the press; that's happened. We have no assurances. Then what about the communists? Do we know all the connections of the communists? We would be fools to think so. From long experience, I know they have connections in Washington. Information gets to them sooner or later. 'Fatso' [a porcine party member, also known as 'Tiny,' who claimed to have entrée to some congressional offices] used to have that job for them.

"There is also an ongoing campaign to use the Freedom of Information Act to ferret out info. The communists are just beginning in that area. The communists' lawyer was censured for being too slow about it... The implications are tremendous both from security and our personal viewpoints. We are in danger of exposure. We have no control over these individuals."

Jack added, "There is a great deal involved here. It's not just the apparatus; it's our families."

Brannigan responded, "We must tell you, as members of our family, that this is what we thought we had to do. Mr. Kelley, all of us, agreed. We cannot give you any guarantees and that is why we are here. We were trying to head off much worse. We were trying to protect you and this operation. This is the most valuable thing the FBI has."

Jack still was not appeased: "The operation is no longer the great secret it was up until now. There were dozens of FBI people involved over the years, but we felt secure. The word of the Bureau was its bond."

Boyle saw that Morris was paying little attention to what anyone said; characteristically, Morris was trying to analyze, to think ahead, and as he did so he mused aloud, speaking more to himself than anyone else. "If they ever found out that we duped all these leaders and the KGB and all the governments that work with them, including Mao, and guys like Gus, they would hound us to the ends of the earth. There is no place on earth where we would be safe. Even the kindest of individuals would want the honor of destroying us... Today Jack received a message from the Soviets to Gus asking, 'Can you see our ambassador?' Tonight I must give the message to Gus. Do you think it is easy for me to see Gus? I am worried. Do I have to carry around a pocket radio to find out when my life is in danger?"

Leavitt interrupted, "I realize this is like being hit between the eyes with a baseball bat, and I understand your feelings." And he

proceeded to list the unique security safeguards protecting SOLO—
the special safes; the armed couriers; the willingness of the highest
people in government to read reports and then hand them back; the
fact that only the president, the secretary of state, and the attorney
general knew about SOLO. He recited all this and stated that the
FBI at any time could "resettle" (i.e., uproot and hide) Morris, Eva,
Jack, and Roz. Meaning to pay tribute, he repeated something Morris had heard at least a dozen times: "This is the most important
intelligence operation the United States has."

Morris said, "But there is something new, is there not?"

Leavitt admitted there was. The FBI could control what it did; it
could not control what congressional committees and their staffs
did. And yes, the KGB or anyone schooled in the history could
deduce from salient portions of the King file the identities of sources
(58 and 69). The Church committee had given its word and thus far
honored it. But it could offer no guarantees about the future.

Morris was scheduled to go to Moscow in February 1976 as a
secret delegate to the Twenty-fifth Party Congress. Failure to
attend this exalted ritual would raise questions and perhaps suspicions. So might Eva's failure to accompany him. By now, the
Soviets expected her to be along, and the wives of Soviet rulers
looked forward to her gifts, her company, and the invitations to
grand banquets. But now Morris was not sure whether they dared
go. "We will play it cool. We have to think things out. In view of
all that's going on in Washington, we better think. If I am able to
go, then we must exert superhuman energy to prevent anything
from happening—even if somebody who is supposed to testify has
to get sick."

During the discussions, Boyle said almost nothing. Headquarters had not consulted or notified him before baring SOLO secrets
to seven people outside the FBI. He understood the necessity of
keeping the committee out of the King files. But, like Morris and
Jack, he felt betrayed. However necessary the revelation, the
Bureau had broken its word and dramatically increased the risks
they were running. For all Boyle knew, the congressional staff
members Wannall briefed might all be honorable, discreet patri-
ots. But he agreed with Morris, who had said, "I think some of

those committees are hiring people who in normal times couldn't have gotten a security clearance to use a government urinal." So what was there to say? Ultimately Morris alone would decide whether to go on.

Morris would of course tell Eva that journeys to Moscow now were much more dangerous and ask if she wanted to go on. Boyle could hear her answer: *It always has been dangerous; how dangerous can dangerous get? If you think it's best to go, let's go. In other words, I'm your wife. I'll accompany you to hell and back, if we can get back. If not, well, there is an end to every story and we have lived a pretty good one. You decide.* For all her cultured grace and coquettish charm, Eva at age seventy-five was still a very tough lady, an American patriot, and a very good spy. If the vote were left to her, it would be "go."

Morris would consult Jack, who was very adept at irreverently giving him, the FBI, and the KGB advice. To the KGB: Stop making these money deliveries in damned blizzards. Stop acting like creeps, spooks, and children. In New York, people don't talk to each other with chalk or crayons or graffiti. They just pick up the telephone. You may have tapped every telephone in the Soviet Union, and I don't give a damn about that. The FBI has sworn to Congress—and they can't lie to Congress unless they want their balls and money cut off—that it has taps on the phones of fewer than two hundred people and I'm not one of them. Morris and I have played a lot of tricks to prove that. To the FBI: We need medical insurance; I need it for my wife and children. I can't run around twenty-four hours a day kissing Gus Hall's ass and screwing the KGB and still run a business. Can the Bureau arrange that? Or does it want to prosecute me for taking 5 percent from all the commie cash I bring in each year?

Outrageous as he may have been, Jack more often than not was right. The FBI came up with the medical insurance. The KGB agreed that if there was a snowstorm everyone could wait until roads were passable, and that phone calls could be made now and then (it never fully abandoned the old-time communications procedures—marks by chalk, crayons, graffiti, and the radio signals that said, "We have nothing to say").

But Jack was a tactician, or as he said in the early days, a "street man," rather than a strategist. In the end, as he had done all his life, he would do whatever his revered brother told him to do.

As the conference adjourned, Langtry asked Boyle, "Do you have time to lift some weights?"

"Absolutely. I need the exercise."

After Langtry's last physical examination, an earnest female medical assistant said to him, "For a man of your age—I mean you are not really old; you're only fifty—but you're in superb condition. You must be an athlete."

"Yes, I am. Almost every night I lift weights."

"I should have guessed from your muscles. What sort of weights do you lift?"

"Scotch on the rocks."

seventeen

TO GO OR NOT
TO GO?

AGAINST A LIGHT SLEET, Boyle threaded his way along streets crowded with shoppers, past storefronts brightly decorated for Christmas. The trumpeters and buglers of the Salvation Army in their operatic uniforms were still at it, just as they had been when Morris studied and tried to learn from them in the 1930s. They blared out carols, compensating with vigor for what they lacked in concert skill, and a small woman, who looked to be in her sixties, added to the volume by pounding an immense drum as if it were the devil himself. Thinking of Morris in the 1930s, he dropped a few dollars into the kettle.

About ten minutes after Boyle entered the cover office, the young agent who had trailed him telephoned, signaling that he had detected no surveillance. Boyle liked the agent personally, but then he tended to be prejudiced in favor of all FBI agents who had served as military officers in Korea or Vietnam. You didn't need a doctorate in personnel management to figure out that past combat and danger prepare men for future combat and danger. It was late, Christmas was near, and Boyle ordered the agent to go home to his family instead of hanging around just to follow him back to the FBI offices.

Eva and Morris came carrying presents she had selected and wrapped for Boyle's children, and they gathered in the back room. Morris as usual seated himself in the tall leatherbound chair behind the big desk, a chair reserved for the chairman, the captain, the boss. During one of the New York conferences, Morris remarked that everyone has "a little vanity," and everyone recognized that by seizing the chair whose occupancy connoted command he was indulging his "little vanity," something he did nowhere else.

Years later, reminiscing in her eighties, Eva offered insights about why Morris behaved differently in the back room. "I think he felt more at ease there than anywhere else. You have to understand that in Chicago we always were careful, just like in Moscow. Going to the office wasn't like going to the market or just anyplace. The FBI, they followed us to see if anybody else was following us. Morris told me they even followed Walt when he came to meet us there. Walt and Morris made the guards and cleaning ladies and handymen think we were retired professors and consultants. We gave them presents around Christmas and were nice to them, and they were on our side. The FBI checked the office to make sure nobody had hidden any bugs, so nobody could listen to us. Then there was Walt. You know, Walt always carried a gun, even on airplanes, and you better not fool around with Walt. If anybody barged in on us, well, that would have been just too bad for them. And if we wanted lunch or supper, we could just call one of the delicatessens and pretty soon it would be brought in. So we could just be ourselves and not be afraid and say whatever we wanted. Morris had a study at home and an office at his phony business but he thought of the back room as his real office."

That late afternoon just before Christmas 1975, Morris from behind the desk assessed SOLO. Time and thought had dissipated the consternation and indignation he had felt in New York, and he was thinking ahead calmly, as Boyle had often observed him do.

He feared that disclosure of SOLO to Church and committee staff members portended the beginning of its end. The question was, when and how would it end? Twenty-three years had passed since he met Carl Freyman and agreed to work with the FBI. During those years, there had been some "goofs," leaks of fragmentary information that could have cost him and Jack their necks, but the Bureau had managed to keep SOLO itself secret from outsiders because everyone followed the rules. With a slight smile, he said, "Maybe Walt, Al, and John along the way now and then made up a few new rules of their own. But we followed the most basic rule: if you want to keep a secret, don't tell anybody." Because the Bureau had to break that rule, SOLO no longer was really secret; experience proved that once a secret is let loose, it multiplies and spreads. Having been breached, the wall of security could not be repaired. The breach dramatically increased the dangers to him and Eva. He wondered if it would be rational to continue missions into the Soviet Union knowing that at any time while they were there the secret of SOLO might reach the press, the party, or the KGB.

Morris paused, perhaps hoping that Boyle would contradict him or present some secret or insight showing he was wrong. Boyle could do neither.

To Boyle, the United States in December 1975 seemed to have sunk to a post–World War II nadir. In the aftermath of the American debacle in Southeast Asia, hundreds of thousands of Cambodians, Laotians, and South Vietnamese were being massacred or enslaved by communist conquerors. If friends of the United States were looking at its disarray with dismay, what might the Soviets be thinking and planning? Now more than ever the United States needed to read their minds through SOLO. Yet how much can you ask of an elderly man and woman? The air force, navy, and Marine Corps withdrew young pilots after they had survived a certain number of combat missions. The FBI had already sent Morris on forty-nine missions into enemy territory, and from 1962 on Eva accompanied him on most. You can only roll the dice so many times without losing, and there was no disputing Morris; events in Washington had worsened the odds.

Boyle said, "Morris, honestly I don't know what to tell you."

"Thank you for your honesty, Walt."

Stepping out of the office building, Boyle instinctively looked around and through a minor maelstrom of wind and sleet glimpsed the agent he had ordered to go home. The agent also had orders to cover Boyle and those were the orders he chose to obey. Boyle thought, *You can take the boy out of the Marine Corps, but you can't take the Marine Corps out of the boy.*

Boyle advised headquarters that Morris was engaged in an anguished debate with himself about whether to quit and thereby terminate the operation. If he were to attend the Twenty-fifth Party Congress, he would have to leave for Moscow no later than February 16, 1976. So he would decide before then.

Although Wannall was about to retire, he retained responsibility for SOLO, and he consulted Kelley about the dilemma that necessitated a fundamental policy decision. Kissinger, doubtless with the concurrence of the president, only recently had ordered SOLO continued, declaring it indispensable to formulation of foreign policy. Wannall believed the Church Committee would protect the secret, but he could not guarantee that to either Kelley or Morris. Undeniably, the dangers of continuing the operation had increased and Morris' new apprehensions were justified.

Kelley remarked, "Ray, as I said, you have the most interesting job in the FBI."

On a dreary Sunday night, February 8, 1976, Wannall flew to Chicago to meet Morris and Boyle in the cover office early Monday to discuss the future of SOLO. They were joined by Section Chief Brannigan, Supervisor Houser, and Special Agent Ronald Fries, then working as Boyle's partner. Brannigan later recalled, "Ray and 58 did almost all the talking. The rest of us just sat there. It was like watching history being made."

Instead of broaching the overriding issue that brought them together, Wannall began obliquely by giving Morris an insider's view of relations between the FBI and Congress. "There are two phases in this work: one is foreign, and one is domestic. They have pretty much left our foreign intelligence activities alone. I know on the domestic side we are going to have problems. You see, one of the problems is that some of those congressional staffers were in the student riots of a decade ago. When the streets were burning, they were part of it. So they say, 'How come you are investigating this stuff?' Not the [terrorist] bombings; they think we should be investigating that."

Fearful of spreading panic, the FBI had not fully publicized the threat posed by terrorist bombings but they represented an increasing danger. "In 1973 there were twenty-four bombings; in 1974 there were forty-five; and in 1975 there were eighty-nine bombings. So they seem to be about doubling every year."

Wannall disclosed highly classified details of how the FBI had prevented bombings by penetrating terrorist organizations. "There were three rented cars, packed with explosives and detonators, parked by an Israeli bank and the El Al warehouse in New York. Experts say that if they had gone off, each would have cleared an area a hundred yards around it. If one had exploded in the middle of downtown New York, it would have killed or injured hundreds, probably thousands of people."

The candor and confidences had the desired effect—a relaxed rapport—and Morris lectured about the history of twentieth-century terrorism and the difference between anarchism and Marxism. "Of course, real Marxists approve of mass terror but not individual terrorism. The same was true of individual expropriation [robbery]. In 1917, they would shoot someone for this individual expropriation. Any real Marxist would fight against individual terrorism." But there were always those individuals who would desert Marxist orthodoxy and try to "speed things up" by fostering "alienation" through indiscriminate bomb-throwing.

Then Morris on his own came to the point, just as Wannall, Kelley, and Boyle hoped. "But we are getting away from the problem of the day. I want to preface my statements by telling you that when I think of our operation, I never separate it from what is happening in the world at the moment. You said, without giving guarantees, that the committee will lay off the foreign aspects pretty much, but we will run into problems on the domestic side."

Everyone had sense enough to say nothing as Morris proceeded to articulate and vent his anxieties and grievances; everyone was willing to listen until midnight if need be.

"The popular idea that the First Amendment can be used by the press to steal confidential government documents" threatened SOLO. "We have a president [Gerald Ford] who was not elected and the power of the president has been eroded... I am not one of those who make fun of politicians; we have to have them in our system." But some politicians were egotists who lusted for publicity. "Such individuals with political ambitions don't always put honor or loyalty above themselves... Be assured the Russians have people going over every line of testimony. I know that their people in this country see congressmen... There is the possibility that a politician who got some information will talk to another politician or to his wife and she will talk to another wife. So you can understand why we are disturbed... In New York, there was a statement about there being no guarantees. I understand that. We have our head in a noose, and we know it."

Morris meandered through the history of SOLO and its successes and, almost pleading, tried to make all understand what he considered now at stake. "This trip or this congress is very important. Most of it will be open. The secret stuff the congress won't hear but I will. And I am experienced enough to analyze a speech and go beyond the words. In addition, when I am in that city [Moscow], I meet party leaders from all over the world, friends, and you get information from them you never could get elsewhere and facts the biggest experts couldn't deduce... Everybody is talking about the defeat of the communists in Portugal. Well, we knew a year ago that the Russians were trying to pull the Portuguese communists back. We knew the Soviets didn't care about a defeat in Portugal, that this is where they didn't want to take us on."

Summing up the long soliloquy, Morris rambled a bit: "Within the next two or three days, pending a final decision, I have to move. Because if we decide that I am going or I should say we are going because Eva has been invited and she has been getting more calls about the trip than I have... because we must go on in the usual way just as if nothing has happened, although we know that some things have happened in the last two months...

"I have been talking a lot, but I want you to know what is in our minds and hearts. I don't expect a yes or no from you about whether we should make this trip."

After some moments Wannall spoke slowly and obviously not from a script. "I don't know of any agent, myself included, who has had in the last twenty to twenty-five years the impact on our government's policies that you have had. I say that to tell you how valuable you have been not just to the FBI, but to the United States. There was no question that we were going to tell you everything that has happened, not just because of moral obligation. You have been a part of us; you are part of the family. I want you and your wife to make this decision knowing what all the facts are. Despite the value we put on this operation, we put a higher value on you...

"Next Sunday if you are not on that plane, you will still be FBI as far as we are concerned. No one could ask anybody to do as much for his country as you have done. Our concern is that you get over and get back, if you go. We know that you have gone beyond your physical endurance many times. But you are more valuable than any mission. I want to tell you that this is the greatest operation we ever have had. You are not only giving information; you are giving yourself. If anything happened to you, I would not be able to live with myself. If you decide not to go, we will still be working together; we still will be associates and friends. I cannot tell you to go or not to go. I have to be as honest and forthright with you as I can be."

The disorganized response from Morris suggested to Boyle that the sentiment and sincerity of Wannall's spontaneous words affected him—maybe decisively: "I talked to my brother and we know that no one can make up our minds for us. There is no such thing here as taking a vacation or stopping temporarily. I should have been in the hospital many times but to those people you never talk about how you feel; that doesn't count... I am glad that you have come here today but I am kind of embarrassed and feel kind of bad that you had to come all the way out here. I raised it with my guy [Boyle]. If it were safe, I would have gone to Washington to see you but that would be the worst place for me today... I must tell you that I am sorry to see you leave [retire]...

"You know, in these discussions we cannot always solve every problem; there is not always a neat solution. I don't want to make the situation worse by quitting. I still feel that unless our government agencies go berserk, there is a need for this operation. I am trying to anticipate the final outcome of the investigations and of things that might seem insane. But I know what our country needs."

Morris then digressed and talked about dying. He recounted the adventures of an old Bolshevik friend, a classmate from the Lenin School, who had spied for the Comintern in China at a time when they chopped off the heads of spies, and later in Nazi Germany, where they did worse things to spies. His friend survived to die peacefully in anonymity. But that was how Morris hoped to die. That was not the way he would die in Moscow. Nor would Eva die in peace and dignity. The betrayed wives, quivering under the lash of their own betrayed husbands, would cry like banshees for a degrading death to prove their loyalty.

No one spoke. No one said, *Come on, Morris, that won't happen; they wouldn't do that to you or Eva*. Everyone knew that the Soviets had done just that myriad times and continued to do it, albeit on a lesser and more discreet scale, in the mid-1970s.

They waited for Morris, the captain, to announce the tentative course. "Well, as things stand now, no one can make the decision for us. For reasons I gave before, there can be no interruption [of his trips to Moscow]. Once there is an interruption, we must expect total stoppage. Despite all the heartaches and thoughts and physical problems, we are going along now as if we are to travel.

"I have asked my son to come from the West Coast to talk to me. I won't give him any details, but he knows what is going on generally. I feel proud I kept him out of the party all his life. So he will come, and we will talk things over. I don't know that it will change anything. At least, we will have seen each other.

"So I am preparing. Until the moment I leave, until Walt says goodbye, we won't know whether we will go. I am not asking for guarantees. I am thinking about what can be done by the people in Washington, by the Bureau. You must be alert. You must make sure accidents don't happen and that in these FOIA [Freedom of Information Act] cases something doesn't get out. The only other thing I can say is let's see what happens in the next few days. Next Monday will be the latest I can leave."

Throughout their deliberations, Eva insisted that Morris decide for both of them and did nothing to influence him. On Saturday he said they could no longer delay and demanded that she tell him what she thought. Eva demurred. Morris insisted.

"You're my partner. I have a right to your judgment."

"Well, we've come a long way. Shouldn't we go all the way?"

Morris dialed Boyle at home and said, "Tomorrow, we're making the first leg of the trip."

They flew to New York Sunday morning for a last visit with Jack, and on Monday Boyle took them to Kennedy Airport. Once their plane was airborne, Boyle called Wannall in Washington. "We've launched."

Representatives of the International Department and Nadezhda, Eva's latest personal escort, greeted them at the airport outside Moscow with hearty embraces. In the limousine en route to their apartment, they as usual were presented with a crowded schedule—appointments with Suslov and Ponomarev, banquets, private dinners, a luncheon hosted by Politburo wives in honor of Eva. Brezhnev hoped to talk with Morris but with so many party leaders in Moscow for the congress, he presently couldn't fix a date. Clearly, in one of the world's most exclusive clubs, Morris and Eva were still members in good standing.

Without any evidence, they assumed that their apartment was honeycombed with listening devices and spoke accordingly. "Everyone is so nice here. I'm sure we're going to have a good time," Eva said.

"Yes. I'm looking forward to seeing all our friends."

During the four weeks in Moscow, anxiety about what might happen in Washington added to the physical stress imposed by a business and social routine that would have exhausted a much younger and healthier man. When they landed in Boston March 13, 1976, Morris looked so drained that Boyle refused to let him board another plane. He telephoned Langtry and asked him to inform headquarters that 58 and 66 (Eva was CG-6653S*) had returned safely and that he was driving them to their apartment in

New York. He also asked Langtry to arrange for a physician to come to the apartment that evening. Of course, asking Langtry if he could help was akin to asking the pope if he is Catholic.

Boyle rented the biggest, most luxurious car available and they set out for Manhattan. As they drove, Morris, despite his exhaustion, related what he had heard and seen in Moscow, and he and Boyle mentally composed the first report to headquarters.

Perhaps the most important report from Mission 54 was, on its face, the dullest. The Soviet Union was suffering grievous economic difficulties, and Morris' Kremlin friends recited a long litany of woes: poor quality control; low worker productivity; an inadequate transport system, which delayed shipments of both raw materials and consumer goods; idle factories and empty store shelves; wastage of grain owing to lack of transport and storage facilities; sloth and indifference on state and collective farms; reluctance or outright refusal by industrial managers to put new machinery and technology into use; and an increasing inability to match Western innovations in computers and electronics.

Every industrial economy periodically runs into bad patches, and Morris had heard of Soviet economic difficulties before. But in the past the Soviets had blamed them on aberrations or transient factors that could be overcome by better management, and they seemed to believe their own propaganda. In fact, the KGB Disinformation Department planted stories of grand economic growth in the foreign press, then presented these stories to the hierarchy as evidence that even Western "experts" admitted Soviet successes and potential economic superiority. At home, the government-controlled media constantly disseminated statistics showing growth and prosperity. All these official data also influenced Western thinking, and thus even sophisticates at the CIA consistently overestimated the gross national product of the Soviet Union while underestimating the proportion of it consumed by military spending.

(Once Morris showed Eva a CIA analysis that the FBI had asked him to evaluate. It concluded that per capita income in the Soviet Union was about to exceed that of Italy. Eva through her own eyes had compared life in Rome, Milan, Florence, and Venice with that in Moscow and Leningrad, and she asked, "Is this some sort of intelligence trick?" A smile from Morris told her it was a serious U.S. government document, and they both laughed out loud.)

Now the men who owned the Soviet Union were acknowledging among themselves that their problems were not temporary and that the economy, upon which their power depended, was steadily deteriorating. And they admitted to Morris that nobody had any idea how to reverse the deterioration.

A second report spelled out in three words—*peace and disarmament*—the themes that would undergird and dominate Soviet foreign policy, propaganda, and "active measures" for nearly a decade to come. Morris stressed that these words did not mean to the Soviets what they meant to Americans. *Peace* meant no armed conflict with the United States, not a surcease of local or regional conflicts instigated or supported by the Soviets in an effort to alter the world balance of power or "correlation of forces."

To Americans *disarmament* negotiations implied "Let's sit down in good faith and rationally discuss how we mutually and gradually can reduce our respective arsenals so that neither of us has cause to fear attack from the other." To the Soviets, *disarmament* meant "Let's stop your young warmongers sitting behind their computers in Silicon Valley, Southern California, around Dallas, Austin, and Boston from designing these hellish new weapons. Let's stop Boeing, General Dynamics, McDonnell Douglas, Texas Instruments, Hughes, Rockwell, General Motors, Ford, and Chrysler from inventing the means to produce weapons more efficiently and reliably. Let's stop the Pentagon from picking out teenage geniuses, secretly paying their way through engineering schools at Purdue or Georgia Tech or Texas A&M, then through doctoral programs at Stanford and MIT so they can contrive ever more diabolical weapons."

The Soviets had no intention whatsoever of negotiating any meaningful erosion of their military power. They had every intention of dissuading the United States from entering into a real arms race, which they were running as fast as they could. "Walt, they know now that they could not win."

Morris credited Eva with inspiring the third report. Between the door of their apartment building and the limousine, she whispered: "Keep an eye on Brezhnev. The girls tell me he's on something."

That had never occurred to Morris. Everyone was getting old, drunkenness was commonplace at Soviet state functions, and it was not unusual for young aides later in the evening to prop up old men they were around to protect. However, on the many occasions when Morris had been with Brezhnev, he never saw him drink too much. Although the private talk suggested at the airport never materialized, Morris twice observed Brezhnev at official functions and, prompted by Eva, realized that he appeared to be in a trance-like state—scarcely functional.

These three reports from Mission 54 turned out in ways to be as seminal as those from Missions 1 and 2 in 1958 and 1959. Analysts in those years did not believe that the breach between China and the Soviet Union was real and irreparable. Ultimately, Richard Nixon and Henry Kissinger did. Analysts in the mid-1970s did not believe that the Soviet economy had plunged into irreversible decline; that the Soviet Union could not militarily match the United States, much less the United States and NATO; that the Soviet Union was an eggshell society waiting to be pierced; or that it increasingly was leaderless. In the early 1980s, Ronald Reagan did believe and act—with results that everyone in the 1990s can see.

THE CHICAGO SAC HAD some good news. For years, Boyle had received outstanding fitness reports or evaluations. They did not, however, specify just what he had done, and personnel managers were suspicious of vague generalities that anybody could write about anybody. And his file still showed that he had been formally censured and demoted for threatening an inspector physically. So for fourteen years he had stayed in the same grade and the same job, the nature of which few at headquarters understood. Evidently, someone—perhaps Wannall or Kelley himself—finally interceded, for now the Bureau wanted to promote and transfer him to "an important supervisory position" at headquarters.

Boyle asked if he still would be involved in SOLO and the SAC said he did not know, but the operation could not continue indefinitely and Boyle should think of his future and the welfare of his family.

On the train home he did think about his family and how pleasant life would be for his six children in the wooded suburbs of Northern Virginia; the educational opportunities; the national museums and galleries in Washington; and the beaches, mountains, and historic sites within easy reach. Transfer to headquarters would erase the old stain on his record and perhaps lead to further advancement. The increase in salary accompanying promotion would increase his pension, and he could retire anytime after reaching age fifty. And in Washington, many an agent had made contacts that resulted in lucrative jobs after retirement.

The SAC, who admired Boyle, asked him if he would like to visit headquarters to discuss his new assignment.

"You said the transfer was not mandatory. I'm not going to Washington."

"I'm afraid if you don't go you won't be promoted."

"There's no way I'll walk away from 58."

"Look! You studied to be an actuary. You know that 58 and 69 can't go on much longer. Walt, SOLO is almost over."

"Maybe. No one, not even Carl or Al or John or I, thought it would last this long. In any case, I'm staying until the end."

eighteen

THE WINDOW
CLOSES

BOYLE SET OUT ON November 30, 1976, with Morris and Eva for the airport well in advance of flight time and the launch of Mission 55 to Prague, Moscow, and Budapest. Traffic was surprisingly light, and having checked in at O'Hare with a couple of hours to spare, they waited in a secluded first-class lounge. Such waits tended to be awkward because there was nothing of substance to say. All preparations had been made, everything that needed to be said had been said, and the apprehension all three shared made small talk seem banal. They said goodbye at the door of the lounge, and Eva kissed Boyle on the cheek. "Cheer up, Walt, we'll come back."

"I know you will. I'll be waiting."

As things began to unravel in Washington, headquarters decreed "no more paper"; Morris and Eva henceforth were not to copy documents or make any notes. Morris, however, during conversations in December with men he had known for thirty or forty years did jot down "TWA"—"tell Walt about"—a few times along with innocent reminders only he could decipher.

He found the Soviets in a state of shock, dismay, and confusion induced by the election of Jimmy Carter as president of the United States. They had been sure that Gerald Ford would win the election, and, contrary to their initial expectations, Ford had emerged in their judgment as a reasonable man with whom they could do business. After all, he had approved the Helsinki Accords by which the West, in return for a Soviet pledge to respect human rights, tacitly acquiesced to permanent Soviet dominion over Eastern Europe and the "Brezhnev doctrine," which in essence proclaimed "What's ours is ours; what's yours is negotiable."

To the Soviets, Carter was an enigma. What did a governor from Georgia know about world affairs? What sort of foreign policy would he formulate? They had heard he might select as a principal foreign policy advisor a Polish professor who didn't even have an American name (Carter soon appointed Zbigniew Brzezinski, a scholar from Columbia University, to be his national security advisor), and *Polish Americans were as bad as*—the Soviets, ever deferential to Morris, caught themselves and stopped. He knew they meant *as bad as American Jews*.

The Soviets were working themselves into a frenzy over the tendency of West European parties now and then to make decisions and set policy independently of Moscow. They likened this "Eurocommunism" to the "American Exceptionalism" of the 1920s and the first stage of Chinese heresy in the late 1950s, and considered it a dangerous phenomenon.

Thank God (despite their professed atheism, the Soviets in talking with Morris used the phrase *slava Bogu* or "thank God") the CPUSA was reliable; the Soviets appreciated its undeviating loyalty and intended to reward it with a $2 million subsidy in 1977. At the same time, they clearly laid down the line they expected the party to follow; *peace* and *disarmament* remained overriding objectives, and they intended to pursue them no matter what Carter did. The unstated but clear message to the American party was *You are to make peace and disarmament your priorities*.

On New Year's Eve 1976, Morris and Eva landed in Boston, and Boyle took them to a motel suite to rest overnight before flying to Chicago. During the night, the racket of men raucously singing or bellowing in Russian awakened them and Eva exclaimed, "I thought we were home! Where are we?" After investigating, Boyle assured them they really were in the United States. The celebration of a visiting delegation of Russians in a nearby room had spilled over into the corridor. Now there was not a sound.

"How do you suppose Walt managed to shut them up?" Eva asked.

Morris said, "Can't you guess?"

In Chicago, after filing the factual mission reports Morris and Boyle undertook to answer the basic question: What does all this mean?

Despite their irrational fears of what Carter might do, and no matter what he did do, the Soviets intended to make the campaign for peace and disarmament the cornerstone of their foreign policy. Why? Morris recalled that, a few years before, someone in the International Department said to him, "Our military intelligence is perfect; our political intelligence is just the opposite." He believed that Soviet intelligence about American science and technology was excellent, and that the Politburo heeded it; the oligarchs, who had no military or scientific expertise, had to rely upon their military and scientific advisors, and they always paid attention to anything they perceived as threatening them personally. To Morris, the Soviets no longer boasted, as they had done in the 1960s, that their weapons were as good as or better than American weapons, nor did they talk about "catching up" with the United States economically. They did talk about the necessity of stopping the United States from proceeding with the development of "hellish" weapons now progressing from computer print-outs toward testing and production.‡

Soviet scientists and generals understood that the Soviet Union could neither match nor effectively defend against these new weapon systems. They understood that, in a real arms race,

---

‡ The Soviets did not specify to Morris any particular weapons system that worried them, and he had no plausible reason to ask. Subsequent evidence shows that they feared the oncoming Pershing and cruise missiles, the neutron bomb, and the B-1 bomber—all spawned by technology and production techniques they could not then, or now, equal.

superior American technology and economic strength would win—by a wide margin—and they so informed the Politburo. Hence, the peace and disarmament campaign. Its long-term aim was to prevent the United States from entering an arms race; the short-term aim was to halt development or deployment of those "hellish" new American weapons.

"If you think like they do, it makes all sorts of sense. If you can't win a race, then don't have a race. If they can make us stand still they can walk ahead and I guarantee you they have no intention whatsoever of reducing their military power. The Party and everybody it can influence will denounce any new American weapon as a threat to peace and disarmament."

Morris did not agree that Soviet political intelligence was "the opposite of perfect." If the Soviets so adroitly could collect information—much of it secret—about American science, technology, and military power, why could they not collect facts about American politics that were mostly not secret? The problem—and danger—as Morris saw it, lay in Soviet misinterpretation of political intelligence. Lacking military or scientific expertise, Soviet rulers had to accept the judgments of their generals and scientists. In political matters, however, they claimed supreme expertise. But their judgments were warped because they had isolated and insulated themselves from reality and because they were prisoners of their own dogma, slogans, and past. As an example, he cited Soviet reaction to the election of Jimmy Carter.

The results of numerous public opinion polls and competent commentary published week after week in newspapers across America before the election indicated that the outcome would be close but that there was a strong possibility that Carter would win. Surely Soviet diplomats and intelligence officers reported what any American reading the papers in the smallest hamlet knew. Ardent adherents of the adage "Better the devil you know," the old oligarchs in Moscow *wanted* Ford to win and therefore he *would* win. When he lost, they were shocked and feared it would be more difficult to deal with a Democratic president than a Republican president. To anyone vaguely familiar with the American political landscape, this view was other-worldly.

"Walt, what this means is that they're capable of going off the deep end."

Headquarters responded: "This is a brilliant analysis and we think it is 100 percent correct. But right now within the [intelligence] community you and 58 are 'pissing into the wind.'"

The FBI in the spring briefed the new attorney general, Griffin Bell, and National Security Advisor Brzezinski about SOLO, its accomplishments, its potential, and the ultrasecret procedures governing distribution of SOLO intelligence. The briefers also explained that leaks and ongoing congressional investigations in Washington made continuance of the operation increasingly dangerous and diplomatically suggested that the political consequences of its compromise would not be good. For security reasons, the FBI was considering ending SOLO. Bell in turn fully briefed his friend, the president. Shortly afterward, headquarters notified Boyle and Langtry that Carter had expressly ordered the FBI to continue SOLO and that he personally accepted responsibility for the consequences. "He thinks it's the greatest thing since ice cream."

THE SOVIET UNION, at some pain to its dwindling treasury, maintained armies of spies and legions of diplomats— most of them intelligent, well educated, and fluent in English—to study and supply information about the United States. They could talk to members of Congress personally, attend congressional hearings, see cabinet officers (even the secretary of state), and read an overabundance of news and commentary about what was happening in the United States. Yet Brezhnev wanted Morris and Gus Hall to come over and tell him what *really* was going on.

They traveled separately to Moscow in late May and saw Brezhnev four times. Morris was in effect the number two man in the American party, and since as far as he knew the party in 1977 had not a single source in the United States government, they could report only what they had read in the press. But Hall made it seem as if their information emanated partially from unregistered sympathizers in the government, and Brezhnev was pleased to get the inside story from men he really trusted, from men who had actually run for public office in the United States. (Hall was a quadrennial candidate for the presidency.) At Morris' suggestion, Hall volunteered that the American party would invest all its resources to promote peace and disarmament and, through Morris, coordinate its efforts with the International Department. Brezhnev responded emotionally. The CPUSA was the only party in the capitalist world that truly upheld the principles of Marxism–Leninism. Ideologically, it occupied in the capitalist camp the same position that the CPUSSR occupied in the socialist camp. The CPUSA could have whatever it needed, whatever it wanted.

Hall and his wife departed in early June, leaving Morris and Eva behind to attend to the details of MORAT. Ponomarev ostensibly was ill, and Morris dealt principally with his deputy, Anatoly Chernayev. On June 9, the day before Morris' seventy-fifth birthday, Chernayev casually mentioned, almost as if by afterthought, that Brezhnev wanted to have a private, "working" dinner with him the next night and that an escort would pick him up in a limousine. Though they had talked many times, Morris had never dined privately with Brezhnev, and he thought it odd that Chernayev did not indicate any topics Brezhnev might want to discuss at the "working" (no wives) dinner.

A well-dressed young man called at the apartment the next evening, introduced himself in faultless English as an interpreter, and led Morris to the limousine. Standing by it, flanked by two bodyguards, was a man Morris knew well—Yuri Andropov, chairman of the KGB. Morris thought, *So this is how it ends. He wants the honor of arresting me himself. Eva, I love you.*

Andropov, who spoke a little English, leaned down and hugged Morris. "Old friend, great comrade. It much pleases me to see you." Through the interpreter, Andropov explained that Brezhnev had asked him personally to escort Morris and to join them at dinner.

Morris called the relatively small Kremlin dining room the "Captain's Cabin" because it was reserved exclusively for the most senior captains of world communism. As Andropov opened the door, a chorus of shouts in English rang out: "Happy Birthday!" There stood Brezhnev, Suslov, Ponomarev, Chernayev,

Mostovets, and about half the Politburo. While an army quartet accompanied by an accordionist magnificently sang, alternately in English and Russian, "Happy Birthday" and "For He's a Jolly Good Fellow," the rulers of the Soviet empire came one by one to hug Agent 58 on the occasion of his seventy-fifth birthday.

Brezhnev placed Morris to his right and gave a toast to "a great man, the last of the true Bolsheviks, our beloved comrade, Morris." The assembled, who had just sat down, stood and applauded. Between courses of the lavish dinner, others offered toasts to Morris, and with such sincerity that Morris had to warn himself: *Don't fall for any of this. Think where you are and who they are. Think about how many millions the men in this room have killed. Think about what Walt and the Bureau will ask.*

While KGB waiters served champagne, brandy, fruit, and cheese, Brezhnev—who remained seated—put on thick glasses and started to read the speech of the evening, the product of considerable research and a talented dramatist.

Morris had joined the party in 1919. Who here has served longer? When the Trotskyites threatened to seize our party headquarters in Chicago in 1927, Comrade Morris organized and led a band of comrades who at the risk of their lives defended and held our headquarters. There was a little truth in this. Obeying orders from Earl Browder, Morris, (the "Red Milkman"), did lead a few scruffy comrades into headquarters and for a few nights they slept on the floor, ready to repel the minions of Jay Lovestone, the heretical "American Exceptionalist." But no one attempted to seize the building, there was no fight or trouble, and Morris had long since forgotten about the incident. But it was recorded in Soviet files, and, in describing it, Brezhnev and his speechwriter made it seem like the battle of the Alamo.

Brezhnev went on rather accurately. As international secretary of the Communist Party of the United States of America, Comrade Morris had won the respect, confidence, and friendship of party leaders throughout the socialist world, and no one had done more to build solidarity among all parties. The CPUSA was the purest of parties, and Comrade Morris for more than fifty years had been a bulwark of that party.

With some difficulty, Brezhnev rose and so did everyone else. He said to Morris, "On behalf of the Communist Party of the Union of Soviet Socialist Republics, on behalf of the Soviet people and of all comrades here, I have the honor of presenting this decoration." He then pinned on Morris' coat lapel a medal, the Order of the Red Banner.

Subsequently, Chernayev told Morris that Jack had also been awarded a medal and that it would be given to him when he next came to Moscow.

In evaluating the ceremony for the FBI, Morris tried to be objective, just as he did in reporting about Soviet persecution of Jews. He thought the Soviets were sincere, or "as sincere as gangsters can be." They ludicrously overestimated the influence of the American party and credited it with causing phenomena, such as the anti–Vietnam War movement, in which it played only a peripheral part. The old doctrine of "Democratic Centralism" from the 1920s still governed their thinking. Once they made a decision and issued marching orders, everyone in all parties was supposed to march lockstep. Morris, Hall, and the American party, unlike the "Euro-communist" ingrates, always did, and the Soviets appreciated that.

Possibly, too, there was some personal warmth and friendship behind the medal. "I've known some of those bloody thugs since the 1930s." The Soviets, logically, believed Morris and Jack were taking extreme personal risks, and like everyone else they admired valor. They also dearly valued MORAT, which is why they awarded Jack a medal. The gesture of having the chairman of the KGB personally escort Morris and the presence of Brezhnev and the main rulers of the Soviet empire at the extraordinary dinner were personal tributes. But the medals also represented tributes to the American party and MORAT. Morris said, "Right now, we're all right in Moscow. It's Washington we have to worry about."

IN THE PAST, SOLO communications between headquarters and Chicago had sometimes been acerbic, and for that Boyle accepted his share of the blame. After receiving the first reports from one mission, headquarters sent a message with the comment, "58 sounds like a communist."

Boyle retorted, "Over there, 58 is a communist. He is virtually a member of the Politburo. He has to think and talk like a communist. What do you want him to do? Go to the embassy, round up a fife and drum corps, pick up an American flag, and parade into the Kremlin singing 'Yankee Doodle' and talking like John Wayne?"

This earned Boyle a visit in his sequestered office, "the hermit's cave," from SAC Dick Held. He realized Boyle was under unceasing stress, that his work was lonely, and that it was supremely important. "But you don't help yourself or 58 when you make senior people at headquarters look like idiots."

Boyle promised to refrain from sarcasm, and by summer 1977 exchanges between the field and Washington had become collegial and cordial. The Bureau designated an agent at headquarters, Michael Steinbeck, to handle SOLO administrative matters and day-to-day communications with Chicago and New York. He and Boyle talked often through scramblers, which garbled words spoken into a phone at one end of the line and ungarbled them at the other end.

Even though the line was secure, they tended to speak elliptically or in their own informal code, and in August Boyle asked if the weather had improved any. Steinbeck said it had not. "Do you think it is safe to fly?"

"We're trying to decide."

The Soviets planned an elaborate celebration of the sixtieth anniversary of the October Revolution, and they fully expected Morris to attend, as did Gus Hall. Boyle wanted to know if the Bureau was willing to risk another mission.

Steinbeck telephoned, in October. "It's a Chicago call. Whichever play you choose, we'll back you up." In other words, the Bureau is willing to take the risk, but let 58 decide. It's his life that's at stake.

Boyle on October 20, 1977, told Steinbeck over the secure line, "We've decided to throw deep." Morris and Eva left for Moscow the next day.

The Soviets initially put them in a suite at the party hotel so Morris could more easily mingle with (and spy on) foreign leaders gathering for the ceremonies. Despite the demands upon their protocol resources imposed by the presence of so many dignitaries, the Soviets assigned a retinue of women to attend Eva and Elizabeth Hall and even arranged for them to have tea with the first female cosmonaut, who to Eva seemed shy and nice.

In the hotel, Morris encountered Fidel Castro, who greeted him heartily and insisted that he and Eva come to dinner at the Cuban embassy.

Castro said the only other guests would be a Spanish couple and pointedly told Morris not to bring a Russian as an interpreter; they would speak English. Castro was an engaging host and especially gracious to Eva. She recalled, "He knew a lot about the United States and he was very interested in our party. He said some snide things about the Russians and I got the feeling he really didn't like them; he wouldn't let any of them come to dinner. They served good steaks and they were a delicacy in Moscow, and after dinner Castro himself poured brandy and asked me if he could smoke a cigar. It was a pleasant evening but he just kept talking and I thought we never would get out of there."

Eva most remembered the sight of Brezhnev at a formal reception. Two men literally held him on his feet; his face was pale and waxen, his eyes glazed, his speech blurred and incoherent. The ruler of the Soviet Union gave every appearance of being comatose and Eva thought, *That man is not going to get well*.

Throughout the four weeks in Moscow, the Soviets were as trusting and friendly as ever. They assembled leaders of South American parties for secret deliberations about how better to coordinate communist activities throughout the Western Hemisphere and invited Morris to participate and make suggestions. Ponomarev said that, despite a shortage of hard currency, they would give the American party $2.1 million in 1978, and he asked Morris to nominate Americans to attend the Lenin School. Except at the reception, Morris did not see Brezhnev, but Ponomarev gave a farewell luncheon for Morris and most of his old acquaintances came.

Eva and Morris started home in mid-November 1977 by flying

from Moscow to Prague. About twenty minutes before the Aeroflot plane was to land in Prague, the pilot or co-pilot came to them with an announcement: By order of the "highest authorities," they must return to Moscow at once. They were not to remove their luggage or other belongings from the plane. While the plane was being refueled, they were at liberty to enter the Prague terminal and speak to the Czech delegation awaiting them. Two comrades would escort them and make sure they did not miss the return flight.

Morris and Eva looked at each other and reached for each other's hand. *They have found out, and we are going to die.*

Flying back to Moscow, they held hands, kissed each other on the cheek, exchanged vows of love, and spoke of the wonderful life they had shared. Eva tried to be cheerful, and once she did make Morris laugh by talking about their visit to the Polish horse farm, Gus Hall's idea of the party selling horse meat as beef, and a communist fast-food chain selling "Gusburgers." She tried to be optimistic. "Walt and John and Jim will get us out."

Morris said, "Listen to me. Nobody will be able to get me out. There may be a chance for you. I will tell them I never let you know, that you were just a good wife who did what you were told. I don't know how much they know. If they show you photographs of Walt or John or anyone else from the Bureau you've seen, you must say, 'Yes, I saw him a few times. Morris said he was a party member.' You are innocent. Maintain your innocence to the last, no matter what."

Before descending the mobile stairway from the plane to the tarmac outside Moscow, they embraced for what they thought was the last time.

Eva imagined that inside the terminal goons would handcuff her or physically drag her away. Instead, beautiful children, bearing bouquets of flowers, and Nikolai Mostovets, chief of the North American division of the International Department, greeted them. Mostovets apologized profusely for interrupting their journey and explained that Hall was on his way to Moscow, and Hall insisted that Morris be present while he was there.

Morris never let the Soviets know when he was ill or in pain but he could not conceal the fatigue that drained his face of color; in consequence, during the return visit, they burdened him as little as possible. Ponomarev told Hall that Morris' health was vital to the party and that because of his conspicuous exhaustion he was ordering him to skip the ceremonial dinners. Ponomarev also gave Morris a number through which he could be reached day or night, and urged Morris to call if he needed anything. The Soviets could not have been more considerate.

Nevertheless, each day in Moscow Morris feared what might happen in Washington, and he suffered heart palpitations and excruciating back pains. Only when he saw Boyle waiting inside customs at Boston on November 20 did the knotting tension begin to subside.

FBI Director Clarence Kelley, while delegating responsibility for daily management of SOLO, monitored the operation closely and came greatly to admire Morris and Eva without ever having met them. In one of his last official acts before retiring, Kelley, on January 13, 1978, traveled to Chicago personally to thank them on behalf of the FBI and the United States. His obvious sincerity, simple eloquence, and the fact that he came with nothing to gain personally touched Morris. Now, within a span of a few months, the chairman of the KGB and director of the FBI had gone out of their way personally to honor him.

STEINBECK IN MARCH ALARMED Boyle and Langtry. Congressional committees seeking evidence of illegalities continued to demand FBI files, and in an effort to prevent a House committee from stumbling onto SOLO, Steinbeck had told three congressmen about it. They pledged silence, but now at least ten people on Capitol Hill knew.

The *New York Times* in April published a column reporting facts that, although they did not compromise SOLO, could only have come from someone with knowledge of it. A senior New York agent who knew was under investigation by the Justice Department, and Langtry suspected that the column constituted a veiled warning from him—back off or there will be worse leaks.

Langtry and Boyle then heard from Steinbeck that on May 1, 1978, this same agent testified in a closed session of the Senate Intelligence Committee. Steinbeck did not know what the agent said but the committee had commanded Steinbeck to appear on May 4 to discuss allegations of illegal acts committed by the FBI in the conduct of SOLO.

Boyle and Langtry of course had committed many acts that, if considered in a narrow context, could be construed as illegal. They had procured medical prescriptions and airline tickets under false pretenses, and they had suborned immigration and customs officials and persuaded them to admit into the country without question people traveling under false names with forged passports.

And for years they had prepared and filed irregular income tax returns on behalf of Morris and Jack. Because Morris and Jack worked full time for the government, the FBI eventually decided to pay them salaries (Langtry recalls that they never received more than $30,000 a year) and insisted that they pay taxes on this clandestine income. Langtry asked, "How do we explain the source of income?"

Headquarters helpfully replied, "That's your problem." Langtry solved his by figuring out how much Jack owed in taxes, obtaining a cashier's check for the amount from a friendly bank, and mailing it to the Internal Revenue Service without explanation. Boyle paid Morris' taxes by a more complicated subterfuge, but still a subterfuge.

Langtry and Boyle also violated laws by participating in a conspiracy to smuggle, hide, and disburse millions of dollars in illicit cash (by 1978, the total was approaching $26 million) on which no taxes were paid.

Certainly, Boyle and Langtry did not act with any criminal intent; neither of them profited personally; and no one was harmed, except avowed enemies of the United States waging covert warfare against the United States. To accuse them of breaking the law because they did their duty in accordance with policies specifically approved by presidents of the United States would be a mockery of the law. But in the prevailing political climate, there was no absolute assurance that some publicity-seeking committee or prosecutor might not, now or later, try to mock the law if given the chance. Boyle and Langtry could defend themselves only if the government and courts approved release of the full SOLO story. In any case, the legal costs to them would be ruinous.

At approximately the same time on the same afternoon, agents from headquarters appeared in the Chicago and New York field offices to show Boyle and Langtry the same letter. Neither man could keep the letter or make notes about it. The original would remain in the Justice Department, and a copy would be secreted at FBI headquarters. But if ever circumstances required, the letter would be made available to them.

The letter was from Attorney General Griffin Bell. It granted Boyle and Langtry immunity from prosecution for any authorized acts perpetrated in discharge of their SOLO duties. No one asked Bell to do this. He grasped the importance of SOLO and of his own initiative did what he thought was right for the United States without any possibility of personal or political gain.

Boyle says, "At the time, we had more to fear from some of our fellow countrymen in Congress and the press than from the enemy. So the letter was very heartening. We were deeply appreciative of the voluntary and noble gesture by Griffin Bell. In retrospect, I only wish I had been allowed to keep a copy."‡

Headquarters in June summoned Boyle and Langtry to Washington to confer with senior Bureau executives about the future of the operation, and none of the factors discussed was encouraging. The *New York Times* had published another article with information obviously supplied by someone with some knowledge of SOLO; the source had not yet betrayed the operation, but how much more would he leak? And Steinbeck in fending off allegations that the FBI was breaking the law had to reveal to the Senate committee many more operational details than Wannall disclosed when defusing the issue of Martin Luther King. Some

---

‡ Because Boyle and Langtry were not allowed to keep copies of the letter, they think—but are unsure—that the grant of immunity applied to all members of the SOLO team.

were exciting, dramatic details—the kind people like to tell wives, girlfriends, journalists, or anyone else they hope to impress. The FBI no longer could be sure how many outside the Bureau knew of SOLO or who all of them were. There was also increasing danger that the operation inadvertently might be exposed through records that had to be produced in response to lawsuits and demands lodged under the Freedom of Information Act. The ongoing attempts of congressional committees to prove the FBI guilty of wrongdoing, any wrongdoing, remained a threat.

MORRIS AND EVA RETAINED all their mental acuity and were intellectually capable of dealing with the Soviets. However, Morris was now seventy-six and in terrible health, and the arduous journeys to Moscow and Eastern Europe exhausted his reserves. When Boyle met him after the last mission, he was bent over and hobbled by back pains, and his voice barely rose above a whisper. How much longer could he retain the necessary physical stamina? How much longer could he even live? How much more could the United States justly ask of these elderly people who for so long had done so much?

Assistant Director James Nolan, who presided over the meeting, concluded it by saying there seemed to be general agreement that the FBI should not further risk the lives of 58 and 66 (Eva), that it should quit while it was ahead. No one dissented, and most nodded affirmatively. Back in Chicago and New York, Boyle and Langtry for the first time discussed with Morris, Eva, and Jack the discontinuation of SOLO.

On June 29, 1978, Steinbeck transmitted urgent messages to Chicago and New York: The president and attorney general have overruled the decision to "disengage." In compliance with their explicit orders, the Bureau must continue SOLO.

Professionally, Boyle doubted the prudence of their order. Personally, Boyle—who in an election between a Democratic dogcatcher and a Republican dog would have voted for the dog—considered it courageous and admirable. Politically, Carter and Bell had everything to lose. By substituting their judgment for that of the FBI, they implicitly accepted responsibility for the lives of Morris and Eva; if Morris and Eva were lost and the public found out, they would be blamed. If SOLO were exposed and only part of the story came out—the part proving that the government long had suppressed irrefutable evidence that the American Communist Party was a wholly owned lackey of the Soviet Union— how would conservatives and anticommunists react? If the Soviets discovered that the FBI for two decades had made fools of their rulers, how would *they* react? Carter and Bell had nothing personally to gain; they believed the United States did.

While the president or attorney general could direct the FBI to continue an operation, only the FBI could determine how to continue it, and on July 25 Steinbeck relayed a terse message from headquarters to Boyle: "No more trips."

Boyle told Morris that he and Eva should maintain relations with Gus and Elizabeth Hall, and if necessary meet the KGB in New York. Jack would go on as before, transmitting and receiving messages, by radio and through drops, and picking up money. But the Bureau had determined that further missions into the Soviet Union would be too dangerous; Morris and Eva could never again leave the United States.

Steinbeck on August 11 sent another alert. Under threat of subpoena, the Justice Department had released to Senate staff members a comprehensive study justifying the legality of SOLO. The study laid bare the operation, and the FBI had no idea how many people might read it. Steinbeck next reported that a retired FBI agent who, as a surveillant in Chicago during the early 1960s, had learned something about SOLO, was blabbing about it to anyone who would listen. The loon had also written a manuscript, a copy of which the CIA had recovered from the debris of the Jonestown massacre in Guyana. Because the former agent seemed daft, apparently no one had paid any attention to him thus far. But if the Soviets got word of what he was saying or saw the manuscript, they would pay attention and understand.

The FBI now judged the operation hopelessly insecure, and on September 15 headquarters unilaterally decided to end it and begin to "disengage." Listen to Eva:

Jack, Morris, Walt, John, and I got together in a hotel suite in New York. Now, Walt and John always were perfect gentlemen. But they were very tough boys; you have to be tough to do what they did. But they still were boys and I always could tell from the way they looked when something was wrong.

They told us that it was too dangerous for us to go on, that the Bureau had decided to close down the operation. Maybe they said slowly or gradually. But it was all over.

I think that at first we—Morris, Jack, and I—were glad. You know, we always were scared. Then I saw that Morris and Jack were sad. This had been their life. They really loved our country. They really were proud to help it. And now it was about to be over. It was a big change for all of us.

Six days later, Steinbeck frantically called Boyle. The attorney general again had overruled the Bureau and ordered it not to stop. "Mike, I've done exactly what you said. I've told the main players exactly why the game is over. I can't go back now and rewrite the rules. You're going to have to tell the coaches that. Tell them what has been said, cannot be unsaid; tell them, you can't put the toothpaste back into the tube."

Steinbeck responded the next day. "We concur. Your comments are appreciated. They will help us explain to those who still want to play."

Morris was supposed to come to Moscow in October for the annual strategic, operational, and budget consultations. Following another FBI script, he went to New York and on October 3 while talking to Hall, he suddenly gasped and bent over, pretending to be disabled by back spasms. He dissuaded Hall from calling for an ambulance; it would be safer if a party doctor looked at him in the apartment. He asked Hall to help him to a taxi. Meanwhile, Eva, following the same script, beseeched Elizabeth Hall, as one wife to another, as a fellow member of their feminist club in Moscow, to help. Morris tried to hide sickness from her; she knew he was very sick and belonged in the Mayo Clinic. The party was Morris' whole life, and he was determined to keep his appointments at the Kremlin. Eva feared he could not survive the journey; would Elizabeth please make Gus order Morris not to go to Moscow, to go to the hospital instead?

Early the next morning, an agent chalked a mark near a subway station signaling the KGB that a message had been deposited in a drop. The message said that because of illness Morris could not travel to Moscow. Pending his recovery, communications could be effected by radio and through drops. That afternoon, Elizabeth called Eva and said Gus wanted Morris to enter the hospital and not to worry about anything else.

The FBI, recognizing that SOLO someday must end, over the years developed a number of contingency plans for ending it. The most basic provided for emergency "evacuation and resettlement" of Morris, Eva, Jack, and Roz. On an hour's notice, agents could bundle them into hiding and then to residences in an area of the country where Soviet diplomatic personnel were forbidden to enter. Boyle scouted for desirable homes in Nevada and Southern California and kept current a list of those available for purchase. However, the sympathetic reaction of Hall to Morris' presumed illness showed that presently there was no emergency requiring Morris and Jack to suddenly disappear.

At an operational conference on October 25, 1978, the FBI tentatively decided to attempt a "field compromise" or ruse that would compel the Soviets to end the operation and make them think they were responsible for its collapse. According to the plan, Jack would request a personal meeting with his KGB handler and make sure their conversation was incriminating. Through a long-range microphone, agents would record the conversation, confront the KGB officer with the tape, and make a clumsy attempt to recruit him. The officer would race to the Soviet Mission and report that the FBI was onto him and Jack. The Soviets would then warn Jack and Morris that they were in danger, cease contact, and wonder what they had done wrong.

The FBI, however, saw no need to try the ploy immediately. Until a clear compromise or crisis occurred, it could continue to milk intelligence from the Soviet radio transmissions to Jack and from his contacts with Hall. Jack falsely told Hall that while in the Mayo Clinic Morris had suffered a "cardiac incident" but doctors expected him to recover. Subsequently, Morris showed Hall a letter from a physician warning him not to make any long flights.

Continuing messages from Moscow did yield some valuable intelligence. One to Hall instructed the party to organize a propaganda campaign aimed at preventing deployment of Pershing and cruise missiles in Europe. Another directed it to discredit and vilify National Security Advisor Brzezinski. Such messages again enabled the United States to read Soviet minds and act accordingly. Carter did order deployment of the missiles, and the Soviets unwittingly enhanced Brzezinski's status.

THE FBI HAD ESTABLISHED an Analytical Unit and staffed it with gifted men and women who tried to solve riddles pertaining to crime and espionage. They also looked at data released pursuant to court orders or Freedom of Information Act demands.

A widow of a party member had filed a lawsuit accusing the FBI of defaming her late husband, and an analyst studying records the court compelled the FBI to give her made and reported a finding, *viz*: On the basis of records now available to the CPUSA, I conclude that Morris Childs of Chicago, former editor of the *Daily Worker*, is and long has been an asset of the Bureau. I also conclude that his brother Jack Childs of New York, known to be a confidant of Gus Hall, probably is and long has been an asset of the Bureau. I do not need or want to know whether these conclusions are correct. I respectfully submit that if Soviet analysts study the same data, they can draw the same conclusions.

Reporting this to Boyle on January 12, 1979, Steinbeck asked if Chicago thought it was time to proceed with the "field compromise." Boyle said he wanted to talk to 58.

Eva in a 1993 interview recalled:

We had a lot of clever ways of talking to each other. We never answered the phone the first time it rang. If it rang a certain number of times, that meant Walt would call back in a certain number of minutes and the number of rings told us what we were supposed to do. I remember that 'four short, then three long' meant that the FBI was coming to take us away, even if I was in my nightgown...

Walt called us to the hideout [the cover office]... Walt was Irish, you know, and he could be very charming and funny. So could John [Langtry]. John was Scottish and Irish... They treated me mostly like I was a queen; sometimes like I was their kid sister. They always made me feel welcome and I sat in on a lot of conferences.

Morris and Walt were very smart, and they really could talk to each other, and they didn't use many words. Walt asked Morris about some trick to end the operation. Morris said, "Why now?" Walt said, "You're right." That's the way they talked. So we kept on going. Of course, we didn't go over there any more.

A telephone call on September 7, 1979, astonished Morris. Nikolai Mostovets was traveling in North America. Surely he was aware that the Royal Canadian Mounted Police and the FBI would not be indifferent to his travels. The Soviets always tried to conceal their relationship with Morris, yet from a Chicago hotel Mostovets called to invite him and Eva to dinner at the Cart Restaurant on the Chicago Loop.

Friendly and solicitous, Mostovets expressed Soviet concern about Morris' health and suggested he come to the Soviet Union and rest in a party sanitorium. Morris explained that, although he would like very much to come, doctors had forbidden him from traveling any long distance. Mostovets said that all of Morris' friends looked forward to the time when he could travel and resume work.

The FBI concluded that none of the SOLO leaks had yet reached or been understood in Moscow. But in late spring 1980, Steinbeck warned that, because of information made public in the suit brought by the widow of the party member, headquarters believed that Morris was in danger, and Boyle alerted him to be ready to flee at any time.

Morris usually kept hidden in Chicago substantial amounts of Soviet cash upon which Hall could draw if for any reason Jack was unavailable. On May 28 in New York he falsely told Hall that neighbors reported men had been making inquiries about him and that he feared he suddenly might have to go into hiding. Therefore, he wanted to return all party funds in his possession, and he gave Hall $225,437 in cash. Hall, himself a former fugitive, understood and agreed that for the time being he and Morris should communicate through their wives or Jack. Elizabeth on June 2 flew to Chicago and collected from Eva the remaining party funds Morris had retrieved from a hiding place.

Jack, who suffered from chronic bronchitis, emphysema, and heart problems, fell ill. In his place Morris five times in June signaled the KGB requesting a personal meeting in hopes of discussing a possible successor to himself. For reasons no one understood, the KGB in New York did not respond.

Worried about Jack, Hall on June 29 visited him at his home and urged him to go to the Mayo Clinic, which seemed to have worked wonders for Morris. On August 11, an ambulance transported Jack to a New York hospital. On August 12, 1980, Steinbeck called Boyle: "69 just died of cardiac arrest."

Eva said, "Morris was very sad. He and Jack were different. But they were brothers for seventy years and they'd been through a lot together and they were close. We all were close. Morris' youngest brother was killed in the war. Ben [the brother who ran the cover business in Chicago] had died. All his brothers were gone."

The FBI could still talk to the Kremlin through the old-time Comintern radio operator, NY-4309S*, and they exchanged messages that culminated in a meeting on August 21 between KGB officer Konstantin Koryavin and Morris. Koryavin said the Politburo and all of Morris' friends in Moscow deeply regretted the death of Jack and inquired about Jack's family. Morris replied that the family was all right but that he feared he might be under FBI investigation. Given that and his failing health, he and Hall were thinking about someone to replace him. Hall nominated a man the KGB code named Caesar, and the Soviets, through radioman "Clip" (NY 4309-S), transmitted detailed instructions for a meeting with him on September 6 in Vienna. There, from the shadows, FBI Agent Charles Knox watched as two men furtively greeted each other on the street. One was KGB officer Anatoly Portyanoy, who had worked with Jack in New York for three years. But Knox did not recognize Caesar, and there were so many KGB counter-surveillants around the rendezvous site that he dared not follow him. After months of detective work in the United States, the FBI finally identified Caesar and tried to recruit him. An old-time Party member, Caesar angrily refused to help. The FBI then laid before Caesar's lawyer the evidence of his clandestine collaboration with the Soviets and warned that if it continued Caesar would be subject to prosecution as an unregistered foreign agent. Thus Caesar instantly became useless to the Party, the KGB, and the International Department.

The Soviets continued to send messages through 4309, and Eva and Elizabeth stayed in touch until the summer of 1981 when headquarters warned it believed that Morris was in imminent danger.

A HUGE VAN PARKED in front of Morris' apartment building and out of it stepped a fine-looking moving crew. Their overalls were immaculate; none had a pot belly; each had a bulge in his pocket, the kind a revolver makes. The chief of the crew was Walter Boyle, and that day he launched Morris and Eva, Agents 58 and 66, on their last FBI mission—this one to a lovely, hidden home watched over and visited by men and women of the FBI.

The window into the Kremlin and the minds of the men in the Kremlin finally had closed.

nineteen

DANGEROUS DARKNESS

WHAT HAPPENED AFTER THE window into the Kremlin closed provides another measure of the importance of Operation SOLO to the United States, and to the world.

A Royal Air Force helicopter on September 16, 1985, landed CIA Director William Casey in the courtyard of an old fortress by the sea in England. It was a redoubt of British intelligence, alternately known as MI-6 and the SIS. Among those awaiting Casey were Christopher Curwen, director of MI-6, and Oleg Gordievsky, who for some sixteen years had spied for the British from the upper reaches of the KGB.

At the apex of his Soviet career, Gordievsky was acting *Rezident* in charge of KGB operations in the United Kingdom; in other words, all KGB officers in London were taking orders from a British spy. In 1985 Gordievsky fell under suspicion, he believes, because of betrayals by one of the most squalid traitors in American history, CIA officer Aldrich Ames (responsible for the execution of at least ten U.S. agents in the Soviet Union; in 1994 he was sentenced to life imprisonment). The KGB recalled Gordievsky to Moscow, put him under virtual house arrest, and began an interrogation. In accord with an emergency contingency plan, Gordievsky signaled MI-6 that he was about to be caught, and, in one of the most daring feats of peacetime espionage ever, the British plucked Gordievsky out from under the eyes and clutches of the KGB. (The rescue plan was so audacious that the British ambassador in Moscow reportedly threatened to resign if it was attempted. Prime Minister Margaret Thatcher is said to have replied, "Chris [Curwen] probably will resign if we don't try it. I need Chris."

While Gordievsky was stationed in London, meetings between him and MI-6 occurred only about once a month and usually lasted less than an hour. Much of that time was devoted to agreeing upon arrangements for the next meeting, and Gordievsky did not have a chance to elaborate on what he was reporting. He did manage to tell the British something about a worldwide KGB operation code-named "RYAN" (*RYAN* is the transliteration of a Russian acronym for the words *Raketno-Yadernoe Napadeni*, which mean "nuclear missile attack"). To the British, the operation sounded crazy—because it *was* crazy.

Casey came to the fortress to glean insights from Gordievsky that might benefit President Ronald Reagan during his first meeting with Mikhail Gorbachev, soon to take place in Geneva. Among other subjects, Gordievsky brought up Operation RYAN and Casey was so stunned that he asked if the remainder of the conversation could be recorded so that Reagan himself could hear it. Gordievsky said he would be honored.

In the Oval Office of the White House, Casey handed Reagan an MI-6 report comprised of forty pages of basic text and twenty-two pages of appendices. Casey told him the report was exceedingly important. The president sat down and without pause but with mounting dismay, read every word. Then, in alarm, he summoned his national security advisors.

One of them, David Major, the first FBI agent ever to serve on the National Security Council, says, "It was a masterful report. What the British had to tell us was incredible, sometimes comical. But they told us in such detail and in such a way that we could see for ourselves that what they were reporting was true."

The British report showed that some of the dangerous possibilities against which Morris warned had come to pass. In the early 1970s, Morris began to discern specific, factual examples of how the increasingly old men who owned the Soviet Union were increasingly isolating or insulating themselves from reality—that they were making themselves captives of their own boilerplate cant and propaganda. Consequently, they could ignore or misinterpret authentic information, just as Stalin did when both British and Soviet intelligence warned him that the Nazis were about to invade the Soviet Union.

They read little from the Western press, and what they did read about political or military affairs they distrusted as propaganda. They were congenitally conspiratorial and gave more credence to what some spy told them than to what some respectable journalist wrote. Morris exploited this ignorance by regularly reading the more enlightening publications of the United States and United Kingdom. He also read newspapers published in Chicago, New York, Washington, and Los Angeles as well as Soviet publications, and he learned to judge which journalists and commentators were the most reliable and astute. Consequently, he dazzled Soviet rulers with the breadth of his knowledge and the depth of his insights. They marveled at the intelligence-gathering capabilities of the loyal American party, and they believed Morris because he was their spy; he was *nahsh*—"ours." Back home, Morris warned that the old men in the Kremlin could misconstrue ordinary and unrelated events into a horrific conspiracy. This is very dangerous, he would emphasize, because they act upon their thoughts. *They are susceptible to dangerous delusions.* And many times in Moscow Morris jotted down "TWAs"—reminders to "tell Walt about" some dangerous Soviet delusion.

At American behest, the British brought Gordievsky to Washington, and David Major ushered him into the Oval Office to talk to the president. Meanwhile, MI-6 and the CIA pooled resources to confirm and expand upon what Gordievsky had reported. The following is a summary of what Gordievsky reported and of Anglo–American conclusions.

KGB Chairman Yuri Andropov at a Politburo meeting in May

1981 announced portentous news. "The new U.S. administration [the Reagan administration] is actively preparing for nuclear war and a surprise attack upon the Soviet Union is a distinct possibility." Andropov somberly explained that the threat was all the graver because NATO, China, and Japan (which had no offensive military capability) were conniving with the United States to start World War III. Therefore, discovery of when this fiendish international cabal planned to strike must henceforth be the overriding priority of all Soviet intelligence. This worldwide operation would be code-named "RYAN."

Senior KGB officers in the field recognized that the underlying premise of RYAN—that Ronald Reagan suddenly had united the entire industrialized world plus China in a plot unprecedented in history to kill hundreds of millions of people—was insane. So, initially, they regarded the operation as a transient absurdity, something not to be taken seriously, something that would soon pass, like a sudden summer rainstorm. That did not happen.

With this seminal information from Gordievsky, the British and Americans traced the paranoia of the Soviets back to the late 1970s when they learned that the United States was perfecting guidance systems that would enable missiles and bombs to hit within a few feet of any target. (During the Gulf War, televised films showed for all the world to see missiles going down the ventilation pipes of buildings or demolishing narrow bridge spans in Iraq.) Then the KGB or GRU learned that President Jimmy Carter, in consequence of the new accuracy of the weaponry, had authorized a study to determine whether it might be practicable to revise American nuclear strategy from "counter-city" to "counterforce." Bluntly put, the question was, *should we blow up Soviet missiles and weapons instead of Soviet people?*

If Morris still had been sitting in the Kremlin three or four times a year, he would have explained to the Soviets: *This is a study. It is not policy. It's like four guys sitting around at their club after a few sets of tennis and drinking iced tea or orange juice and speculating with each other. You know I am not a military man and your generals will know best and if you want our party to find out more, we will try. I have the impression that generals when they have nothing else to do always are gabbing with each other about what might be.*

But Agent 58 was no longer sitting down three or four times a year in the Kremlin.

The imminent advent of two new American weapons systems, the cruise and Pershing missiles, magnified the paranoia. The cruise missile flew only at about the speed of a commercial jet airliner. But a combination of new technology—space, photographic, computer, and microelectronic—empowered any one of the U.S. armed forces to program it to fly so low over water, hills, and dales, through any weather, that no Soviet radar could detect it. The Pershing flew fantastically fast, so fast that if launched from West Germany, the Netherlands, Italy, or the United Kingdom it could hit Moscow or any target in the western Soviet Union within ten to twelve minutes. No Soviet interceptor or missile could stop it. Both the cruise and Pershing missiles carried miniaturized thermonuclear warheads many times more powerful than the atomic bombs that obliterated Hiroshima and Nagasaki in 1945. The men who owned the Soviet Union had constructed for themselves lavish underground shelters stocked with provisions to survive nuclear war. What they proposed to do upon emerging from their caves into a devastated and depopulated land is unclear. But now Soviet scientists told them that no shelter, however deep and heavily armored, could withstand the accuracy and blasts of the new American missiles. And the Soviet oligarchs needed more than twelve minutes' notice to get themselves and their families to the bunkers. Hence, the potentates felt personally threatened.

Other factors joined to feed the paranoia. From 1977 or so until 1984, the Soviet Union essentially was leaderless. As Eva reported to the FBI, Brezhnev by 1977 was almost comatose. Upon succeeding him, Yuri Andropov soon became mortally ill and nonfunctional. His successor, Konstantin Chernenko, was both a nobody and senile and soon died. Boris Ponomarev and Mikhail Suslov also died.

Then came Ronald Reagan. The Soviets dismissed his anti-Soviet rhetoric during the 1980 presidential campaign as political demagoguery. They anticipated that if elected he would privately come to terms with them in the mutual interests of the Soviet and American "ruling classes." To their astonishment, Reagan once in office appeared to them to mean what he said and to be setting about doing what he said he would do. Quite openly, he set about rejuvenating the United States military into a force capable, if necessary, of fighting and winning a war against the whole world. He publicly called the Soviet Union an "evil empire"; more terrifying to the Soviets, he privately called it a "cancer" to be excised from the body of mankind; and most terrifying of all, Reagan was matching his words with deeds, and more and more Americans seemed to be applauding what he said and did.

Then the Soviets learned, principally through their satellite Polish intelligence service, of an American program to develop a system to protect the United States and its allies against missiles launched against their people. The program was called the "Strategic Defense Initiative," or SDI. Some American journalists, happily joined by Soviet propagandists, succeeded in pejoratively labeling it "Star Wars"—by implication, a mad, diabolical scheme to turn the heavens into a battleground and thereby defile the universe.‡

Whether SDI was a good or impractical idea is irrelevant to this story. Relevant is that Ronald Reagan considered he had a duty to protect the American people from enemy attack, and the Soviets (as Morris had warned that at any time they might) misconstrued the motives of his support of SDI. The Soviets had a reverence for American technology, ingenuity, and productive capacity. They believed that, if Americans put their heads together and decided to do something, they probably could do it. Landing American men on the moon in 1969 may have contributed little to science; maybe

---

‡ For more than twenty years, Soviet and American missiles had been pointed at each other. They would all sail through the skies at approximately the same altitudes and on the same trajectories. The interceptors the SDI program hoped to develop would fly no higher than Soviet missiles except when they intercepted them at launch. (As the best research indicates, no American journalist or politician has referred to Soviet missiles flying through the same space as "Star Wars.")

the grand voyage through space was a political stunt. Stunt or not, it was a technological feat the Soviets could not duplicate. The Soviets, rightly or wrongly, believed the Americans could through SDI construct a system of defenses against ballistic missiles and thereby endow the United States with the capability of striking first against them in confidence that whatever missiles the Soviets had left after a first strike could be intercepted.

Failure of the KGB and GRU in the summer and fall of 1981 and throughout 1982 to uncover any plans by anyone to attack the Soviet Union did not alleviate fears in the Kremlin or at KGB headquarters, which officers in the field called the "Center." To the contrary, it intensified them. To the Kremlin, the absence of evidence meant either that its many conspiratorial enemies were being devilishly clever in concealing their war plans or that the KGB and GRU were being dangerously indolent.

Consequently, the Center progressively increased pressures on *Rezidencies*, or outposts around the world, to produce evidence of the existence of a plot that did not exist. In February 1983, the Center warned them of a "growing threat of war." It emphasized that "prior discovery" of enemy attack plans had "acquired a special degree of urgency" because the Soviet Union had to have advance warning *so it could strike first*. In June 1983, the Center cabled: "U.S. continuing secret preparations for nuclear war." And in November 1983 the KGB formed at the Center in Moscow a special section staffed by more than fifty KGB officers to magnify RYAN.

Still, the legions of KGB and GRU officers and all their subsidiary spies in all the capitals of the West could not come up with a single conventional indicator of an impending attack—unusual mobilizations, evacuation, or government decrees reordering civilian life. In London, Paris, Bonn, Washington, Miami, San Francisco, and Tokyo life seemed to be merrily rolling along as usual. The KGB and GRU reported they could discern no evidence, no fact hinting of an impending attack, but the same crowd in Moscow, which had doted on every word of an American spy and heeded his advice, disregarded the reassuring reports from their own people.

Instead, the Center ordered foreign outposts to look for "seemingly unimportant developments in the civilian sector" and issued a long list of "indicators" to be spotted. It also conveyed a message that chieftains in the field interpreted to mean *Tell us what they (the Center) want to hear or you will suffer.*

Continuously goaded, the *Rezidencies* scraped up bits and pieces of trivia, usually from newspapers or television newscasts. The London *Rezidency* reported that some roads and bridges outside the city were being repaired. Officers in the special RYAN section at the Center, who felt that their careers depended upon telling the Kremlin what it demanded to hear, rated this revelation quite important. After all, missiles could be transported over the roads and bridges undergoing repairs. The Center commended the London *Rezidency* for the report but censured it for transmitting such vital information by pouch rather than by instant cable.

According to the Center, unusual activity during nonworking hours was likely to occur in government buildings, and KGB officers were to stand on the streets to keep watch "for lights burning late at night." Thus, if the president and his wife invited their children or old friends up to the private quarters of the White House late at night for a chat and a snack; if harried men and their secretaries stayed late at night to finish a report or assignment; if some janitor or cleaning woman forgot to turn off the lights in offices at the Pentagon, CIA, or FBI—war might be drawing near. Efforts to arouse "anti-Soviet sentiment" constituted another danger sign. Thus, any Western politician or publication taking exception to the Soviet tactics of maiming children in Afghanistan with explosives disguised as toys also fanned paranoia in Moscow.

The Soviets and their communist allies joined in one of the most massive propaganda campaigns ("active measures") in history to prevent deployment in Europe of the cruise and Pershing missiles. Ronald Reagan, in effect, said "to hell with you"; the British, West Germans, Dutch, and Italians, in effect, said "bring them [the missiles] on over." They were "brought over" and made ready to fire, and now at KGB headquarters the pronouncements regarding RYAN bordered upon the hysterical.

Morris Childs never saw the British report that so shocked both

William Casey and the president. It would not have shocked him; he, like they, would have been very alarmed, but not surprised. "TWA-DD"—tell Walt about dangerous delusions.

According to the report, Vladimir Kryuchkov, the head of the First Chief Directorate, the man in charge of all foreign KGB operations, made the following statements at a conference of the KGB leadership in January 1984. (Morris warned that Soviet rulers had made themselves prisoners of their own "cant and propaganda," and, with the exception of a few technical references, what Kryuchkov said could have come from a Bolshevik manual Morris studied at the Lenin School in 1930.)

> Reactionary, imperialist groups in the U.S.A. have openly embarked on a course of confrontation. They are increasing tension in literally all sectors of struggle between the two opposed socialist [political] systems and in consequence the threats of outbreak of nuclear war have reached dangerous proportions... American monopolies would like to recover the positions they have lost in recent decades and conquer fresh ones... The White House is advancing in its propaganda the adventurous and dangerous notion of survival in the fire of thermonuclear catastrophe. This is nothing else than the psychological preparation of the people for nuclear war.

The Center in February 1984 cabled to the *Rezidencies* a directive that evoked wide-eyed disbelief. Declaring that nuclear war might erupt at any moment, it ordered officers to recruit spies in banks, insurance agencies, hospitals, church organizations, and slaughter houses:

> In order to restore and regulate the stability of the country to function in the period after a nuclear missile strike, the political–military leadership of capitalist states will pay particular attention to seeing that the system of financial credit operates uninterruptedly...

More intensive activity may take place in the period of
preparation for RYAN at branches of banks involved in
insurance and credit operations. Banking personnel *at
any level* [emphasis added] may have information of
interest to us about the action being taken.

Post offices were sure to know when the attack was coming
because "these institutions are used to make a preliminary check
on addresses of mobilization contingents and for measures to
ensure stable functioning of national communications." As "mass
slaughter of cattle" would precede the attack, butcher shops and
slaughter houses needed to be watched. The Center was sure that
Western governments would tip off "leaders of national and international religious organizations, the Vatican, and institutions
abroad" about their war plans.

The directives conjured up this surrealistic scenario: *The whole
Western world, plus China and Japan, was plotting a surprise
nuclear attack. Everyone had been so secretive that the Soviets
could not find any clue about the impending attack. However, on
the eve of the attack, government, military, or security emissaries
throughout the West would drop by the bank or the post office, or
call their insurance agent, and say, in effect, "We're going to attack
the Soviet Union next week. Make sure the mail gets through; get
my credit card statement out on time; keep my policy in order." To
meat packing companies or their local butcher: "We're going to
attack the Soviet Union next week, so we'll need some extra meat."
And of course the French, British, or American ambassador in
Rome would request an audience with the pope: "Your Holiness, I
just stopped by to let you know that next week we're going to blow
up the Soviet Union. We thought you might want to say a prayer
for all those commie bastards we're going to kill."*

Some honest KGB officers in the field protested to their superiors that Operation RYAN had become insane. But the operation
had gained such powerful patronage and momentum in Moscow
that no one in authority dared try to stop it. On the contrary, some
KGB bosses or *Rezidents* in the field cynically inflamed Kremlin
paranoia by forwarding ridiculously meaningless reports.

Having been rebuked for making insufficient contributions to RYAN, London *Rezident* A.V. Guk on March 9, 1984, a Soviet holiday, summoned a subordinate to the nearly empty Soviet embassy. According to a radio report, British and American troops that day were conducting a joint exercise at Greenham Common where cruise missiles were based. The fact that the British press and radio publicized the exercise made clear that it was routine, that there was nothing secret about it. Nevertheless, at Guk's orders, the junior officer flashed to the Center a message assigned the highest priority and labeled "of strategic importance." It said: "In connection with our task to watch for signs of enemy preparations for sudden nuclear missile attack against the Soviet Union, we report that on 9 March the U.S. and British armed forces conducted the first field exercises with cruise missiles based on Greenham Common."

For reporting what the British press and radio had reported, the London *Rezidency* received a commendation, and a few days later it won another. The Center had explained that nuclear explosions burn people and that treatment of burns requires blood plasma; therefore any attempt to increase supplies of blood plasma was a prime signal that the West was about to pounce. Great Britain annually asks public-spirited citizens to donate blood. In several reports the *Rezidency* represented this yearly well-publicized appeal as a sinister phenomenon related to RYAN and for that received praise.

Not being fools, other *Rezidents*, like Guk, sensed the message: *Show us what we want to see and you prosper; show us nothing and you will suffer.* Hence, the KGB locked itself and its masters into an accelerating cycle of fear and increasingly strident alarms.

In April, then again in May 1984, the Center warned that war was about to erupt at any minute. On July 4, 1984, it ordered *Rezidencies* to report every two weeks on RYAN *even if they had nothing to report*, and its levies grew even more unrealistic. For example, officers in the field were to report at once any infiltration into the Soviet Union of "sabotage teams equipped with nuclear, bacteriological, and chemical weapons." It was as if the Center expected Western governments to invite KGB officers out to a military airfield or submarine base to wave farewell to the departing saboteurs, who presumably had shown them the nuclear weapons they had in their hip pockets.

It got worse. The Soviets estimated that no more than ten days would elapse between the time the West finally decided to attack and the attack began. They concluded that, even if they learned of the decision to attack the moment it was made, ten days would not be enough for them to organize and launch a first strike of their own. Therefore, on a wall at KGB headquarters, they put up a kind of doomsday graph. A number of red bars on the graph represented separate "indicators" that the West was about to strike. If reports caused enough bars to rise to a specified level on the graph, the Soviets automatically would launch missiles in a massive preemptive strike against North America, Western Europe, China, and Japan.

Former National Security Advisor Robert McFarlane recalls that Americans returning from Moscow reported that Soviets told them they knew they were about to be attacked. He says, "The idea was so preposterous that we couldn't make any sense out of those reports and we dismissed them."

Having escaped to London in 1985, Gordievsky detailed the full history of RYAN. He said that, after Mikhail Gorbachev assumed power in March 1985, L.P. Zamoyski, deputy director of the KGB's Analytical Directorate, declared that RYAN was "absolutely useless"; the KGB admitted it had failed to gain insights into "the real thinking of NATO and the U.S." But as far as he knew, the operation continued and the doomsday graph with those awful red bars still was on the wall.

In October 1985, Ronald Reagan arrived in Geneva early and before meeting Gorbachev walked around the estate where they were to talk. He looked inside a charming chalet on the grounds and told the Secret Service men guarding him that by 10 A.M. the next morning he wanted a fire blazing in the fireplace.

Upon being introduced the following day, Reagan told Gorbachev that prior to their formal discussions he wished to speak to him alone, man to man. He invited Gorbachev to bring his own interpreter and take a walk with him. Alone with Gorbachev and the interpreter before the fire in the chalet, Reagan declared that the United States had no intention of attacking the Soviet Union and that it was dangerous to everyone for the Soviets to think otherwise. He insisted that Gorbachev come to the United States and see for himself that there were no preparations for an attack.

In large part, thanks to a British spy and loyal allies, Operation RYAN, which ultimately menaced all mankind, was finally put to an end.

Had Operation SOLO still been alive, RYAN never would have been born.

EPILOGUE

JACK CHILDS ENTERED A New York hospital August 11, 1980, and died the next day at age seventy-three. The Soviet Union in 1975 awarded him the Order of the Red Banner (awarded only to those who distinguish themselves in battle); the United States in 1988 posthumously awarded him the National Security Medal. Had it not been for Jack Childs, Operation SOLO would never have occurred.

Alexander Burlinson, who worked with Jack for twenty-four years, lived the life of a country squire after his retirement in 1975. He continued to smoke cigarettes, rub his ulcer, play the piano, and compose poetry almost until his death October 10, 1990. He was eighty-five.

Carl Freyman, who recruited and developed Morris Childs into Agent 58, still lives with his wife of more than half a century in the same pleasant house outside Chicago where many SOLO sorties were planned and analyzed. He retains his mental acuity and good spirits, and for a man in his eighties enjoys good health. Those privileged to study the secret history of SOLO regard Freyman, along with Burlinson, as a legendary figure of the FBI.

John Langtry lives in New York, where his son is an outstanding young FBI agent. Although physicians have forbidden him to "lift weights" ("Scotch on the rocks"), he still meets his many friends in neighborhood taverns and attends monthly luncheons where active and retired agents gather to renew friendships and to talk about what the FBI has done right and wrong, and what it ought to do. As throughout his FBI career, Langtry always is one of the most popular men present.

James Fox, as assistant FBI director in charge of the New York field office, also became popular among union, business, religious, and political leaders, and most of all among the FBI personnel he led. Fox often appeared on national television to answer questions after agents under his direction arrested terrorists ultimately convicted of bombing the World Trade Center in New York in 1993. He planned to retire January 3, 1994, and on December 4, 1993, a New York television station interviewed him about his FBI career. Toward the end, the interviewer asked about the public statements of an FBI informant who claimed he had given the FBI advance warning of the bombing. Fox said, "Salem did not warn us. Nobody warned us. If we had been warned, we would have prevented the bombing." (Testifying under oath, the informant later admitted that he had never given the FBI any forewarning, just as Fox said.)

FBI Director Louis Freeh on December 10 telephoned to inform Fox that in consequence of these three sentences he was placed on administrative leave as of 5 P.M. that day until his official retirement. In other words, he was to clear his desk, get out, and never come back.

Freeh had ordered that no one comment on the case of the bombing of the World Trade Center pending the trial. Fox agrees that by impulsively telling the truth, he violated an order. Few others, in or out of the FBI, think that by telling the truth in nineteen words Fox harmed the FBI. Nevertheless, two weeks before Christmas his long and luminous FBI career ended suddenly and sadly.

Before his suspension, between 250 and 300 people had registered to attend a retirement dinner in honor of Fox. Now he expected only about half that many, and he understood that friends still in the FBI might consider it imprudent to come. When Fox entered the banquet hall at the New York Hilton Hotel, more than a thousand men and women stood to applaud. Among them were clergymen, union leaders, financiers, corporate executives, politicians, and hundreds of men from the FBI, including a defiant delegation from headquarters. The Democratic governor of New

York, Mario Cuomo, and the Republican mayor of New York
City, Rudolph Giuliani, led the tributes to the son of a Chicago
bus driver, to Eva's "favorite Baptist Indian." Fox silently prayed,
Please let mother and father see what they have done.

Today Fox is executive vice president of the Mutual of America
Life Insurance Company, a columnist for *Forbes* magazine, a consultant to the Columbia Broadcasting System, and a member of
the board of directors of several major corporations.

Walter Boyle officially retired in January 1980 after twenty-six
years in the FBI. In declining a promotion and transfer to headquarters, he had said, "There is no way I ever will walk away from
58." So the day after his retirement, Boyle returned as a "consultant" working out of the cover office in Chicago, doing what he
had been doing since 1962. He stayed eighteen more months until
Morris and Eva were safely hidden and until SOLO ended or at
least until it seemed to have ended.

Today Boyle works in corporate security for a large conglom-
erate and fights gangsters. He lives in an attractive home with a
lovely wife and at sixty-six remains in superb physical condition,
weighing about the same as when he joined the Marine Corps
forty-five years ago. He dotes on his children and grandchildren,
whose happy lives have been made possible by him and Catholic
Charities of Chicago, to which Morris and Eva donated the
$10,000 bonus from the FBI. He is also close to his brothers and
older sister, who has been a nun for more than fifty years. John
Langtry and he talk often. As Eva said, "We always had a lot to
talk about."

Boyle and other agents packed Morris and Eva off in August
1981 to a condominium apartment high in an elegant building
north of Miami. It gave them spectacular views of the Atlantic
Ocean, the Inland Waterway, moored yachts, and the lights of
Miami. The apartment was spacious enough to allow each a study
and to accommodate guests. Guards patrolling the lobby twenty-
four hours a day permitted no one they did not recognize to go
near it without first consulting Morris or Eva.

FBI agents visited often, and they formed special friendships
with three of them: Ivian C. Smith, Wesley Roberts, and Barbara

Moser. Smith first called upon them after taking charge of the Miami field office, and he realized he had stumbled onto a gold mine of intelligence that still could be mined. Eva recalled, "After I.C. [Smith] became boss, it was kind of like we were back in business. People started coming down out from Miami and down from Washington, and they brought us up to Virginia and treated us like royalty. They asked Morris lots of questions about what was going on in Russia, and they asked me about wives and people we knew in Moscow, and sometimes they asked about things that happened a long time ago. These talks perked Morris up; he could stay up explaining things all night without getting tired."

Since his first heart attack in the 1940s, Morris long had beaten both the medical and actuarial odds. Many times ambulances rushed him to hospitals and physicians feared for his life, yet always he came home. In late May 1991, Eva had to summon an ambulance and this time she sensed that he would not be coming home. She stayed at the hospital, and when he died on June 2, she was holding his hand.

Eva in June 1991 was eighty-one or ninety-one or somewhere in between and there was nothing more she could tell the FBI. However, Smith had secured a written commitment from Washington that the FBI would provide for Morris and Eva for the rest of their lives, and it did. The Miami office arranged for Eva to have a female companion; Agents Roberts and Moser visited often; Jim Fox called regularly from New York; and nieces and nephews from Chicago came to see her. Still, the FBI and Eva were careful to conceal her whereabouts from all but the most trusted people. As late as 1993, Gus Hall made inquiries in Chicago in an effort to discover where she was.

Eva very much looked forward to publication of the story she and Morris lived, and she was prepared, in secure surroundings, to talk to journalists and historians about it. Having heard that she had been in the hospital, I in June 1995 telephoned her, and she assured me she was going to be all right. Three days later, Eva died.

Some one hundred relatives and friends, including quite a few young people, gathered in the same Chicago chapel where services for Morris were held. There was no longer any reason to conceal

the truth, and a eulogist announced the presence of five representatives of the Federal Bureau of Investigation—Barbara Moser,
Wesley Roberts, Carl Freyman, James Fox, and Walter Boyle.
Characterizing Eva as an American heroine, the eulogist told
something of her feats as a spy and her contributions to the United
States. This time the gasps from the congregation expressed awe
and pride rather than shock and anger. After the service, many of
the mourners, especially young people, crowded around to shake
the hands of the FBI agents.

I remarked to Wes Roberts that it was especially sad that Eva
did not live to see the book she made possible. "She read every
word of the manuscript," he replied. "She died a happy and
fulfilled woman."

APPENDIX A:
SOLO MISSIONS

MORRIS CHILDS (CG-5824S*) accomplished fifty-two missions under FBI control into the Soviet Union and other communist countries; Jack Childs (NY-694S*) accomplished five. Eva Childs accompanied Morris on all but two of his missions from 1962 onward. Listed below are the dates and destinations of each mission. The five missions made by Jack Childs are designated "Agent 69"; otherwise, the missions listed were made by Morris Childs. The list does not include missions to Canada and Mexico.

First Mission	4/24/58–7/21/58	Moscow, Peking
Second Mission	1/18/59–2/26/59	Moscow
Third Mission	9/23/59–11/11/59	Moscow, Peking, Shanghai
Fourth Mission (Agent 69)	2/3/60–3/10/60	Prague, Moscow
Fifth Mission	5/5/60–5/10/60	Havana
Sixth Mission	7/9/60–7/30/60	Prague, Moscow
Seventh Mission	8/1/60–8/25/60	Havana
Eighth Mission	9/22/60–12/17/60	Moscow

Ninth Mission (Agent 69)	6/18/61–7/13/61	Moscow
Tenth Mission	10/2/61–12/5/61	Moscow
Eleventh Mission	10/16/62–12/19/62	Moscow, Prague, Budapest
Twelfth Mission (Agent 69)	4/28/63–5/21/63	Moscow
Thirteenth Mission	8/7/63–8/25/63	Moscow, Prague
Fourteenth Mission	11/1/63–12/2/63	Moscow
Fifteenth Mission (Agent 69)	4/19/64–6/5/64	Moscow, Havana
Sixteenth Mission	10/19/64–10/29/64	Moscow
Seventeenth Mission	11/30/64–12/31/64	Moscow
Eighteenth Mission	2/19/65–4/26/65	Moscow
Nineteenth Mission	10/19/65–11/12/65	Moscow, Prague
Twentieth Mission	3/18/66–4/25/66	Moscow, Prague, East Berlin
Twenty-first Mission	8/7/66–10/15/66	Moscow, Prague, Berlin
Twenty-second Mission	1/8/67–1/30/67	Moscow
Twenty-third Mission (Agent 69)	4/2/67–4/18/67	Moscow
Twenty-fourth Mission	10/19/67–12/4/67	Moscow
Twenty-fifth Mission	2/21/68–3/16/68	Prague, Moscow
Twenty-sixth Mission	4/17/68–5/6/68	Prague, Budapest
Twenty-seventh Mission	6/8/68–6/29/68	Moscow
Twenty-eighth Mission	8/23/68–8/29/68	Moscow
Twenty-ninth Mission	9/27/68–10/10/68	Budapest, Moscow
Thirtieth Mission	11/15/68–12/2/68	Budapest, Moscow
Thirty-first Mission	2/22/69–3/31/69	Budapest, Moscow
Thirty-second Mission	5/17/69–6/30/69	Budapest, Moscow
Thirty-third Mission	9/5/69–9/18/69	Moscow
Thirty-fourth Mission	11/30/69–12/18/69	Moscow

Thirty-fifth Mission	2/20/70–3/5/70	Moscow
Thirty-sixth Mission	4/8/70–5/7/70	Moscow, Budapest
Thirty-seventh Mission	11/24/70–12/13/70	Moscow, Berlin
Thirty-eighth Mission	3/14/71–4/19/71	Prague, Moscow
Thirty-ninth Mission	9/5/71–9/17/71	Moscow
Fortieth Mission	11/24/71–12/16/71	Moscow, Warsaw
Forty-first Mission	2/5/72–2/16/72	Moscow, Poland
Forty-second Mission	3/19/72–4/30/72	Moscow
Forty-third Mission	6/2/72–7/5/72	Moscow
Forty-fourth Mission	10/4/72–10/26/72	Moscow
Forty-fifth Mission	12/11/72–1/6/73	Moscow
Forty-sixth Mission	4/9/73–4/30/73	Moscow
Forty-seventh Mission	11/21/73–12/12/73	Moscow
Forty-eighth Mission	2/18/74–3/7/74	Moscow
Forty-ninth Mission	4/22/74–5/23/74	Moscow
Fiftieth Mission	9/6/74–10/3/74	Moscow
Fifty-first Mission	11/25/74–12/13/74	Moscow
Fifty-second Mission	6/2/75–6/16/75	Moscow
Fifty-third Mission	10/14/75–11/5/75	Moscow, Poland
Fifty-fourth Mission	2/16/76–3/13/76	Moscow
Fifty-fifth Mission	11/30/76–12/31/76	Moscow, Budapest
Fifty-sixth Mission	5/24/77–6/25/77	Moscow
Fifty-seventh Mission	10/21/77–11/20/77	Moscow, Prague

APPENDIX B:
SOVIET PAYMENTS
TO THE U.S.
COMMUNIST PARTY

THE SOVIET UNION BEGAN supplying money to the U.S. Communist Party through SOLO in 1958. Initially, representatives of the Canadian Communist Party gave the money to Jack or Morris Childs in Toronto or New York. Beginning in 1960, KGB officers handed the money to Jack Childs during clandestine meetings around New York. Listed below are the amounts the Soviets paid each year. Occasionally, when Morris Childs was in Moscow, the Soviets gave him in foreign currencies the equivalent of a few thousand dollars. Some of the amounts listed are odd because of the conversion of these currencies into dollars.

1958	$75,000
1959	$200,000
1960	$298,885
1961	$370,000
1962	$172,000
1963	$583,606
1964	$739,032
1965	$1,054,616
1966	$743,829.19
1967	$1,049,069.90

1968	$1,141,354.80
1969	$1,516,808.90
1970	$1,066,742.80
1971	$1,043,440.12
1972	$1,634,370.80
1973	$1,260,344.26
1974	$1,832,376.80
1975	$1,792,676
1976	$1,997,651.28
1977	$1,981,594
1978	$2,355,612
1979	$2,632,196
1980	$2,775,000

APPENDIX C:
KGB OFFICERS IN SOLO

THE KGB FOR TWENTY-FIVE years assigned officers posing as diplomats at the United Nations to deal with Jack and Morris Childs—to pass messages, documents, and money, and to receive messages from them. Listed below are the names of these officers and the years they worked in SOLO (which the Soviets called MORAT) while posted in New York.

1958-61	Vladimir Barkovsky
1962	Valenin Zaitsev
1962-63	Aleksei Kolobashkin
1963	Grechchukin (first name unknown to author)
1964	Aleksei Kolobashkin and Vladimir Chuchukin
1965-68	Nikolai Talanov (assisted by Ivan Belov)
1968-74	Vladimir Chuchukin (assisted by Yuri Germash and Vladimir Tulinov)
1974-77	Yuri Zhuravlev
1977-80	Anatoly Portyanoy
1980-82	Konstantin Koryavin

APPENDIX D:
SECRET COMMUNIST
DOCUMENTS

THE DISPARATE DOCUMENTS reproduced below illustrate secret communications and relations between the communist parties of the Soviet Union and the United States. Two also illustrate how Morris Childs exploited his knowledge of communism to manipulate the Soviets.

Confidential

Memorandum to Comrade Dimitroff: 187

    Another personal question I must raise, because of its
possible future political importance. For about 7 years my
younger sister, Marguerite Browder, has been working for the
foreign department of the NKVD, in various European countries.
I am informed that her work has been valuable and satisfactory,
and she has expressed no desire to be released. But it seems
to me, in view of my increasing involvement in national political affairs and growing connections in Washington political
circles, it might become dangerous to this political work if
hostile circles in America should by any means obtain knowledge
of my sister's work in Europe and make use of this knowledge
in America. The political implications of such possible
danger will be clear to you, being directly *connected with* the
relations between USSR and USA, as well as to the work of our
Party in America. I raise this question, so that if you agree
to the existence of this danger, and consider it of sufficient
importance, steps can be taken by you to secure my sister's
release from her present work and her return to America where
she can be used in other fields of activity.

                        Fraternally

                        Earl Browder

Moscow, Jan.19, 1938

"Memorandum to Comrade Dimitrov"

    Earl Browder, head of the American Communist Party, addressed this memorandum to Georgi Dimitrov who in 1938 was chief of the Comintern. Dimitrov forwarded it to Nikolai Yezhov, chairman of the NKVD (predecessor to the KGB) with a recommendation that Browder's sister be relieved of espionage duties in Germany. The willingness of the Soviets to accede to Browder's request is an indicator of the importance they attached to Browder and the American Party. Historian Herbert Romerstein discovered the memorandum in Soviet archives.

<u>*Fond 495, Opus 74, Delo 465, page 5*</u>

To Comrade Yezhov,

I am sending you Comrade Browder's note (General Secretary of the American
Communist Party); from this end I consider it politically expedient to dismiss his
sister from her position in the Foreign Bureau of the NKVD. 24 January 1938 with
Comradely greeting, G. Dimitrov

No. 153/LD

Browder's note in English was sent to Comrade Yezhov, copy was not kept

Translation of carbon copy from Comintern files.

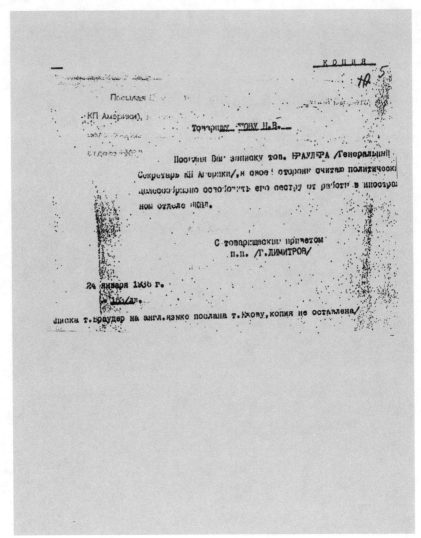

Carbon copy from Comintern files.

Совершенно-секретно

Товарищу ЕЖОВУ Н.В.

Посылая Вам записку тов. БРАУДЕРА /Генеральный
Секретарь КП Америки/, я своей стороны считаю политическ
целесообразно освободить его сестру от работы в иностра
ном отделе НКВД.

С товарищеским приветом

ря 1938 г.

Original letter from KGB files. Signature is G. Dimitrov;
the letter is marked top secret in upper right hand corner.

1.

Complaints about special privileges in the socialist countries.

Memorandum

In March 1965 on a brief visit to the GDR and Czechoslovakia I heard
considerable talk among economists and other professional people about the
indifferent or negative attitude of workers to the leaders and to socialist
production objectives. Special privileges of top leaders, and, to a lesser
extent, of burocrats, were referred to as a major cause of these attitudes.
I was told about special stores in Prague where only high functionaries
could make purchases of superior products unavailable elsewhere. One person
I talked to claimed to have visited such a store together with somebody privileged to buy there. This and similar complaints were made here in New York
by the wife of a Czechoslovak employee of the United Nations.

I spent the month of October 1965 in the USSR. From the interpreter and
some other people I heard comments indicating a negative attitude towards
leadership which, however, could simply reflect their personal bitterness over
something or other.

Two days before leaving the USSR I spent the evening with a Soviet
journalist, an "angry young man" type, who talked very bitterly about the
Party and Trade Union leadership. He charged they were predominantly careerist,
bureaucratic types completely indifferent to the welfare of the workers and
that the workers had no use for them. He also charged that the top party
officials and government leaders get extravagant special privileges, making
themselves into a spe cial caste. He mentioned, among other things, special
stores at which top leaders could buy things unobtainable elsewhere, and at
lower prices than charged for inferior goods bought at ordinary stores.

The next day I had lunch with a Pravda correspondent who is anything
but an "angry young man" type. I asked him x about this. He said it is
rather true. He did not know if the special stores are still in existence.

"Complaints about special privileges in the socialist countries"

Like virtually everybody else, Morris Childs knew well that in communist
countries the *Nomenklatura*, or ruling class, enjoyed privileges, perquisites,
and luxuries denied the general populace. Morris himself frequented one of
their special stores where he could select quality imported products for free.
Yet to burnish his image as an old-time, idealistic Bolshevik, Morris submitted this memorandum to the International Department of the Central Committee, as if he had discovered something shocking.

2.

But, he said there was more resentment over special allowances that top
leaders and officials get for vacations, over and above the regular
trade union contributions to the cost of vacations. He also said he
thought the special privileges were less than they had been.

It was too late to arrange to discuss this with any leading people
in the USSR, but the following week I met with the director and staff of the
higher Party School in Budapest, and asked them about special privileges in
Hungary. The director said the problem had been greatly reduced in Hungary.
It is less evident now in Budapest. But in some of the provinces the local
chiefs set themselves up with fine mansions, and act as if this were
their private duchy . It was his understanding that there were more
extreme special privileges in some othersocialist countries, including the
USSR.

In February, 1966, I was visited by a professor from Bulgaria, a former
minister of Finance who had been imprisoned at the time of the Traicho Kostev
case. I asked him about special privileges in Bulgaria. He said it is
a serious problem, and gave the following examples:

In smaller towns where the electricity supply is inadequate all Party
functionaries and actives live in a particular section of town. That section
continueds to get electricity on the frequent occasions when there is none
in the rest of town.

Central Committee members and other highly plaaed people have 600 square
meters of living space in their homes. They have at their disposal private
resorts, staffed with service people who could care for 50-100 guests, but
in practice only service the one family and their friends for a few weeks
a year.

He claimed that in the USSR the special vacation allowance given to high
functionaries is 2,000 rubles a month.

Certainly these word of mouth accounts are not wholly authentic, and must

3.

contain inaccuracies. Yet I do not believe they are wholly inventions.

Obviously there is a line beyond which appropriate differential incomes for top contributions to society become special privileges, losing their historical function and creating a bad relationship between the people and their leaders; which in turn can undermine efforts to involve the masses wholeheartedly in socialist construction, corrupt the recipients of the privileges, and provide propaganda ammunition to the world's capitalists.

I am in no position to judge where that line is. Yet, some of the examples mentioned above, and some of the occasional better documented charges in the capitalist press (e.g. Gromyko's private traveling cook), give me the impression that this line may well be exceeded. Apparently the problem was worse in the past, and is receding, but perhaps not decisively or speedily enough. £

I think that this problem should be reviewed on a high level. Also, material advantages of top leaders should be controlled in a democratic way within the Party, and not permitted to reach levels which have to be kept secret because of possible adverse public reaction.

Able Kit   Hill — CONFIDENTIAL

The case of -----. is related to a rather serious political
probl.. that we face. It is not a new problem for the
revolutionary movements of the world. In general terms the
problem is petty bourgeois radicalism. As we know it is a part
of the overall process of radicalization and mass upsurge. It
reflects the nature of the crises of capitalism. The problem
of petty bourgeious radicalism becomes once acute when the petty
bourgeoasia elements, students and youth become frustrated, the
petty bourgeois radicalism turns to individual acts of teroor
and to anarchism.

There is a dialectical interrelationalship between the rise
of reactionary terror by the state of monoply Capitalism and these
acts of terror by left individuals and left groups. These acts become
the excuse for more reactionary policies and they also become obstacles
in mobilizing ma..ses for a strugle against bourgeois terror. These
left groups are infiltrated by the police and the FBI they are very
often the instigators of violent acts by left groups. This interre-
lationships of the two processes is creating some very real and difficult
problems for the revolutionary movement.

ITS RELATED TO A NEW FASCIST DANGER FOR OUR COUNTRY

----- ----- has been a member of our Party for about 3 years. But she
always leaned in the direction of the petty bourgeois radical groups
She was and has remained a follower of Marcuse. She has been involved
with groups like the Black Prnthers. One of the New theories of
Petty Bourgeois radicalism is that all Negro prisoners are Political
Prisoners. ----- ----- became involved in an attempt to force some of
these Negro prisoners who were in prison for ordinary crimes. We have

"Able Kit—Hill—CONFIDENTIAL"

Morris Childs could talk and write like a communist, as well as think like
one. In this rough draft of a memorandum to the International Department,
he displays the mastery that helped convince communist dictators that he
truly was one of them. ("Able Kit" was the contemporary code for the Central Committee of the Communist Party in the USSR.)

as a sister of one of the prisoners. The plan to free the
prisoners was worked out during these trips. It seems that she
bought the guns and the getaway car.

She is now in hiding. While we do not agree with her
actions, we agree that we will have to help her get out of the
country. But the people working with her feel that now is not
the time to make the attempt. We think she should be gotten into
some Socialist country. She is a very intelligent young person
who has gotten hung up on petty bourgeois radicalism.

PAT Greetings

obk

Reo

AbcCox

To the Communist Parties in the capitalist countries,
newly independent countries, and the courtries under
the domination of imperialism:

The struggle against the escalated U.S. imperialist aggression in Indo-China
has now emerged as the most urgent and crucial issue in the struggle for world peace
and against nuclear war.

Serious as the moment is, there is no need for any attitude that this must
necessarily be the beginning of a new world war. The danger is very grave, but the
possibilities of turning back from this path are still present.

In fact, there is every reason to believe that the Johnson Administration can
still be brought to its senses and to calling a halt to this present direction of policy.

The people of the United States are not supporting this aggression. At no
time in our history has there been such opposition amongst the broad masses to a
major government policy as there is against this aggression in Indo-China. This
opposition is growing and will become ever more vocal.

The anti-war actions around the war are of key importance in this struggle.
Amongst the other activities now going on, we would like to suggest the organization
of a "people's boycott of goods and products made in the U.S.A." This can, and has
been in the past, a very effective additional means of concrete actions by the masses.
This is a very sensitive area. It is sensitive because of the critical nature of the
difficulty U.S. capitalism is having with its trade balance and the outflow of gold.
It is sensitive because U.S. capitalism knows that the World War II boycott against
Japanese and German-made goods, even to this day, still affects the buying habits
of some sections of the people of the United States that would not like to see such
a development even started.

The boycott should be organized and supported by the broadest possible
peace forces. Because of the crucialness of the moment, it should be done as
soon as possible. For the moment, this effort should be on the level of a people's
boycott movement.

This can quickly add to the pressures already exerted against the policies
of U.S. aggression in South Vietnam.

"To the Communist Parties in the capitalist countries..."

The Soviets regularly issued instructions to Communist Parties throughout
the world and expected them to be obeyed. This order received by the American Party is typical.

To Gus Hall

It would be desirable for us to know your estimation
of the state of public opinion in the United States - the
attitude towards Nixon's administration. What are the changes
in the mood of the opinion - what are the main tendencies?
We should like to know particularly your estimation and that
of your party leadership, of the attitude of various strata
of U.S. people toward the USSR.

"To Gus Hall"

The Soviets repeatedly asked Hall to analyze public opinion and political
trends. Most of the responses actually were composed by Morris. This is a
deciphered request to Hall.

Anxious to receive from Oak, his evaluation of the Nixon
Administration etc. (Question that was asked of him on
2/16/71). It is to be evaluated by cc. It will have influence
on Brezhnev report to the 24th Congress.

Closed channel to be busy from now to end of 24th Congress.
Watch Roosevelt Avenue every day.(Except Sat. and Sunday).

Shoe delivery March 18 - 7:30PM in Westchester (possibly 200
pairs of shoes.

Need two more meeting places, lower Manhattan

Need more drops.

Delegation (both CP,USA and Puerto Rico) must arrive Moscow
six days before Congress starts. Must have smallpox vaccination
before, leaving US. If not can be vaccinated in Moscow but
must arrive 12 days before Congress. (Anyone going to USSR
must be vaccinated.

Gave Spring two new shoe delivery spots for his OK.

Improved micro transceiver will be given at later date (to Spring).

Did Spring have any more information concerning memoirs of Leon
Trotsky which :are to be published.

"Anxious to receive from Oak"

This is a representative operational message radioed by the KGB to Jack
Childs on behalf of the International Department. This version has been deciphered but still contains some code words: "Oak" means Gus Hall; "Spring"
means Jack Childs; "Shoe" means money; "200 pairs of shoes" means
$200,000. In the first paragraph, "cc" stands for Central Committee.

INDEX